Brokering Belonging

LISA ROSE MAR

# Brokering Belonging

*Chinese in Canada's Exclusion Era, 1885–1945*

UNIVERSITY OF TORONTO PRESS
Toronto

First published in Canada in 2010 by University of Toronto Press Incorporated
Toronto
www.utppublishing.com

ISBN: 978-1-4426-1022-4

Copyright © 2010 by Oxford University Press, Inc.
Published by arrangement with Oxford University Press Inc.

A cataloguing record is available from the Library and Archives Canada.

University of Toronto Press acknowledges the financial assistance of the
Canada Council for the Arts and the Ontario Arts Council.

University of Toronto Press acknowledges the financial support of its publishing
activities by the Government of Canada through the Canada Book Fund.

9 8 7 6 5 4 3 2 1

Printed in the United States of America
on acid-free paper

*Dedicated to the memory of Edgar Wickberg*

ACKNOWLEDGMENTS

D OING RESEARCH AND WRITING a book is a labor of love, and I was fortunate to enjoy the generous help of many colleagues, friends, and family members.

*Brokering Belonging* is dedicated to the memory of Edgar Wickberg of the University of British Columbia. Ed was a kind mentor and incisive critic in my journeys through Chinese Canadian history since my undergraduate student days. Ed's intellectual generosity, broad approach to knowledge, and commitment to community history have guided my own academic work. Following his example, I learned to read modern and classical Chinese. These skills revealed new evidence so compelling that I put aside my dissertation and started an entirely new book organized around the insight that Chinese Canadians had approached Canada, the United States, and China as a single field of opportunity. Ed's critical readings of this book's early chapters reflected his deep immersion in Chinese diaspora, Chinese, Canadian, U.S., and Asian American history.

My dear friend Andrea Goldman, a China historian at the University of California, Los Angeles, proved a steadfast intellectual companion throughout the research and writing process. She read through a number of early draft chapters, and we discussed *Brokering Belonging* from start to finish, including during many late night phone calls. Andrea helped to strengthen the book's connections to China studies, and she was a helpful critic of Asian American history. She offered both theoretical and practical suggestions which helped the book reach its full potential.

Timothy Brook, a China historian at the University of British Columbia, was my graduate advisor at the University of Toronto. I am grateful for his gracious collegiality, his professional support, and his critical reading of both early chapters and the full manuscript. Tim's comments improved both the Canadian and Chinese aspects of the book, as well as its organization. *Brokering Belonging*'s conceptual structure is most strongly inspired by modern Chinese history, particularly local elite-society relations. As a mentor, Tim continues to have an important impact on my intellectual development.

Patricia Roy, a Canadian political historian, British Columbia specialist, and race relations expert at the University of Victoria, read several early chapters. She offered invaluable criticisms, editorial advice, and guidance. Every page of *Brokering Belonging* builds on Pat's foundational research into Canada's Asian-white race relations. Pat's impressive breadth of knowledge strengthened this book, and she generously shared tips about relevant archival collections. I am grateful to her for being a model colleague and scholar.

I also appreciate Gordon Chang, an Asian American historian at Stanford University, for being a mentor since I first ventured into Chinese Canadian research as an undergraduate student. I benefited from his sage counsel and his scholarly mastery of Asian American, U.S., and China studies. Gordon read the entire manuscript, and he offered extraordinarily helpful criticisms that made *Brokering Belonging* into a better book.

My editor, Susan Ferber of Oxford University Press, contributed helpful advice in the developmental years of the project, and she also helped to guide the mature manuscript toward more effective focus. Susan's thoughtful edits and responsive feedback have made *Brokering Belonging* a stronger, leaner, and more accessible book. In addition to Susan, I would like to thank the readers and editors from three university presses, who greatly improved this book's content, concepts, and organization. These included six very generous anonymous readers who offered many criticisms and suggestions. At Oxford University Press, I enjoyed working with helpful production editor Jennifer Kowing and copy editor Merryl Sloane, whose careful reading and insight made this book better throughout. Len Husband of the University of Toronto Press, and Stacy Wagner of Stanford University Press also greatly contributed.

Many of my colleagues at the University of Maryland, College Park, also read chapters, and I am grateful for their help. As a mentor, Julie Greene offered helpful feedback on the introduction and book proposal. Her advice also helped to guide my navigation through the book publishing process. Gary Gerstle helped to sharpen the project's conceptual framework. Robyn Muncy encouraged a deeper exploration of social movements. Saverio Giovachinni contributed the concept of an alternative public sphere. David

Grimsted's provocative questions about preliminary findings pushed me to investigate fragmentary evidence to the fullest extent. David Freund helped with the introduction. Alison Olson's reading of drafts improved the book's clarity. Rick Bell's and Peter Wien's comments on a conference paper about the Chicago School of Sociology helped me to better communicate.

Chairs on both sides of my joint appointment, Richard Price (history) and Larry Shinagawa (Asian American studies), gave me the time to complete *Brokering Belonging*. Their attentive mentoring, support, encouragement, course releases, and coordination made this book possible. Previous chairs Gary Gerstle (history) and Timothy Ng (Asian American studies) also arranged a semester of research time.

Henry Yu of the University of British Columbia and Roger Daniels of the University of Cincinnati provided helpful suggestions and encouragement.

I would like to thank Mae Ngai of Columbia University for inviting me to present my work on the Chicago School of Sociology at a 2006 American Studies Association panel that she organized on the history of Asian American brokerage. The attendees, especially Donna Gabaccia of the University of Minnesota, provided helpful feedback.

I very much appreciated an opportunity to preview *Brokering Belonging* at a conference titled Refracting Pacific Canada, which was organized by Chris Lee and Henry Yu of the University of British Columbia. The preview generated a helpful dialogue with scholars from Canada, the United States, and East Asia, as well as students and community members. Thank you also to editors Henry Yu and Robert Macdonald and to two anonymous readers for the journal *BC Studies* for helpful feedback on the subsequent article.

Thank you to the following Chinese Canadian community members for their help and hospitality during my research: Larry Wong, Quan Lim, Vivian Wong, Josie Lee, Howe Lee, Chris Lee, Jim Wong-Chu, and Dora Nipp.

My assistants on this project also deserve credit. University of Maryland doctoral student Rebecca Wieters read and formatted the penultimate manuscript. Rebecca turned out to be an excellent critic and natural copyeditor. Her fresh look made the manuscript tighter, better organized, and more transparent to a nonspecialist audience. Begin Zen and Claudia Cole helped with gathering research data. David Estrin provided editorial assistance.

Many archivists and librarians also assisted with my research, especially George Brandak (UBC Rare Books and Special Collections), Ralph Stanton (UBC Rare Books and Special Collections), Eleanor Yuen (UBC Asian Library), Sheldon Goldfarb (Alma Mater Society Archives), Kelly-Ann Turkington (BC Archives), Carolyn Soltau (Pacific Newspaper Group Library), Keith Bunnell (UBC), the Special Collections Department of the Vancouver

Public Library, the staff at the National Library and Archives of Canada, and the University of Maryland's Interlibrary Loan Department.

Although this book is not a revision of a dissertation, it builds upon my earlier work and draws on one-tenth of my earlier data. Therefore, I would like to thank my other graduate teachers at the University of Toronto who laid this book's foundation: Franca Iacovetta, who introduced me to immigration history, and Carolyn Strange, Michael Szonyi, Michael Bliss, and R. Craig Brown.

Funding and hosting support for *Brokering Belonging*'s research came from the University of Maryland's Graduate Research Board, the Institute of Asian Research at the University of British Columbia, the Queen's Fellowship of the Social Sciences and Humanities Research Council of Canada, the Andrew W. Mellon Fellowship, the University of Toronto, Cornell University's East Asia Program, the U.S. Department of Education's Foreign Language and Area Studies Fellowship, Green College at the University of British Columbia, the American Historical Association, the International Council of Canadian Studies, and the University of Toronto's Chinese Canadian Culture and Chinese Railway Workers of Canada fellowship.

The following permitted use of their copyrighted material. The last and the 17th paragraph of the introduction, chapter 1's endnote 120, chapter 5's discussion of the Chinese workers' movement, the conclusion's endnote 2, and the second paragraph of the conclusion originally appeared in *BC Studies* 156–157 (Winter 2007–Spring 2008). The quotation from the David C. Lew Fonds comes from the Royal British Columbia Museum, British Columbia Archives (E/D/L58). The picture of Yip On is a detail from a photo by the Chinese Empire Reform Society, Vancouver Public Library (VPL26691). The photo of Thomas Moore Whaun from the 1927 *Totem* is reproduced courtesy of the Alma Mater Society Archives. Alphonse Savard took the cover photo of Chinese Empire Reform Association members in Vancouver with Liang Qichao, a visiting scholar and reformer from China. It comes from the University of British Columbia, Rare Books and Special Collections, Won Alexander Cumyow Fonds (BC-1848-14).

Above all, I would like to thank my family for their love and encouragement. I would especially like to thank my parents, Linda and Jerry Mar, for inspiring in me a love of learning, and my brother, David Mar, whose friendship I treasure. My mother's comments greatly improved the book's flow, and she helped to distill my approach to legal history. My father and brother helped me to calibrate my manuscript to be accessible to a broader audience. In British Columbia, Jack and Arlene Mar, as well as Coreen and Georges Rivard, welcomed me into their homes. Finally, my beloved husband, Troy

Goodfellow, read every draft of this book from start to finish. As a Canadian political scientist and freelance writer, Troy gave me feedback on both my analysis and my writing. He also coined the title, *Brokering Belonging*. I am grateful beyond words for Troy, who is a strong comfort, an intellectual soulmate, and a beacon of wisdom in my life.

CONTENTS

*Note on Translations and Terms* xv

Introduction 3

ONE Negotiating Protection: Illegal Immigration and Party Machines 15

TWO Arguing Cases: Legal Interpreters, Law, and Society 49

THREE Popularizing Politics: The Anti-Segregation Movement as Social Revolution 69

FOUR Fixing Knowledge: Pacific Coast Chinese Leaders' Management of the Chicago School of Sociology 89

FIVE Transforming Democracy: Brokerage Politics and the Exclusion Era's Denouement 111

Conclusion 131

*Notes* 135
*Bibliography* 191
*Index* 217

NOTE ON TRANSLATIONS AND TERMS

THIS BOOK RENDERS CHINESE NAMES according to their English spellings, with Mandarin romanization given when Chinese characters are available. Consequently, the transliteration of Cantonese terms reflects immigrants' idiosyncratic romanization from local subdialects. A Chinese character glossary for *Brokering Belonging* is available at the University of British Columbia Library Rare Books and Special Collections.

I refer to British Columbia's European population in a variety of ways that reflect Chinese Canadians' understanding. These terms describe a history of relations as most people perceived them, through a lens tinged with ideas about "race." British Columbia's mainstream population is most commonly called "Anglo," defined as Anglophone Europeans who belonged to the province's dominant British American power structure. I also use the terms "white" and "European" when they are most relevant to the context at hand.

Brokering Belonging

# Introduction

MIDDLEMEN ARE NEVER HEROES. EVERY immigrant community has middlemen because they serve an important function: they help immigrants deal with the larger society. Their work is often controversial. They may expect payment in loyalty, coin, tribute, or souls. Often, middlemen became immigrant communities' most visible public figures, but their profile in history does not match their prominence in life.[1] This book explores some of the most controversial political middlemen in the history of Canada and the United States: Chinese immigrant leaders during the Chinese Exclusion Era.[2] It also probes the mystery of why their past became obscured.

Between the 1880s and 1940s, Canada and the United States implemented policies that excluded and harassed Chinese immigrants. In the face of immigration exclusion, anti-Chinese laws, and mob violence,[3] Chinese sought political power to combat this discrimination. The Chinese Exclusion Act (1882–1943) barred the entry of all Chinese workers to the United States. Canada implemented a Chinese head tax (1885–1924) on entering Chinese workers, followed by the total exclusion of virtually all new Chinese immigrants (1923–1947).[4] In this setting, Chinese political middlemen improvised, creating unofficial ties to mainstream institutions. Their persistence heightened public unease about nonwhite immigrants, as many Canadians and Americans felt that Chinese political middlemen threatened democracy. Frequently, they saw the middlemen as exploiters of non-English-speaking Chinese workers, who treated the workers more like "yellow slaves" than free men and women.⁵ The popular media often depicted middlemen as despots who ruled Chinatowns rife with Oriental intrigue. The media also described them as mediators so alluring that few of their non-Chinese neighbors could resist their supposed corrupting influence.⁶ Fearing Chinese political power, Canada and the United States denied nearly all Chinese the right to vote.⁷

Many ordinary Chinese saw the immigrant power brokers as complex figures. Chinese greatly respected individual leaders, regarding them as effective community representatives and as patrons, but they also criticized particular leaders as compromised collaborators with Anglo society, deeming them exploiters. Perhaps because of this complexity, some historians have described Chinese middlemen, but very few have explored the process of brokerage itself.⁸

*Brokering Belonging* traces the history of some Chinese brokers, individual ethnic leaders who acted as intermediaries between the Chinese and Anglo worlds of North America's West Coast. Examining the work of these leaders in the brokerage relations between Chinese and Anglo institutions provides a new view of West Coast society. This book will reveal a process of making history from the middle, from neither a top-down nor a bottom-up perspective. Against the backdrop of a rapidly changing landscape of politics, law, and institutions in the early twentieth-century Pacific world, several generations of ethnic leaders aspired to claim power as the dominant representatives of their Chinese immigrant communities to Anglo institutions. Analysis of their work offers a new view of the boundaries between the Chinese and Anglo worlds and the political interactions between them. A unique but fragmentary body of Chinese-language documents has provided a record of the politics that sustained North America's first illegal immigrant group.⁹ Canada's authorities could not read Chinese newspapers and letters without Chinese brokers' help. Secure behind the language barrier, Exclusion Era Chinese created an alternative public sphere,¹⁰ where they openly debated the politics of brokers, brokerage relations, and illegal immigration.

*Brokering Belonging*'s story has no heroes or villains but documents a restless struggle for power amid great change and instability. Chinese power brokers' political world was competitive. They worked hard for the support of Chinese and Anglo constituents, who often had conflicting interests. If one failed, a more effective broker would take his or her place. The history of Chinese brokers reveals mainstream and minority politics as inextricably linked. First, the brokers' story helps to reconfigure top-down histories of exclusion, which have focused on politics, the state, and the law. *Brokering Belonging* shows Chinese as more than excluded victims or resisting outsiders.¹¹

Through brokers, Chinese immigrants actively joined in the central politics of their time: party machines and social reformers, labor and capital, immigration debates, and conflicts over a more interventionist state. Second, *Brokering Belonging* traces how brokers' negotiating power within both the Chinese and Anglo worlds often was rooted in Canadian, transpacific Chinese, and transnational North American ties. Third, *Brokering Belonging* explores transformations over time in brokerage. I eschew the common approach to immigrant leadership as the domination of naïve new arrivals by English-speaking merchants, labor contractors, interpreters, and professionals.[12] *Brokering Belonging* instead focuses on the changing political relations between ordinary people, their leaders, and their institutions in the Pacific world.[13]

The story begins in the nineteenth century with elite-oriented politics dominated by businesspeople. After the First World War, new charismatic leaders mobilized ordinary citizens to participate in mass politics, challenging both traditional brokers and the subordinate place of Chinese in Canadian race relations. These mass movements culminated during the Second World War, when Chinese protests for equality helped to transform brokerage relations, contributing to the Exclusion Era's postwar waning. Throughout, *Brokering Belonging* explores how Chinese immigrants who could not vote wielded considerable influence, successfully navigating a period of anti-Asian sentiment and exclusion at all levels of society. Community power brokers often succeeded in winning resources for the Chinese community. Consequently, they became significant players in race relations, influencing policies that affected all Canadians.

Chinese Canadians' situation was unique because they were Canada's first group of immigrants from Asia, having arrived during an era of "white Canada" policies. They were also one of Canada's largest visible minorities. As late as 1941, Canada's population was 98 percent European; the overwhelming majority was of British or French ancestry.[14] British Columbia, where most Chinese Canadians lived, differed. In 1885, only one third of the province's 49,459 people were European. Two-thirds were First Nations and Chinese. By 1945, ninety-two percent of British Columbians were European, but the province remained exceptionally diverse. Asians numbered five percent of the total 817,861 population, and Chinese were two percent. At the time, many Europeans saw Chinese as racial "others." In British Columbia, these political pressures forced Chinese into a separate, unequal status.[15]

Thus, the story of Chinese brokers' work contributes a new perspective on the process of political integration. Most studies of foreign migrants' political integration focus on immigrants who could eventually become citizens.[16]

While this was the norm for European immigrants, policies in Canada and the United States did not allow Asian immigrants the same privileges. Legally, most Chinese had no choice but to remain permanent foreigners and nonvoters. British Columbia did not allow Chinese Canadians to vote. Canada also made it difficult for Chinese immigrants to become naturalized citizens. The United States denied all Asian immigrants the right to naturalize. Many Chinese also lacked legal immigration status.[17] The ways in which Chinese brokers wielded political power also reflected their roles as representatives of a migrant community that stretched across Canada, China, and the United States.

Particularly, brokers helped to create conceptions of Canada and the United States as immigrant nations deeply rooted in the Pacific world.[18] Chinese brokers often drew on their wider Pacific world to alter Chinese-Anglo relations. For example, Yip On (*Ye En*), a Chinese merchant and immigration interpreter in Vancouver, British Columbia, made his leadership in protests against anti-Chinese laws the foundation of a secret alliance with Canada's ruling Liberal Party between 1899 and 1910.[19] As an orator, Yip traveled across North America, China, and Hong Kong to urge Chinese to show their displeasure with foreign discrimination by boycotting U.S. and Japanese goods. He also helped to found and lead a Chinese political party, the Chinese Empire Reform Association (CERA, *Baohuanghui*), which claimed five million members.[20] Yip's passionate attacks on anti-Chinese laws encouraged ordinary Chinese to wield their power as consumers to compel concessions from world powers.[21] Sometimes, they made gains, and the elected leaders of the United States, Canada, and Mexico had to meet with them.[22]

In Canada, Yip won influence through the interplay of political and economic power. He managed his political party's business investments, which ranged from a modern newspaper in Shanghai to a streetcar line in Torreon, Mexico. In 1904, he parlayed this influence into a patronage appointment as Canada's official immigration interpreter in Vancouver. Yip enforced anti-Chinese immigration laws, but he also undermined them by admitting great numbers of illegal immigrants. Through bribes to Anglo officials, who passed money along to Liberal Party officials, the Yip family's emigration business sent many Chinese workers to Canada.[23] However, Yip's secret alliance was illegal, and he had no formal political standing, a situation that opened him to competition from rivals.[24]

My examination of the brokers' work counters common perceptions of oppressed Chinese as a monolithic "race," shows that they responded to a politically complex Anglo politics of prejudice, and reinserts Chinese Canadians as part of a more integrated political history. When a young rival, legal interpreter David Lew (*Liao Hongxiang*), attempted to depose Yip in 1910, conflict broke out between the two leaders' Chinese and Anglo supporters in Canada, the United States, and China.[25] At the time, Chinese illegal immigration was an open secret.[26] Many Chinese Canadians complained, however, that Vancouver's immigration officials, including Yip, extorted excessive amounts of cash from new arrivals.[27] Taking advantage of the situation, Lew brought together leading members of the city's anti-Asian movement with Chinese Canadian businesspeople who feared Yip's dominance. To the Chinese Canadian public, Lew offered himself as a more effective defender of his people than Yip. In 1910, he arranged to meet with Canada's prime minister, Wilfrid Laurier, to discuss Chinese immigrants' concerns.[28] However, Lew had garnered his political access through a devil's bargain. Prominent white members of Vancouver's anti-Asian movement made a deal with Lew to expose Vancouver's immigration officials' misdeeds. Lew hoped to secure a political appointment as the port's new Chinese immigration interpreter, whereas the anti-Asianists wanted to expose Yip's protectors, their rivals in Canada's ruling Liberal Party.[29] This clash of Chinese power brokers and their Anglo allies bears little resemblance to the oft-told story of Anglo discrimination and Chinese response.[30] Instead, Chinese consistently interacted with and exercised influence upon their non-Chinese neighbors.

While *Brokering Belonging* traces Chinese immigrant power brokers' ongoing negotiations with Anglo society, it roots their continuing work as actors in a larger Pacific world. The maxim "all politics is local" frequently applied, but in British Columbia, the local was often global. There, Canada met a Pacific world that included the British Empire, the United States, and East Asia. British Columbia's chief city, Vancouver, housed one of North America's largest Chinese populations and was a gateway for Chinese slipping illegally into the United States. Both Chinese and Anglos shared a West Coast culture that crossed the U.S.-Canada border. They also felt keenly aware of distinctions between Canada, which was a dominion of the British Empire, and the United States.[31] West Coast Chinese also shared common origins in Guangdong, China.[32] For both Chinese and Anglos, Vancouver's role as the "Chinese capital of Canada"[33] made it a pivotal site in West Coast struggles over Chinese migration's future. The resulting Chinese-Anglo brokerage relations involved local contexts, but also ties to the larger Pacific world where Canada strived to make its mark.

Indeed, Chinese Canadian power brokers played an unacknowledged role in the foundation of immigration studies through collaborations with social science interviewers. In 1924, they organized a community campaign to manage visiting U.S. researchers from the Chicago School of Sociology who were conducting a pioneering research project to determine whether or not West Coast Asian immigrants could assimilate. The researchers' interview pool was largely made up of Chinese brokers. Fearing further discrimination, brokers schemed to hide their transnational activities behind a façade of their yearning to assimilate, laying the foundation of two major myths in U.S. and Canadian immigration scholarship: the idea of Asians as a patient and diligent "model minority" and the belief that immigrants seek complete assimilation into the wider community.[34]

Further, Chinese brokers' performances helped to encourage a heroic myth about their communities. They inspired the researchers to conceive of them as tragic "marginal men," the leading edges of their people's Canadianization and Americanization.[35] They presented themselves as immigrants with a heroic faith in their adopted homes, patiently waiting to fulfill their new land's democratic promise. This domestic story of heroic assimilation without troubling racial confrontations became celebrated as national myth. By bridging ethnic studies with the fields of political and intellectual history, this book argues for a more expansive vision of transnational immigrants and nonwhites as shapers of Canadian society—and, at times, as influencers of U.S. society as well.

For over a century, scholars have been fascinated with the Exclusion Era's central paradox: despite anti-Chinese laws, Chinese kept coming to Canada and the United States. *Brokering Belonging* explores this puzzle of Chinese resistance. The story of community power brokers closely relates to the U.S. experience, so my interpretation at times speaks to both countries. Two major schools have shaped the debates engaged by this book. The consensus school's roots lie in the identity politics of the 1960s with ethnic minorities' claims that "we, too, are Canadians," and their insistence that discrimination be recognized. Consensus historians often focus on racial barriers and the nation-state. They interpret anti-Chinese laws as central expressions of larger race relations, national politics, imperial identity, legal culture, and bureaucratic state-building. They often trace Chinese dealings with Anglo institutions. Most see Chinese resistance as expressing a universal immigrant process of assimilation.[36]

The historians of exclusion of the China school often employ a Sinocentric lens that foregrounds migrants and their transpacific connections. The majority of early Chinese immigrants were men who supported families in China. These historians explain Chinese resistance as a product of migrants' transpacific culture, society, and economy.[37] *Brokering Belonging* employs underutilized Chinese-language historical documents[38] to build on both the China and consensus schools, while it also unifies and expands these schools.

Both schools treat Chinese and Anglos as mostly separate groups. How different would the history of the Chinese Exclusion Era look through an immigrant-centered lens that focused on the shared dimensions of Anglo-Chinese political life?

The story begins in 1885, when Canada implemented its first anti-Chinese immigration act, the head tax, just as Chinese workers were completing the new nation's first transcontinental railway. At the railway's Pacific terminus, Vancouver became an instant city as British Columbia transformed from a mainly First Nations western frontier into a British Canadian settler society. Vancouver, its regional center, served as a hub for a steamship and rail network that helped to bind together the globe-girdling British Empire to which Canada belonged. Vancouver's Chinatown, a rustic collection of wood buildings built in a tidal swamp, underlined the marginal position of Chinese residents in the new Exclusion Era order.[39]

Crossing back and forth across the Pacific, as well as moving between Canada and the United States, many Chinese led what scholars term a "transnational life" that did not conform to Canada's immigrant settler ideal.[40] Chinese Canadians included legal and illegal residents, foreigners and citizens, settlers and temporary migrants, China-born and Canadian-born.[41] Given this mix, Chinese often felt a deep sense of personal connectedness to more than one nation, whether through kith and kin or the imagined ties of culture and memory.[42] Most Anglos imagined Chinese as permanent foreigners, but Chinese were also assimilating and developing deep roots in Canada.[43] At the same time, many Chinese Canadians kept open minds about their ultimate destination. The majority of Chinese left Canada for the United States or China. Departure rates ranged from half to over two-thirds of arrivals.[44] Even those who stayed in Canada continued to send money to relatives in China.[45] Chinese Canadians also had close ties to the United States—ties made tighter by illegal Chinese emigration to that country.[46] Even Chinese children born in Canada saw life as something that involved moving across borders.[47] By the early twentieth century, generations of Chinese Canadians had approached Canada, China, and the United States as a single field of opportunity. Chinese noted that Canada's other immigrants from Europe and Asia behaved similarly.[48] Neither anti-Chinese laws nor repeated acts of Anglo racial violence would drive the Chinese out of the Pacific West.

The first and second generation of brokers, backed by wealthy Chinese merchants, acted as representatives for the disenfranchised, establishing themselves among the community. These traditional brokers prioritized assuring a steady stream of Chinese immigrants. With corrupt or sympathetic partners in Anglo politics and business, the brokers helped many Chinese newcomers to evade anti-Chinese immigration laws. Even the legal route through Canada's borders was tightly controlled by these brokers and their allies in China. To this end, Chinese brokers often secured official immigration interpreter posts by making alliances with ruling party factions and by bribing politicians.

A rivalry between two brokers, Yip On and David Lew, provides the focus for chapter 1, "Negotiating Protection." To evade the Chinese head tax, both Yip and Lew formed alliances with factions of Canada's ruling Liberal Party.[49] They swayed powerful politicians with both financial boons and international threats.[50] The Yip-Lew conflict stands out because its public exposure provoked national scandal. However, it was part of a larger pattern of covert Chinese-Anglo political alliances that were prevalent during the Exclusion Era in both Canada and the United States. Party machines helped to integrate disenfranchised groups.[51] Ultimately, public scandal imperiled but did not destroy the founding bargain between Chinese and Anglo factions to permit illegal immigration that ruling parties across the political spectrum would honor.

Chapter 2, "Arguing Cases," demonstrates how brokers merged their Chinese clients' aspirations with British legal institutions. Chinese Canadians contended with laws and a justice system that frequently treated them unfairly. When Chinese appealed to Canadian and British Empire courts to rectify these wrongs, judges often upheld the white majority's right to discriminate against them.[52] Despite these challenges, Chinese Canadians found ways to influence the larger legal culture. Chinese brought from China and the United States strong traditions of litigation, so they often turned to Canadian law to resolve external and internal disputes.[53] Because British Columbia did not permit Chinese to practice law, Chinese legal interpreters worked as unofficial "Chinese lawyers" and were often involved in legal negotiations that expanded the Canadian state's influence in Chinese Canadian affairs. Chinese in the United States similarly dealt with popular demands for the rule of law and with racial barriers in the legal profession. The final act of the Yip-Lew rivalry involved a contest of legal virtuosity between 1922 and 1925. It began in Nanaimo, a small coal-mining town in Vancouver's hinterland, and ended in London, England, as the House of Lords judged the case's import for the British Empire.[54] In the midst of these machinations, an assassin murdered David Lew, leading to an investigation that created an extraordinary record of his legal dealings.[55]

Starting in the 1920s, traditional merchant brokers and legal interpreters faced new challenges from a third generation of charismatic brokers: intellectuals, labor leaders, and civil rights activists. The new brokerage was based less on wealth or patron-client relations and more on the active consciousness of thousands of Chinese. Chapter 3, "Popularizing Politics," explores how these new leaders burst onto the political stage in 1922 with a year-long mass protest movement against public school segregation. While this protest has been regarded as a local Chinese-Anglo conflict, Chinese evidence reveals it to be a transpacific event, rooted in global anti-colonial nationalist movements after the First World War.[56] Anti-segregation leaders joined new social movements across the Pacific world that mobilized ordinary people to political protest. Besides making British and Canadian claims, leaders alluded to mass protests against British colonialism in China and India. Their efforts paralleled rising labor unions and emulated related campaigns by Chinese Americans. Their populism provoked severe backlashes from some Chinese and Anglo business leaders, but the social movement's power to bring ordinary people into brokerage politics could not be undone.

Chapter 4, "Fixing Knowledge," examines how astute intellectuals among these new brokers attempted to reshape public discourse about Chinese in Canada and the United States. As the first major academic survey of East Asian immigrants' opinions began in 1924, its director, Robert Park of the University of Chicago, opined that Asians appeared to be more like blacks than whites.[57] Chinese Canadian leaders in Vancouver believed that they could not leave the Survey of Race Relations' outcome to chance, so they coordinated the interview data that researchers would find.[58] Chinese leaders countered Park's assumptions that Asians adapted more slowly than European immigrants by claiming that their own lives heralded Chinese Canadians' future as an educated, assimilated, deferential, and hard-working model minority. Their performance built on and added to nascent U.S.–Canada debates about factoring immigrants into more pluralistic visions of national life, rather than enforcing Anglo conformity. Chinese in Victoria, Seattle, and San Francisco then did likewise, planting the seeds of enduring immigrant myths in the United States and Canada.[59]

The new brokerage coincided with an era of intense racial pressures. In 1923, Canada's Parliament ended legal Chinese immigration.[60] Still, in the 1920s, Chinese Canadians were more integrated into greater Vancouver than in the past. Despite racial segregation in most public schools, workplaces, neighborhoods, and public accommodations, over half of Chinese spoke English.[61] Chinese were scattered across more than forty integrated city blocks of Vancouver's East Side. They often lived among other outsiders: non-British European immigrants, lower-class Anglo migrant workers, Jews, Japanese, and African Canadians. Chinese also mingled with non-Chinese in gambling houses, saloons, soccer fields, and movie theaters.[62] Only Chinatown's center, a nine-block area of Chinese shops, residences, and association headquarters, was an ethnic enclave. Even there, the many European grocery shoppers and diners testified to Chinatown's integration into wider city life.[63] The increased integration inspired Chinese Canadian beliefs that they might eventually win more equal status. However, the Great Depression (1929–1939) and Canada's Chinese exclusion law darkened these hopes. Most Chinese later recalled the 1920s and 1930s as a time of great Anglo discrimination, futile resistance, and unfulfilled assimilation.[64]

Chapter 5, "Transforming Democracy," discusses brokers' ongoing negotiations with Anglos and brokers' actions within the Pacific world during the Second World War (1939–1945). The waning of exclusion is typically attributed to liberalizing Anglo attitudes and Chinese Canadian lobbying. This chapter shows how mass protests also contributed. Unpopular war policies put the traditional brokers favored by the Canadian government on the defensive. Charismatic brokers mobilized thousands of Chinese Canadians to combat war policies that made it difficult to send relief remittances to relatives in China. Thousands of Chinese workers also organized within their larger Canadian labor unions, protesting tax regulations and demanding equal pay. These protests pushed reluctant labor unions to combat Anglo racial discrimination just as new industrial relations policies made unions into more powerful political machines than in the past. An anti-conscription movement inspired thousands of Chinese to boycott military service to protest their disenfranchisement. This protest also built on the larger conscription crisis, which bitterly divided British and French Canadians. This Chinese Canadian action highlights an overlooked dimension of the conscription crisis: a majority of Canada's nonwhite population refused to serve. *Brokering Belonging* ends in 1945, as Chinese Canadians' new alliances began to shift their legal status from aliens to citizens and as the rise of Communist power in China ushered in a new era of Chinese Canadian transpacific relations.

Brokerage relations provide a new lens that transforms common views of the Exclusion Era as it has been understood in the Americas, China, and the Pacific world. Particularly, this book revises the Exclusion Era's larger context: a global turn away from unrestricted entry into the immigrant settlement nations of the Americas and the British Empire toward policies of gatekeeping designed to keep undesirable immigrants out.[65] This new regime of global border controls first focused on Chinese, but it later expanded to encompass all immigrants.[66] Arriving at a time of vast global international migrations, Chinese found themselves on the cusp of a transition from immigration freedom to immigration restriction in the Americas and Australasia. Most histories of this transition focus on the gatekeepers and their institutions, a perspective that renders invisible much of Chinese agency and Chinese internal tensions. The story of the Chinese brokers points toward another side of this gatekeeping story: its persistent failures, its gate continually left ajar. Throughout the Exclusion Era world, Chinese developed a global system of illegal immigration and secured local political protections that made continued migrations possible. Chinese Canadians achieved a true but unequal political integration. This history of trading for power brings Chinese connections with the Pacific world back into the center of domestic histories of North America.

My analysis of Chinese brokers' work challenges conceptions of immigration history which have viewed Asians as marginal compared with European settlers during the great age of migration from the mid-nineteenth to the early twentieth century. Exclusion laws did significantly constrain Chinese immigration. However, continuing interactions between Chinese and Anglo worlds, as well as ongoing transnational and transpacific connections, underline the limitations of an immigration history which has been shaped by a methodological nationalism—a desire to tell histories of permanent settlement even when one-third of the global Canadian-born population had moved to the United States.[67] *Brokering Belonging* embraces Chinese migrants' mobility and global gaze as typically Canadian. It challenges conceptions of transnational migrants as "nowhere" in national history,[68] demonstrating how mobile, cosmopolitan peoples created a distinctive history of Canada.

Still, *Brokering Belonging* holds no illusions about the ways that white racial prejudices divided the Chinese and Anglo worlds. The hardening boundaries between these worlds created a Chinese Exclusion Era almost entirely unknown to Canadians today. This book chronicles the daily difficulties of Chinese Canadian life, as well as Chinese brokers' relations with Anglo Canadian allies, which made the situation tolerable. At the time, immigration and racial policies expressed a European nation-building intent. The Chinese Exclusion Era coincided with the displacement of First Nations people and with the aggressive recruitment of European immigrants to the Canadian West. *Brokering Belonging* contributes a new Chinese-centered view of the operation of Canada's racial policies, but it also challenges common views of past race relations as expressive of white racial hegemony.[69] Chinese Canadians worked with a significant minority of Anglo Canadians to develop unofficial multicultural, transnational spaces of politics and law.

My research in Chinese-language materials shows that Chinese Canadians did not merely react to Anglo dominance: they took action and they adapted. Through political brokerage, this disenfranchised group mitigated even the most direct processes of exclusion. They were shapers of their own presents and futures, as well as those of the surrounding society. The history of the Chinese in Canada can only be properly understood if scholars explore interactions as much as exclusions. We will see that the official settler story of Canada as a nation of immigrants coincided with an unofficial story of Canada that was written through global migrations at the crossroads of the Pacific, North American, and British worlds.

ONE | **Negotiating Protection**
*Illegal Immigration and Party Machines*

ONE OF THE MOST CURIOUS aspects of anti-Chinese policies was officials' practice of hiring immigrant Chinese interpreters, thus foiling exclusionary laws. The clash of two titans, Yip On and David Lew, shows how political alliances across racial lines compromised enforcement of anti-Chinese immigration policies.[1] Both leaders sought to control Vancouver's Chinese immigration interpreter post. Like generals, they marched with powerful political machines. They battled from Ottawa's halls to Vancouver's backrooms. They attacked along fronts in Canada, the United States, and China. In 1910 and 1911, Lew's efforts to reform Chinese immigration thrust the open secret of Chinese Canadian influence into the public eye. The resulting Royal Commission inquiry created a unique record of Canada's unofficial political history. Through brokerage, Chinese immigrants who could not vote found ways of influencing policy; in an era of "white Canada" policies, they helped to make Canadian party politics covertly multicultural.

The study of interpreters and the politics through which they won, held, and lost their posts creates a new understanding of how immigration policy was made. As an ethnic collaborator, the interpreter engaged in policy making from a distinctive position. He had a duty to carry out the mandates of Parliament, but he gained political leadership from supporters who viewed anti-Chinese laws as illegitimate. On a daily basis, he had to reconcile national politics with ethnic community dynamics. Thus, the story of interpreters brings together these two often separate histories. While other studies of Canada's Chinese head tax treat the policy from a legislative perspective and some scholars emphasize the law's passage as a symbol of racism, this chapter moves beyond the legislative and takes into account how the head tax was enforced. By my focus on the day-to-day implementation of the law, disenfranchised Chinese Canadians appear as key political players in determining the head tax's significance for Canada's Chinese immigrant community. In contrast to the letter of the law, enforcement of the head tax was arbitrary, and Chinese Canadians in British Columbia found many ways to influence enforcement of the head tax policy.

The Chinese head tax did more than levy a fee of two years' wages on all new Chinese immigrants who were not merchants, students, or diplomats. It created Canada's first policy to closely screen individual immigrants, and it set precedents that would have a lasting impact on national policy.[2] To that end, Canada's officials modeled the Chinese head tax on the U.S. Chinese Exclusion Act of 1882.[3] Both systems treated Chinese as suspected illegal immigrants. Both countries detained arriving Chinese for questioning and held them indefinitely, while Europeans entered without undue hindrance.[4] Most Chinese who did not speak English—or who spoke it poorly—felt "deaf and dumb" as they dealt with Anglo officials.[5] For these immigrants, the Chinese interpreter became their ears and tongues. Their salvation or damnation rested in the interpreter's hands. Interpreters served as crucial conduits for communications, but they were rarely impartial.

Canadian historians have presumed that party patronage appointments to civil service jobs only involved voters; the Yip-Lew clash shows how the disenfranchised could also exercise influence.[6] As with most patronage politics, the participants were careful not to leave any embarrassing documents to posterity.[7] The official record often only lists the results of political struggle: appointments to and resignations from civil service posts.[8] The daily thrust and parry of patronage politics belongs to the unofficial history of Canada's democracy. Often, these backroom deals defined later official acts. They helped to meld local community politics with national public policy.

Chinese Canadian patronage politics involved not only race relations, but also balancing local, national, and transnational politics in the struggle. The close connections between political parties and society enabled a few Chinese leaders to interact as Pacific world citizens and to participate in Canada's economy. These leaders made themselves valuable to Canadian corporations and political parties through their ties to transpacific commerce. To win allies, these leaders proffered cash, connections, and the promise of a stronger Pacific Canada. Much of their bargaining power came from transpacific contexts and, sometimes, they won an audience.[9] Without votes, however,

Chinese had to negotiate from a position of weakness. Because Chinese Canadians would pay almost any price for minor political access, party leaders could afford to alienate them, yet still draw on them as a source of party funds. In general, parties did not permit direct contributions from Chinese Canadians.[10] Chinese had to work through Anglo intermediaries, such as influential local Liberal Party members or Anglo corporate business partners. Every hand through which Chinese Canadian contributions passed profited. Between 1907 and 1911, the money trail associated with Chinese interpreter appointments stretched across Canada and even to China. In these arrangements, each political broker brought his or her network's politics to the table.

The enforcers of the Chinese head tax served at the pleasure of the ruling political parties, which profoundly affected their handling of policy.[11] Before the First World War, the spoils system reigned in the civil service. The local branch of the ruling party rewarded supporters with posts, charging civil servants with the sometimes contradictory objectives of buttressing both the party and the state. At the time, the federal cabinet determined the hiring, firing, promotion, salary, and benefits of all customs and immigration personnel at Canada's borders.[12] Candidates for civil service positions often campaigned for support within their local party associations, seeking to win the nomination from their member of Parliament (MP) and regional cabinet minister.[13] Likewise, Chinese Canadians who wanted interpreter positions importuned the ruling party's leaders. They also campaigned to depose rival incumbents in Vancouver, Victoria, and Nanaimo.[14]

The populace considered interpreters' appointments to be at-will jobs. Since the inception of the Chinese head tax in 1885, newspapers had reported public campaigns for and against particular Chinese interpreters. The first appointee, former U.S. Chinese immigration interpreter John Vrooman Gardiner, bested Won Alexander Cumyow (*Wen Jinyou*) in a competition debated in Victoria newspapers.[15] Interpreters frequently dealt with challenges from rivals. Between 1908 and 1910, Lim Bang (*Lin Bang*), a merchant in Victoria, approached British Columbia's cabinet minister, William Templeman, about deposing interpreter Lee Mongkow (*Li Mengjiu*) and taking his place.[16] Lee kept his post until 1920, despite evidence of misconduct.[17] In 1908, David Lew proffered a $1,500 bribe in exchange for being appointed as Yip On's replacement, but failed to dislodge him.[18] Still, Chinese Canadian political appointees had no constituencies of voters to support them, so they were less secure than their European counterparts. As a result, Canadians approached Chinese interpreter appointments as matters of continual—and often public—politicking.

Because interpreters' political appointments came from alliances between Chinese and Anglo political machines, many factions felt entitled to try and control the outcome. This context magnified the Yip-Lew conflict into a broader struggle that affected both Chinese and Anglo populations. In the English-language press, the conflict made news across Canada and in California.[19] Liberal Party factions, unions, corporations, Chinese political parties, anti-Asian groups, and fraternal associations all vied for advantage. Chinese across North America also followed the contest. For many Chinese, evading immigration laws at Vancouver had been a first step in an illegal journey to the United States.[20] Even the Chinese in New York City reportedly discussed Yip and Lew in their shops.[21] Eight Chinese-language reporters covered the story, printing stories in Chinese newspapers that circulated throughout North America.[22] Yip On was known as a visionary nationalist leader in much of the Chinese world, especially among the Chinese diaspora in the Americas, Guangdong, Hong Kong, and Southeast Asia.[23] David Lew, on the other hand, appeared to be known mainly in Canada. Behind the scenes, members of Canada's political elite, including Prime Minister Wilfrid Laurier and cabinet minister William Templeman, struggled to control the controversy.[24] Pressure also arose from the grassroots. White labor unions opposed to Asian immigration donated money to support Lew's side.[25] As accusations of Liberal Party graft in Chinese immigration burst into public view, Laurier attempted to control the political damage by creating a Royal Commission.[26] Under the public spotlight, neither side could gracefully withdraw.

## The Titans: Competing for Vancouver's Chinese Interpreter Post

To many Chinese Canadians, Yip and Lew had heroic stature because of their work as political brokers. They also came to represent the tragic result of Chinese Canadian leaders' unofficial pursuit of power: compromised positions that corroded even the most idealistic of men.[27] The incumbent interpreter, Yip On, was a striking example of the apparent contradiction between the head tax's aims and its implementation. In 1904, the ruling Liberal Party appointed Yip, an implacable foe of anti-Chinese immigration laws, as the nation's de facto chief enforcer of the Chinese head tax.[28] Just one year after his appointment, Yip traveled to China and led a national boycott of U.S. goods to protest that country's anti-Chinese immigration laws.[29] As a director of the Guangdong boycott efforts, Yip helped to blanket the province's cities with pamphlets and placards denouncing Americans' ingratitude toward the Chinese pioneers who had developed the West.[30] "When the virgin land was opened in former years, [they were] recruited as coolies," went one popular boycott song. "Now that the forest road has been opened up [they are] thrown away like worn shoes."[31] Boycott literature also denounced the "painful" U.S. detention of legitimate Chinese on reentry as "even worse than a prison."[32] Speakers at boycott rallies also noted that the United States and Canada were just two of many immigrant settlement nations that mistreated Chinese.[33]

Chinese Canadian popular thought followed similar lines. As *Da Han Gong Bao* writer Zhou Chi Zhu later lamented, after the hardest taming of Canada's wilderness was done, the British tried to drive out the Chinese: "Canadians should ask in their hearts, would it not be more virtuous to treat overseas Chinese kindly?"[34] Not surprisingly, the Chinese in British Columbia "energetically" supported Yip's cause. In 1905, they boycotted U.S. goods, and they refused to work for any U.S. citizen. Chinese Canadians also raised funds to support dock workers in China who refused to unload U.S. ships.[35] Many regarded Yip as a nationalist hero. He had helped to guide China's people to stand up against the United States, and the boycott's representatives twice won audiences with U.S. president Theodore Roosevelt.[36] The boycott did not succeed in repealing anti-Chinese laws, but it won concessions that improved the treatment of arriving Chinese.[37] Roosevelt ended the humiliating Bertillon system, canceling its requirement that every arriving Chinese's limbs, fingers, toes, and genitals be measured. He also ordered port officials to accept Chinese merchants' certificates of exemption from the U.S. Chinese Exclusion Act. The exemption certificates, produced by China's government and approved by U.S. consuls, were not reliable. Nevertheless, Roosevelt ordered that officials treat holders of exemption certificates courteously and admit them without question, or be dismissed.[38] Canadian officials, likewise, enacted similar reforms in their own immigration system.[39] After the 1905 boycott, Yip returned to working for the Canadian immigration system he opposed. As an enforcer of Canada's anti-Chinese policies, Yip was not unique. Between 1885 and 1910, Canada's ruling political parties often appointed Chinese interpreters whom they knew handled anti-Chinese policies ambivalently.[40]

As a leader, Yip had an exceptional ability to inspire trust and a bold vision of China as a nation defined by people power more than monarchs.[41] He repeatedly led mass, nonviolent boycotts of foreign goods, espousing the anti-imperialist credo "China for the Chinese."[42] His boundless energy and sharp mind impressed observers. The *Vancouver World* wrote that Yip translated between Chinese and English as rapidly as a "linotype."[43]

FIGURE 1.1. Yip On. Detail from a photo by the Chinese Empire Reform Association, 1899. Vancouver Public Library, VPL26691.

As a Chinese diaspora leader, Yip spent much of his time in China and Hong Kong attending to political matters relating to modernizing China.[44] Nevertheless, he always returned to his immigration interpreter post in Vancouver. No document records how Yip felt about his work for a system he despised, but he probably felt unease. Perhaps he saw it as a way to soften a harsh system; maybe he understood the political appointment as a way to represent his community. Or perhaps he saw collaboration as a form of domination too dangerous to leave in the hands of others. He almost certainly felt obligated to protect his family's Chinese immigration business, which traded on his fame.[45] Nonetheless, no one could participate—much less prevail—in the interpreter position's sordid politics for long without compromise.

Political machines on both sides of the racial divide influenced the politics of Yip's appointment. In 1910, Yip On's family had controlled the Vancouver Chinese immigration interpreter's position for twenty-three years.[46] To that end, the Yips had maintained good relations with both ruling political parties, the Conservatives (1887–1896) and the Liberals (1896–1911). The Yips' faction also had dominated, and to a large extent controlled, Chinese Canadian community life.[47] However, by 1910, the political base of Yip On's brokerage alliance had frayed. The Chinese political party that he once led had collapsed into acrimony, assassination, and recriminations from his fellow Chinese Canadian merchants. Revolution in China bitterly divided the Chinese diaspora.[48] At the same time, the Yips' Anglo allies in Vancouver's Liberal Party machine also came under siege. Dissident local leaders split from the party's executive, alleging excessive graft.[49] A series of immigration scandals and a controversial trade policy alienated many voters.[50] Seeing Yip's vulnerability, David Lew chose to target "Liberal machine" corruption (in the language of early twentieth-century political reform).

Even tarnished, Yip On was a political giant, whereas Lew's fame came from his reputation as a daring, brilliant legal warrior. The handsome, ever-fashionable Lew was a charming, fast-moving, smooth-talking rogue—and

FIGURE 1.2. David Lew. Artist unknown. Detail from "Artist's Impressions at Inquiry," *Vancouver World*, 18 January 1911.

he spoke fluent, unaccented English. He had studied Canadian law and was not afraid of challenging established power to protest injustice. Unlike most Chinese, he felt that he could say anything to anyone. He championed the underdog, loved the spotlight, and felt drawn to the shadowy underworld between the Chinese and Anglo societies.[51]

Chinese Canadians admired Lew much as they admired China's unofficial lawyers, the "litigation masters" (*songshi, zhuangshi*), who were able, literate men who could sometimes win justice for the powerless.[52] In the courtroom, Lew "had a mind like a bear trap" and a quick wit that delighted audiences. Chinese Canadians also considered him among the best writers of legal briefs among Chinese Canada's unofficial lawyers.[53]

David Lew cast his campaign against Yip On as a crusade to reform Canada's Chinese immigration system. Drawing on early twentieth-century reform movement politics, he called for a more professional, nonpartisan civil service that would advantage Canadian-oriented brokers like him.[54] Referring to immigration, Lew said, "This matter is too serious to be within the control of party politics." With proper procedures, he argued, the Chinese could avoid the exactions of arbitrary officials. Chinese who won entry also would be freed from suspicion of illegal immigration.[55]

The question of Lew's sincerity divided observers at the time. Like Yip, he had a flair for strategic self-presentation.[56] His backers also included Chinese Canadian business titans who competed with Yip's family for the profits of migration: Chang Toy (Sam Kee, *Chen Daozhi*), Shen Man (*Shen Man*), Lee Saifan (Lee Kee, *Li Shiqi*), and Loo Gee Wing (*Luo Ziyong*).[57] Most likely, Lew and his Chinese backers hedged their bets. If Lew succeeded, they would be ready for reform. If not, they would continue to work within the patronage system.

Three Liberal rising stars also joined Lew's side: lawyers Thomas McInnes, Gordon Grant, and John Wallace de Beque Farris.[58] They defied Vancouver's federal Liberal Party and its machine head, Robert Kelly, because of his alleged excessive graft in Chinese immigration. Kelly also faced criticism at the time for the patronage appointments of judges. All three lawyers had worked with Lew for years on Chinese Canadian legal cases.[59] McInnes was Prime Minister Wilfrid Laurier's agent on Asian immigration matters. Grant and Farris, former members of the Vancouver Liberal Party's executive, possessed inside knowledge of graft, which Lew planned to expose and which they hoped would discredit local party leaders.[60] Grant, a former vice president of Vancouver's Asiatic Exclusion League, also brought into Lew's alliance the Vancouver Trades and Labour Council (VTLC), a long-time opponent of Asian immigration.[61]

Going public with criticism of the Chinese immigration system was a desperate action—and to understand it, it is necessary to explore the circumstances that made Lew and his backers feel desperate. In 1910, a series of events tightened the control of Yip and his Anglo allies over Chinese migration. Canada and the United States moved toward more closed immigration procedures, which isolated arriving Chinese.[62] Court rulings limited Chinese entrants' rights to legal appeal.[63] Competition between various Chinese-Anglo alliances seeking to profit from Chinese migration also escalated into a bitter bidding war. Meanwhile, a backdrop of rising anti-Asian sentiments in British Columbia encouraged officials to extort increasing sums from both legal and illegal Chinese immigrants.[64] Only a few years earlier, in 1907, white mobs had taken to Vancouver's streets, attacking Asian neighborhoods to drive the immigrants out of Canada.[65]

Amid these rising tensions, Lew staked his challenge to Yip On's control. No clear evidence proves whether Lew organized the plan against Yip, or whether he acted solely as the front man. Regardless, the young legal interpreter, who was struggling to pay his debts, found the plan's daring and danger irresistible.[66] As an independent, he worked at the beck and call of the wealthy Chinese merchants who hired him. If he could topple a titan, he would become a titan himself. In any case, Lew's exposé of Yip touched a nerve among Anglos and Chinese who were concerned with the arrogance of established power, shaking both political worlds.[67]

## The Stakes: Chinese Head Tax Enforcement, Collaboration, and Resistance

From the start, enforcement of the Chinese head tax depended on Chinese collaborators, which deeply affected its character. Interpreters handled most communications between arriving immigrants and Anglo officials. Interpreters faced the challenge of carrying out the law within a harsh system, an institutional expression of anti-Chinese racism, while at the same time attempting to mitigate the law's effects for some Chinese. To that end, interpreters often allied with Anglo institutions seeking to profit from Chinese migration, but their own position was fraught with competing tensions. Foon Sien Wong (*Huang Wenfu*), a Chinese Canadian leader who would later work to repeal anti-Chinese immigration laws, never forgot his first impression of Canada. Wong arrived in Vancouver, Canada, in 1910, at the age of nine.[68] When his ship landed, British Canadian guards herded all Chinese passengers into an immigration detention shed while the European passengers disembarked.[69] The guards locked Wong in a cell with iron bars until his father, a shopkeeper in Cumberland, British Columbia, could travel to Vancouver to claim him. Wong had never been outside China and was terrified. The British guards teased him mercilessly, calling him a "pig" and other names he did not understand. They also cut off his queue, the long hair worn by Chinese males as a sign of loyalty to China's government.[70] As each day passed in jail, Wong and other Chinese passengers grew more anxious, fearing that they would be sent back to China. To free his son, Wong's father first had to bribe the Chinese interpreter, Yip On.[71] Next, Yip On interviewed the father and son separately in the presence of Anglo official J. Mackenzie Bowell, who did not understand Chinese. Yip declared that the father's answers matched those of his son and that the father was a legitimate merchant whose family was exempt from paying the head tax.[72] Wong was free to go, but Canada's sorting process had left an unwelcome message. Many Canadians, he later wrote, treat the Chinese as "devils" and "dogs."[73]

Anglo officials seeking to collect the head tax often asked for the Chinese interpreter's advice to help them decide cases. Otherwise, they had great difficulty determining whether Chinese deserved exemptions. The legal categories were ambiguous. The law exempted merchants from the head tax but gave little guidance about how to verify claims.[74] The law also stipulated that each Chinese should pay only once and that British subjects, such as naturalized citizens and Canadian-born individuals, were exempt.[75] Many Chinese attempted to evade the head tax by making fraudulent claims.[76] In addition, the law sometimes seemed to imply contradictory actions. While officials were supposed to reject any Chinese likely to become unemployed, the law instructed them to deny entry to any immigrant with a prearranged job.[77] Officials also had the power to turn back any entrant deemed "unsuitable."[78] China's government provided no reliable documentation on any of these factors, and Chinese interpreters became key actors in determining how the law affected individual immigrants.

As a result, Chinese regarded Canada's immigration system as arbitrary. In the detention shed, the young Wong probably heard other Chinese talking about Yip On. Chinese who made their travel arrangements through Yip's brother in Hong Kong found entry to be smooth and easy. For these Chinese, Yip On did not even translate British Canadian officials' questions, and he lent them "show money" to prove their bona fides as good immigrants.[79] Other Chinese faced more prolonged investigations of their class status and identities. In 1908, Lum Ching Ling, an English-speaker and twenty-nine-year resident of British Columbia, returned to Canada after a visit to China. Yip and Lum knew each other, but Yip denied all evidence of Lum's merchant status and naturalized citizenship. Yip On detained Lum until he paid the $500 Chinese head tax as if he were a newly arrived Chinese laborer.[80] Like Lum, a great many Chinese returning from visits to China struggled to prove their identities. Most Chinese had even more difficulties returning because, unlike Lum, they did not speak English well. No Anglo immigration officials could speak or read Chinese. The language barrier made it especially difficult for Chinese Canadians to prove their previous residence.[81] Historian Edgar Wickberg described their dilemma:

> Many Chinese were semiliterate in English, had never standardized Romanized equivalents of their Chinese names, and were easily confused and intimidated by the situation. As if that were not enough, the names of the Blue Funnel steamships on which many Chinese came to Canada (some examples are: "Philoctetes" and "Protesalaeus") seemed to be fiendishly designed to defeat comprehension in memory of both Chinese passenger and immigration agent.[82]

One Chinese detainee in Victoria carved his anguish into the detention shed's wall in 1919: "When I think of the foreign barbarians, my anger will rise sky high. They put me in jail and make me suffer this misery. I moan until the early dawn. But who will console me here?"[83] Ensnared in the head tax's bureaucratic maze, they hoped that the official interpreter would help free them—or at least not hinder them.

## Controlling and Exploiting Chinese Migration

Estimates suggest that Yip On may have helped Chinese to defraud Canada of $1 million in head taxes between 1906 and 1910 in addition to allowing in as many 2,000 entrants on false papers.[84] Workers who impersonated established Chinese residents had a greater chance of entry; they also avoided the $500 head tax.[85] Fraudulent Chinese merchants paid a price in bribes that was higher than the head tax they avoided, but in exchange, they gained a more secure status.[86] Chinese certified in Canada as "merchants" could legally enter the United States, the destination for two-thirds of Vancouver entrants.[87] Merchants' wives and children also did not have to pay Chinese head taxes. In contrast, Chinese workers often found bringing families from China unaffordable. Further, fraudulent merchant papers allowed Canadian Pacific Railway (CPR) steamships to exceed Canada's legal limit of one head-tax-paying Chinese passenger per fifty tons of ship's weight.[88] Most Chinese arrivals continued to pay the head tax, but Yip's control of the interpreter post enabled him to preside over extensive graft and fraud.

When David Lew challenged Yip On, he also challenged the Yip family's backers on both sides of the racial divide. Chinese regarded the head tax as unjust, creating a market for its evasion, and they saw Yip as a dominant broker to Canadian corporations and political parties. This mingling of interests helped to create an unofficial political economy of migration, which Yip and Lew fought to control. The long-term strength of Yip's alliance with the Liberal Party came from his family's business, which sent a steady stream of Chinese passengers and freight on the Canadian Pacific Railway's train and steamship lines.[89] The Yip family's alliance with the CPR began during its construction, when Yip On's uncle Yip Sang (*Ye Liansheng*) parlayed his railway-building experience into an exclusive position as Vancouver's Chinese CPR ticket agent. Steamship and railway lines profited greatly from Chinese passenger traffic, and at election time, these corporations donated generously to political parties that supported their business interests.[90] They also aggrandized favored Chinese brokers by appointing them as exclusive Chinese ticket agents. Yip Sang probably arranged through the CPR for his nephews Yip Yen and Yip On to become Vancouver's Chinese immigration interpreters.

Like the Yip family, other Chinese immigration interpreters usually leveraged their official power to become steamship and rail ticket agents. In Victoria and Vancouver, they earned three to four times their official salary from commissions.[91] Their control over Chinese entries and exits made them powerful and rich. They could also steer passengers to their favored shipping lines. The CPR backed Yip, while Chinese merchants in Lew's alliance sold tickets for the rival Blue Funnel, Weir, and NYK steamship lines. No Anglo CPR agents would sell train or steamship tickets to Chinese, so Chinese ticket agents/interpreters effectively controlled emigrants' ability to return to China.[92] The practice followed Chinese diaspora precedents from the United States and Southeast Asia. In these places, as in Canada, Chinese ticket agents and interpreters collaborated with governments, transportation companies, and local Chinese associations to "tax" returning Chinese or to prevent their return to China if they had unpaid debts.[93] Canada's ruling parties also protected the Yips despite repeated complaints about irregularities in the handling of Chinese immigration.[94]

Like its U.S. and British steamship competitors, the CPR's *Empress* steamship line did little to enforce immigration laws. During the early 20th century, the CPR brought in thousands of Italian and Japanese contract workers in defiance of Canadian, Japanese, and Italian laws.[95] The CPR also helped to conceal many indebted Chinese immigrants who might otherwise have been rejected for entry by paying Canadian head taxes for nearly all Chinese passengers in one lump sum.[96] Illegal entry increased ticket sales and made immigrants even more dependent on the brokers who knew their secret.

Thousands of Chinese chose to enter as illegal immigrants, a legal limbo that made their position even more precarious; they looked to leaders like Yip for protection. Before 1913, Canada's Chinese entry documents lacked photos, so a black market in used immigration papers flourished.[97] Officials noted that over 99 percent of Chinese immigrants "lost" their entry documents.[98] Moreover, Chinese exit certificates lacked photos until 1 October 1910.[99] In Canadian ports, Chinese sailors on Pacific liners changed their clothes in town, applied for exit certificates under new identities, then sold the certificates to smuggling rings in Hong Kong. Older Chinese across the province claimed to be merchants, sometimes falsely, so that they could sponsor the head-tax-exempt entry of younger men as "paper sons."[100] Illegal migrants without papers came in considerable numbers as well; they hid from often indifferent Canadian authorities with the assistance of ships' Chinese crews.[101] They climbed down anchor chains, jumped out of portholes, and disembarked at remote lumber mills and coaling depots, where steamers docked beyond the view of immigration officials.[102] Thus, through black markets in immigration papers, invented identities, fraudulent relationships, and human smuggling, Chinese found many ways to evade Canada's immigration laws.

This unofficial political economy of migration also depended on business networks in China and Hong Kong. Canada's unpredictable officials made Chinese immigrants anxious to prearrange screening by a friendly interpreter in Vancouver. For ordinary men, emigration required borrowing what was, by Chinese standards, an enormous sum (Can$600–700) to cover the head tax, travel, and emigration assistance. Families saved for years to sponsor a single immigrant. To borrow money from emigration firms required raising a 25 percent cash down payment. In 1902, unskilled workers in China made an average of 3.5 Canadian cents per day.[103] Estate records and oral histories suggest that immigration costs exceeded most immigrant workers' total net worth even after many years in Canada.[104]

The political economy of international migration brought together immigrants, Chinese local elites, and Canadian brokers in a web of interdependent relationships. For example, in 1910, Mak Wai of San Chuen in Taishan County, Guangdong, wanted to go to Canada. In China, he gave his name and photograph to unnamed "gentlemen" in his village. These gentlemen arranged for a Chinese passport stating that Mak was a rice merchant, and the British consul approved his claim to Canadian status as a head-tax-exempt merchant. When Canadian officials in Vancouver questioned him without Yip On's expected aid, Mak cracked under the pressure. He admitted that his father was a Chinese laundryman in Philadelphia, which was his most likely destination.[105] Mak had bought his papers and steamship ticket through one of the many Hong Kong emigration firms active in Guangdong's Pearl River Delta. Yip On's brother operated one of these firms. Yip Yen sold CPR tickets, arranged immigration to the Americas, handled immigrants' banking, and conducted transpacific trade.[106] The presence of his famous brother, Yip On, as Vancouver's interpreter, would have helped sales considerably. To Yip On and David Lew, the interpreter post was more than a job: the victor could partly control and channel the profits of Chinese migration.

## Gatekeepers Who Left the Door Ajar

As Yip On discovered, Canadian officials' procedures made head tax evasion through impersonation simple. Chinese immigrants could easily memorize a coaching book of right answers to the standard questionnaire. Most false papers came with these coaching books, along with contracts that required immigrants to maintain a consistent appearance of belonging to their paper family.[107] According to the records of Canada's Department of Trade, which administered the Chinese head tax as part of its customs mandate from 1885 to 1911, officials judged whether merchant status was warranted through a two-step process.[108] The first step examined the prospective merchant's documentation. Before 1907, Canada's officials depended on British consular affidavits. Agents of the Yip family then began to sell "genuine" Chinese viceroy of Liangguang passports that certified Chinese merchant status. Emigrants purchased these passports, obtained Canadian visas from the British consul in Hong Kong, and then entered Canada under aliases.[109] In Guangdong, China, a network of local brokers affiliated with the Yip family marketed these immigration packages in Taishan County's cities, towns, and villages and in Guangzhou.[110] For example, Ng Yik met a scholar outside the Liangguang viceroy's court. For Mex$90, the scholar arranged for a merchant passport that certified Ng exempt from the head tax.[111] At first, Canadian customs officials were surprised that merchant immigrants arrived with only Chinese-language documentation of their status.[112] In 1908, Vancouver customs collector J. M. Bowell consulted his superior in Ottawa, immigration controller Francis C. T. O'Hara. O'Hara concluded that the Chinese passports, which no Anglo official could read, were sufficient proof. To maintain Bowell's cooperation, Canada's cabinet subsequently voted to raise his annual salary from $400 to $700, despite the fact that he was the son of a former Conservative Party prime minister.[113] The raise indicated that backers of illegal immigration had substantial influence within the Liberal Party.

The second step in judging Chinese merchants' claims, the interviews, also left ample room for officials' interpretation. Canadian officials used standard questionnaires to ask simple questions about entrants' business activities. The form that recorded their answers had room for only cursory replies.[114] Officials also examined each entrant's appearance, clothing, hands, and intonation for clues to his class status.[115] The entrant also had to display sufficient cash and credit to convince officials that he could start a business in Canada. Fathers and sons had to give the same answers to a standard questionnaire about their family in order to share a head tax exemption. Officials also asked fathers to pick their "sons" out of a group of boys.[116] Returning Chinese had to match answers to questionnaires filled out at the time of their departure. Their height, weight, and identifying marks also had to be similar to their exit certificate.[117]

The increasing standardization of Canada's head tax system paralleled trends in the United States' enforcement of its Chinese exclusion law.[118] However, Canada's system diverged from the U.S. model because the ruling parties did not attempt to create a strong Chinese immigration system. They did not hire full-time Chinese interpreters. Frontline Anglo officials were also part time; they devoted most of their time to handling customs.[119] In addition, the Canadian government relied on the CPR for Vancouver's Chinese detention shed until 1914 or 1915, allowing the CPR's Chinese ticket agents free access to all detainees.[120] The simple, underfunded system prompted Anglo officials to rely on Chinese interpreters' judgments. As a result, politically appointed interpreters became the head tax's *de facto* chief gatekeepers.

## *Opportunity for Challenge: Contests over Chinese Diaspora Leadership*

Yip On's Chinese Canadian political machine maintained his dominance as a power broker only as long as it was united. Between 1899 and 1906, his leadership in the Chinese Empire Reform Association (CERA) lifted him to the peak of Chinese Canadian authority.[121] This organization promoted democratic reform of imperial China's politics.[122] It also helped to transform

China's urban citizenry, mobilized mass protests against U.S. anti-Chinese laws, and fostered civil society through the publication of China's first modern newspapers.[123] Many of British Columbia's wealthiest Chinese merchants, including Chang Toy, Lee Saifan, and Loo Gee Wing joined CERA. Despite the fact that their individual businesses competed with the Yip family's firms, Yip persuaded Chinese Canadian merchants to buy a great number of shares in CERA's investment fund. They trusted that Yip would invest their money wisely, and in the fund's first few years, investors enjoyed dividends.[124]

Yip's political influence also came from the Chinese Freemasons (*CF, Chee Kung Tong, Zhigongtang*), a Chinese brotherhood (triad, secret society) that dominated British Columbia's Chinese communities. The CF was Canada's first pan-Chinese organization, uniting a community divided by dialect and region. It soon became a central organization for community governance, support, and protection, enrolling at least half of all Chinese Canadians as members. By 1914, it had over forty branches and claimed between 10,000 and 20,000 members.[125] Chinese along the West Coast both admired and feared Yip's clout with the CF and its North American federation of tongs, along with his CERA leadership. Few Chinese dared to oppose him by speaking publicly of revolution in China.[126] The Chinese Freemasons' power also helped to keep Yip's graft alliance with the Liberal Party quiet and provided a mechanism to enforce contracts and debts and to maintain the secrets related to illegal immigration.

Between 1907 and 1910, however, divisions began to sunder the CERA/CF political machine's power in Canada—and some of Yip's former allies turned on him. The collapse of CERA reduced Yip's stature across the Pacific world and in Canada. It is possible that Lew's challenge to Yip's leadership may have been related to settling scores within Chinese exile politics.[127] For example, Yip On had arranged for the CERA fund to invest in the building of the Canton-to-Hankow railway in Guangdong. Under pressures associated with the 1905 boycott, China had ejected its previous U.S. and Belgian owners. Yip now helped to supervise the construction. To many Chinese, his railway-building efforts made him a hero of national development. However, the railway firm's slow progress in laying track elicited fierce attacks from disappointed U.S. and Mexican CERA investors. A Hong Kong newspaper accused Yip of fraud, but U.S. consular officials noted that the railway's lack of "any substantial accomplishments" arose from local political conflicts in Guangdong.[128] In 1907, a financial panic caused recessions in the United States, Canada, and Mexico, bankrupting CERA's banks in New York and Torreon. As CERA investments began to fail, expected dividends to party shareholders disappeared along with any hope of recouping their initial outlay.[129]

Chinese exile politics of reform and revolution further divided Yip's once-mighty machine. As bungled investments caused CERA to implode, Chinese Canadian merchants sustained the worst losses.[130] Yip On also had borrowed $129,000 from the party's investment funds, which he never returned, leading to accusations of embezzlement.[131] He had strong influence within Guangzhou's and Hong Kong's militantly nationalistic Canton merchants' Self-Governing Association (SGA, *Yueshang Zizhi Hui*).[132] Yip helped to lead the SGA and CERA in a popular boycott of Japanese goods between 1908 and 1909, which involved both China and the Chinese diaspora.[133] In 1910, the SGA boycotted the city of San Francisco to protest the opening of the Angel Island Immigration Station, a new U.S. detention center for arriving Chinese.[134] In 1909 or 1910, the Yips quit CERA and endorsed Dr. Sun Yat Sen's (*Sun Zhongshan*) plan to overthrow China's monarchy. Apparently, Yip still held strong influence within the CF, because his endorsement freed many West Coast Chinese to declare their own revolutionary intentions.[135] Sun's revolutionaries, however, regarded Canada's CF and the Yip-allied SGA as his rivals.[136] In short, China's exile politics provided no shortage of motives. Indeed, Lew's ally Tom McInnes said that he tried to depose Yip in order to curry favor with unspecified powers in China.[137] Whatever the cause of their dispute, Lew and Yip became bitter rivals who used their allies in government to strike at each other.

## *Competing Chinese-Anglo Alliances and the Quest for Political Checks to Power*

Vancouver's Liberal Party machine took advantage of the divisions between leading Chinese Canadian brokers to foment a bidding war. In 1907, the party's chief fixers, Robert Kelly and MP Robert Macpherson, pitted Yip and Lew against each other for control over Chinese illegal immigration.[138] As an Asiatic Exclusion League chapter formed in Vancouver and began to plan a terrible night of violent racial terror, Macpherson publicly "demanded that 'Canada be kept a White man's country' and that 'the influx of Asiatics . . . be stopped.'"[139] Meanwhile, Macpherson and Kelly privately raised the cost of Chinese immigration. Many Chinese transactions required a bribe: merchant entry, certificate to visit the United States, entry of family members, reentry. Even real Chinese merchants had to pay $100 for their sons' admission at Vancouver.[140] The threat of anti-Asian violence prompted Yip and Lew to increase their bribes in hopes of winning political favor, which raised the price of illegal immigration by at least one-third. The bidding war continued into August 1907, when the Liberal Party executive apparently made a deal with Yip.[141]

In September, a white anti-Asian riot in Vancouver increased the political risk to Yip's Anglo allies. Ten thousand whites marched in a protest parade against Asian immigration. As leading Liberals addressed the crowd, white rioters split off and attacked Chinese, Japanese, and East Indian neighborhoods in two nights of racial terror, broken glass, fire, and pitched street battles.[142] Higher bribe costs followed. By 1910, Chinese had to pay Mex$1,100 (more than Can$500) to arrange fraudulent entry as head-tax-exempt "merchants,"[143] including steamship tickets, fraudulent documents, coaching, and prearranged bribes. Anglo protectors enjoyed the most profit from the bribes. For example, a Chinese worker entrant who "reused" another immigrant's head tax papers paid Can$120 in bribes. The lower price reflected that his "worker" status did not confer the benefits of "merchant" status. Yip On himself collected only one-sixth of the bribe (Can$20) per Chinese worker "reusing head tax papers" whereas Anglo customs officials split Can$100.[144] Anglo officials probably garnered even larger bribes from fraudulent Chinese merchants. The number of Chinese head-tax-exempted immigrants entering at Vancouver rose dramatically from double to triple digits between 1904 and 1910.[145] The increase in Chinese merchants also was dramatic: 12 arrived in 1904 and 169 came in 1910.[146] In any case, leading Liberals who condoned Yip's deal expected that Anglo beneficiaries would return a good proportion of Chinese bribes to the Liberal Party. The receivers of bribes' apparent failure to abide by the unwritten rules of the patronage game suggested a complacent sense of entitlement.[147] Disaffected Liberals probably felt that Yip's Chinese race made him a softer target for striking at Kelly's machine.

Two U.S. events increased pressures on Lew's alliance. In 1909, the U.S. government had handed over *de facto* control of legal Chinese immigration from Canada to Yip On, which suggests that Yip had powerful U.S. supporters. Henceforth, all Chinese arriving in Canada who wished to enter the United States legally had to be certified by Canada's Chinese immigration officials at Vancouver as part of a U.S. policy to deter Chinese Canadians' entry.[148] Moreover, in 1910, the United States closed all other border crossings to Chinese. Until then, thousands of Chinese had traveled by rail from Vancouver to eastern Canada to slip over the border into locales in New York and Vermont where officials and courts appeared friendly to Chinese claims to be U.S. citizens.[149] The Vancouver monopoly on processing U.S.-bound Chinese Canadians also cost Canada's railway companies—and their Chinese ticket agents—considerable revenue.[150]

The changing legal conditions of the Chinese head tax's administration provoked Lew's challenge. In 1910, Chinese Canadians suffered a devastating legal defeat. Following U.S. precedent, the courts declared in the Chinese Canadian *habeas corpus* case of *In re Lee Him* that immigration officials' judgments were not subject to legal appeal. The decision gave official interpreters like Yip On even more power.[151] The court's verdict came as head tax enforcement in Vancouver shifted toward a more closed system. Whereas during the previous decade, third parties like Anglo lawyers often participated in Chinese immigration interviews, by 1910, Canadian authorities had grown suspicious of outside helpers. Legal interpreters like David Lew could no longer provide help from the outside by marshaling Anglo lawyers, business associates, and political connections to free their clients. Court cases and testimony from lawyers and legal interpreters involved in resolving detainees' problems documented this trend.[152] Even before *In re Lee Him*, Chinese had few legal rights to appeal immigration officials' decisions. Between 1905 and 1910, David Lew's allied Anglo lawyers had attempted to check immigration officials' power through a series of habeas corpus court cases. The most notable victory came in 1905, in *In re Chin Chee*, which strengthened immigrants' rights to return to their established homes in Canada even if they left for brief visits to the old country.[153] However, by 1910, Lew's allies had exhausted the possible legal challenges to the head tax system. Only through politics could they hope to check immigration officials' power.

## *Power Brokerage from the Top Down: Prime Ministerial Conversations to Bureaucratic Infighting*

David Lew began the fight in Canada's capital, Ottawa, where he sought Liberal Party support while trying to show Chinese that he could represent them better than Yip On. To that end, Tom McInnes introduced David Lew to Prime Minister Wilfrid Laurier.[154] The prestigious audience conferred great honor on Lew as a broker. Between 1885 and 1945, few Chinese Canadians directly spoke with national political leaders. As late as the 1950s, British Columbia Chinese regarded a leader who achieved direct access to Ottawa as extraordinary.[155] McInnes was Laurier's trusted advisor on Asian immigration matters.[156] Laurier's view of CERA was positive, and Lew was a CERA member.[157] McInnes also had represented CERA in negotiations about possible Pacific trade ventures with a number of Canadian corporate executives from Montreal and the West.[158] Thus, Lew's audience with Laurier gave him instant credibility as a leading political broker as it demonstrated the power of his Chinese and British allies.

Lew's request to Laurier echoed a personal appeal made by CERA president Kang Youwei to U.S. president Theodore Roosevelt during the 1905 boycott. Lew argued for a mutual treaty to limit immigration, like Canada had with Japan. He claimed that repealing the head tax system would improve Canada's trade relations with China. No record exists of any public response, though Lew and McInnes believed that their appeal would have a significant effect in the near future.[159]

Lew's attempt to depose Yip On also involved him in the internal power struggles of Canadian and U.S. immigration officials. His rising star opened doors within the civil service bureaucracy. For ten days in Ottawa, Lew met with high-ranking Liberals to discuss improving the handling of Chinese immigration. To override Kelly's machine in Vancouver, he presented evidence of Yip On's immigration frauds directly to senior officials, including Chinese immigration controller F. C. T. O'Hara.[160] O'Hara launched a dominion Secret Service investigation of Chinese frauds at Vancouver.[161] Detective work was Lew's specialty. He had worked extensively with the U.S. immigration service and with British Columbia's provincial police; so O'Hara arranged that Lew meet with Colonel Percy Sherwood, head of Canada's Secret Service, to plan a dominion police investigation into Yip's conduct.[162]

Lew next headed to the United States to rally support against Yip On and to collect evidence of his alleged smuggling.[163] Lew's aims in the United States appeared to be twofold. He wanted to find evidence to discredit Yip On, and he wanted to break Yip's power over Chinese migration to both the United States and Canada. To block Lew, Yip denied him a Chinese merchant's certificate that would permit him to legally visit the United States.[164] When Lew's train crossed the border, U.S. immigration authorities detained him for three days, until Colonel Clark, a U.S. immigration official in Montreal, secured his release.[165] Lew's first stop was Chicago, where he visited U.S. immigration inspector Dr. P. L. Prentiss. In 1909, Lew had brought to Prentiss's attention that Yip On had unfairly denied a group of Chinese Canadian merchants certificates needed to visit the Seattle World's Fair, which Prentiss reversed.[166] Most likely, Lew hoped that discrediting Yip might force U.S. officials to reverse the policy of making Vancouver officials the arbiters of Chinese entry from Canada.

Lew then crossed the continent, seeking evidence of Yip's involvement in smuggling Chinese into the United States, which involved Chinese merchants in Vancouver and CF lodges in the United States that coordinated

Chinese illegal immigration.[167] In Washington state, Lew sought evidence against Yip by helping U.S. immigration officials to decipher coded letters seized from Chinese illegal immigrants.[168] He returned to Vancouver without definitive proof, but with stronger political allies in both the U.S. and Canadian immigration services.

## Battle of the Transnational Networks and Their Local Chinese-Anglo Alliances

Lew then escalated to direct challenge, setting off a battle between the two leaders' Chinese-Anglo alliances and their larger transnational networks. When Lew returned to Vancouver, he worked with Edward Foster, a dominion Secret Service agent from Ottawa, to gather evidence about Yip On's smuggling ring.[169] Lew suggested a ruse to trap Yip On. Yip routinely met Vancouver Chinese passengers aboard CPR ships in Victoria, a port eighty miles from Vancouver. Here, Yip prepared Chinese immigrants for their upcoming Vancouver interviews.[170] Lew asked the government to temporarily remove Yip On. Lew would stand in and gather incriminating evidence.[171] Pretending to be Yip's agent, Lew collected letters from arriving Chinese on the CPR steamer *Empress of China* that detailed their plans to pose fraudulently as merchants and evade the head tax.[172] The documents Lew gathered showed that three parties within the Yip family arranged immigration frauds: Yip On's firm, his brother Charlie Yip Yen's firm in Hong Kong, and his uncle Yip Sang's Wing Sang Company (*Yong Sheng Gongsi*) in Vancouver.[173] Yip On himself had brought in typesetters and an editor for the CERA newspaper, *Xin Bao*. He also brought in workers for various Yip companies.[174] The Yips, however, quickly recovered from the surprise of Lew's ruse. As the *Empress of China* sailed from Victoria for the two-hour journey to Vancouver, they prepared a counterattack.

When the *Empress of China* arrived at Vancouver, Yip On orchestrated chaos, enabling his family members to speak with arriving Chinese passengers.[175] Guards delayed steering Chinese passengers to the detention shed, allowing them to mix with the crowd at the docks. Once the Yips had gathered the information they needed, the guards hustled the male Chinese to the shed. The Yips told the Chinese passengers to retract the statements they had made to Lew. Yip On's partner, Yip Sue Poy, also cabled to Yip Yen in Hong Kong, warning him to stop sending so many fraudulent merchants, "Strictly select a few come. Don't bring letters."[176]

Later that evening, Lew and Foster saw a Chinese man lurking on the wharf, waiting to throw a package of tea through the window of the immigration detention shed. They seized the package and found the following letter inside:

> It is rumoured that you have stated the amount of money paid for guarantee landing. How did you come to leak that out. If you are asked why did you write to Yip On, this shows some secrecy, you must answer, "I do not know Yip On," but say this man Lew instructed me what to write in order to be landed so I wrote accordingly. You must remember this.[177]

To Yip, the investigation signaled that his Liberal Party backers had been outfoxed in Ottawa. He had to change the political arena to a more favorable setting fast. In September 1910, Yip left Canada for an unspecified foreign country.[178] He asked his allies to rally his supporters in Canada, Hong Kong, and China. At community meetings in Vancouver and Victoria, Yip's allied Chinese Canadian merchants raised funds to pay for his legal defense. The meetings also resolved to appeal for help from China. Yip's supporters sent cables to the SGA, to Hong Kong's Sei Yap Board of Labour and Trades (SBLT), and to the Chinese viceroy of Liangguang.[179] As a matter of respect, they demanded that any Chinese who had merchant credentials issued by China's government and approved by the British consul should have his status honored.[180] Put simply, Yip's allies hoped for a repeat of the 1905 U.S. boycott's impact. They wanted to force Canada to halt its inquiry into Chinese merchants' credentials, saving Yip On and protecting the channels for head tax evasion. Surviving English Canadian newspapers do not record whether the SGA or SBLT replied, and Chinese Canadian coverage has not been preserved. However, to Canadian corporations involved in Pacific trade, like the CPR, the threat would have been clear. The 1905 boycott, as well as the two SGA boycotts, won national attention in the United States and Canada.[181] The SGA's boycott of Japanese goods from 1908 through 1910 caused a 24 percent drop in Japan's trade through Hong Kong and affected Japanese shipping lines serving Canada as well.[182] In the fall of 1910, as the Royal Commission prepared its investigation, SGA's embargo of San Francisco over U.S. immigration policy—particularly its protest against the treatment of Chinese "merchants"—reduced U.S.–China trade 20 percent.[183]

Given this context, Yip On's appeal to the SGA evoked a boycott threat to Canada's, and perhaps the British Empire's, trade with China. This threat to Canadian corporate interests, including the CPR's *Empress* line, may have started a groundswell for Yip that eroded Lew's Liberal Party backing.[184] Surviving records from Canada's Department of Trade related to head tax administration do not reveal any formal government reaction to the boycott threat.[185] However, it appeared to dampen Canada's sudden ardor for enforcing immigration law.

In Canada and China, the Yips' allies also mobilized against Lew by appealing to Guangdong migrants' local identities. Among his supporters, Yip described the conflict as part of a "tong war" between Chinese from two regions of Guangdong's Pearl River Delta over controlling the interpreter post.[186] The two regions differed by dialect, class, and legacies of domination. Like the Yips, two-thirds of Chinese in Canada came from *Siyi* (Sei Yap), the Four Counties region.[187] *Siyi* supplied mainly migrant workers to North America's Chinese diaspora; these people spoke dialects unintelligible to speakers of standard Cantonese. The more affluent *Sanyi* (Sam Yap) came from the Three Counties region, which lay closer to Guangzhou and Macau, and spoke standard Cantonese. During the pioneer days, *Sanyi* merchants who had brought capital from China dominated Chinese life in the United States. By the early twentieth century, *Siyi* struggled to break free of *Sanyi* power; to that end, *Siyi* in the United States, led by Yip On, had boycotted *Sanyi* merchants.[188] If Lew's faction succeeded, both of Canada's Pacific ports would fall into *Sanyi* hands. (The Chinese interpreter at Victoria, Lee Mongkow, was *Sanyi*.) Except for Lee Saifan, Lew's backers all came from *Sanyi's* Panyu County, a suburban district of Guangzhou. Most likely, their tong was the Chong Hoo Tong (*Chang Hou Tang*), run by merchants from Panyu County.[189] (Lee, a *Siyi*, probably joined the effort because his businesses competed with the Yips'.) Fearing *Sanyi* power, *Siyi* merchants held citizens' meetings in Vancouver, Victoria, and Nanaimo, organizing a See Yip Benevolent Association (*Siyi Huiguan*) to defend Yip.[190] They also organized a boycott of Lew; its enforcers probably came from the CF.[191] The boycott cost Lew both Chinese and Anglo business.[192] Vancouver's Chinese Board of Trade, the Chinese Chamber of Commerce, and British Columbia's *Siyi* Board of Trade also contributed funds for Yip's legal defense. The meetings intimidated opponents and reminded *Sanyi* of the *Siyi* majority's power.

Yip also worked to deflect Lew's blow through his allies in the Liberal Party and the CPR. Arguing that Lew could not be trusted, Yip managed to arrange that the ordinary practice of interviewing Chinese arrivals in seclusion be suspended. When David Lew conducted immigration interviews with Chinese "merchants" who had arrived on the *Empress of China* on 30 September 1910, thirteen official observers watched his every move. They included the dominion counsel, an attorney for the applicants paid for by the

Chinese Board of Trade, the Chinese consul, the president of the Chinese Chamber of Commerce, the president of the Chinese Citizens Association, Edward Foster, Won Alexander Cumyow, a stenographer, the general Vancouver CPR passenger agent, and a CPR attorney.[193] Yip's supporters hired an Anglo lawyer, S. S. Taylor, and three Chinese Canadian interpreters to help the Chinese "merchants" counter Lew's accusations of immigration fraud.[194]

Lew refused to be intimidated when he conducted the Chinese passengers' interviews. He immediately moved beyond the government's short standard questionnaire, exposing its inadequacy. He probed every story, displaying the virtuosity of a trial lawyer as each man's case crumbled into inconsistencies, evasions, and lies. Lew's discoveries strengthened his claim that the head tax system should be based on truth rather than farce. The merchant candidates, all men from Taishan County, Guangdong, in *Siyi*, brought with them Chinese viceroy's passports and invalid "drafts" for cash to be drawn from local Chinese firms as proof of their merchant status.[195] For example, Chung Kwong, twenty-six, of Tai Shee Wo, Taishan, claimed to be a merchant from Kong Moon City in Xinhui. Under questioning from Lew, he admitted that he did not know Kong Moon well. He could not recall any firms, people, or steamers there. When immigration officials searched his luggage, they found many white cloth coats of the type worn by cooks.[196] The men admitted that local gentry in their villages and towns had helped them to obtain viceroy's passports, get British consul visas, and obtain their steamship tickets. Many had purchased their CPR tickets through the Chung Hing Company, probably an affiliate of Yip Yen's emigration business in Hong Kong. Chung also carried a letter from Yin Lung Tong, stating that he and eleven or twelve other passengers from "Fong Kin Show's place" were "guaranteed passage." The letter included the statement, "I received from Fong 30 small gold pieces, bade me when landed to hand to interpreter for his own use. Fong has a letter for each individual to bring along to be handed to Yip Ting Sam."[197] "Yip Ting Sam" was another name for Yip On.[198] These interviews proved extremely damaging to Yip; the power struggle within the Liberal Party over which faction would prevail intensified.

Victories and losses for both sides rapidly followed, showing the fluid nature of each Chinese-British faction's political influence. Shortly after Yip's dismissal, party leader Robert Kelly convened a meeting of the local Liberal Party executive in Vancouver to address Lew's accusations of political corruption. Fearing discovery of their own involvement, the Liberal executive complained that its prerogative to advise on appointments in Vancouver had been overridden. Moreover, it claimed that Lew was dishonest. Members alleged that Lew wanted the position for his own profit and for the foreign Blue Funnel line's advantage over the Canadian-owned CPR.[199] The claim attempted to neutralize Lew's image as a reformer and to make the contest about supporting Canada's economy.

Kelly's party machine also fought to protect Yip, resulting in a struggle in both the ruling party and the government bureaucracy. With Kelly, cabinet minister William Templeman allegedly visited dominion policeman Edward Foster late at night. They reportedly told him to back off from investigating Yip and "not to harm the Liberal Party." Bowell then reinstated Yip On as Vancouver's interpreter.[200] On 14 November 1910, Lew reported to the minister of customs that prominent members of the Liberal Party in the cabinet and the Vancouver party executive had thwarted his investigation because of their involvement in Yip On's Chinese immigration frauds.[201] The charges reached Prime Minister Laurier, resulting in Lew's reinstatement and a second dismissal of Yip.[202] Shortly afterward, the federal government dismissed Lew again and hired a new Chinese interpreter for Vancouver, Poon Shang Lung, at the recommendation of Yip's faction.[203] Poon promptly resumed Yip's illegal immigration scheme.[204] Meanwhile, the CPR ordered that Lew not be admitted to its facilities so that he could not report on Poon's activities.[205] However, Lew's accusation that a cabinet minister had impeded a police inquiry to protect his own graft forced public scrutiny of the alleged cover-up.

Laurier ordered a Royal Commission to explore the handling of Chinese immigration at Vancouver, with Lew as the expected star witness. Yip's allies then stepped up the pressure on Lew. At first, Chinese who resented Yip On had rejoiced at his downfall, but the fierce counterattack quickly silenced them.[206] Yip's allies in the CF probably provided the intimidation. Unnamed Chinese men attempted to bribe Lew to halt his inquiry. He refused. The men then threatened Lew with death if he pursued the matter further.[207] The two Vancouver Chinese newspapers owned by the Yips printed editorials denouncing Lew as a "traitor to the Chinese." The Chinese newspapers also reported that the merchant Wong Lung, one of Lew's former legal clients, had offered a $3,000 bounty for Lew's murder.[208] The two newspapers also called for a public boycott of Lew. Enforcers levied fines on and threatened to boycott persons dealing with Lew. Chinese and Anglos, even people Lew thought were friends, cursed him as a "squealer." Wherever he went, Chinese threw mud at him, calling him a "dirty spotter," a "spy," and more profane epithets. Colonel Sherwood, head of Canada's Secret Service, heard that Lew would be killed by Christmas.[209] Eventually, personal betrayal appeared to break Lew's resolve. In November 1910, Lew's Chinese house servant tried to blind him by poisoning his eyewash with carbolic acid. After that, Lew backed down. He burned all of his correspondence relating to Yip On. By the time Lew testified at the Royal Commission in January 1911, he still had criticisms of Yip, but he could no longer recall any details about the "rumors" of Yip's actions that could lead to a criminal charge.[210] Possibly due to Liberal Party pressures, Edward Foster also destroyed his correspondence and retracted part of his earlier findings about Kelly's Liberal machine's protection of Chinese immigration frauds.

During those same months, the Chinese and their Liberal Party allies battled over control of Chinese illegal immigration elsewhere in British Columbia. In January 1911, Tom Chue Thom, the former immigration interpreter at Nanaimo, wrote to immigration controller O'Hara:

> [T]he old interpreter with dozen of Chinese merchants use financial skime influence the prominent Liberal lawyers to get the appointment of this new interpreter in Vancouver. Well, I know this, as much, your new interpreter got to obey these Chinese merchants.[211]

Thom accused the new interpreter, Poon, of having a criminal record that included fraudulent immigration. The Royal Commission also discovered that Poon and Yip On had been partners in a Toronto opium-dealing business. Thom blamed the strife between the Chinese merchant factions of *Siyi* (Yips) and *Sanyi* (Lew, Chang Toy) for the removal of Lew and the hiring of the "thief," Poon. "Both of them are greedy," Thom wrote. "I know have no chance for the appointment, because, I will not spent money for it, and I did not go through the right party."[212]

The Chinese-language *North American News* condemned Thom's revelations. It called for a public boycott of Thom, his mission school, and his Sunday service. They warned that any Chinese who attended would be fined $30, a month's wages, by pro-Yip enforcers. Chinese notices calling Thom "a traitor to the Chinese" also appeared on telegraph poles in Nanaimo. The flyers stated that neither Thom nor his children were welcome in Nanaimo's Chinatown.[213] Even Thom's Chinese friends tried to organize a "citizens' meeting to denounce him."[214] In the battle for interpreter posts, Chinese and Anglo politics were inextricable.

As the Royal Commission prepared to meet, Yip's ties to Kelly's Liberal machine entwined the two men's fates. Both Yip's and Lew's factions lobbied for their allied Anglo lawyers to win patronage appointments as the Royal Commission's judge and crown counsel.[215] Laurier appointed neither faction's favorites. Neither judge Denis Murphy nor crown counsel George McCrossan appeared to have extensive ties to either side. Nevertheless, their Liberal Party loyalty mattered: Murphy and McCrossan treated their mandate as narrowly defined.[216] They felt reluctant to call all of their party's political appointees to account, though they knew some disclosure was inevitable. If scapegoats had to be found, they would be Chinese because, as Vancouver Liberal executive president Harry Senkler put it, they were "proverbially dishonest."[217]

## Political Accountability and Political Cover: Managing Conflicts over Immigration Frauds at the Royal Commission

As a strategy to manage political conflict, the Royal Commission offered a public, quasi-judicial investigation. Judge Murphy presided over the Royal Commission's public hearings first before a large audience at Vancouver's O'Brien Theatre and later in Victoria and Nanaimo. The Royal Commission's charge mandated that Murphy investigate alleged Chinese frauds and recommend actions to the federal government.[218] To that end, it granted him the power to compel witnesses to testify and to subpoena documents.[219] George McCrossan led the government's inquiry. As the commission opened, McCrossan believed that Yip On was guilty, but he regarded Lew's evidence as possibly tainted.[220] Lew's lack of compliance with the commission's subpoena, particularly the burning of his papers, and Lew's inability to recall the names of his informants made McCrossan suspicious. He subpoenaed both the telegraph office that Lew used to communicate with his co-conspirators and the transpacific cable companies that Yip's allies used to send messages to Hong Kong. McCrossan found that both Yip's and Lew's factions had sent coded messages about their political intrigues.[221] As the commission staff attempted to collect the facts, Yip and Lew fought to redeem their reputations.

Yip On came to the Royal Commission expecting to win. After lawyers for both sides submitted their evidence and lists of witnesses, Yip felt certain of victory, so he returned to Canada to testify in January 1911.[222] Every time McCrossan asked Yip a question at the trial, Yip deflected it with idiocy, playing to Anglo stereotypes of Chinese as simple and childlike. He pretended not to understand English, dropping his usually commanding persona. When McCrossan handed Yip some incriminating cables to read, "His mind, which heretofore was the delight of his countrymen, refused to work. He could not recall a thing." Slowly, he said, "I no send." The cables in question had advised his brother Yip Yen in Hong Kong not to send more illegal immigrants.[223] After his testimony, which fooled no one and said nothing, Yip On sat in the audience, smiling, as David Lew took the stand. A great number of Chinese spectators took out pencils to write down every word that Lew said, and they let it be known that each represented a Chinese organization that would hold him accountable.[224] Despite the fixed fight, Lew was unwilling to be totally destroyed.

David Lew testified in perfect English, dancing around his opponent, parrying incoming blows, but landing only light strikes upon Yip himself. "Did you ever hear any complaint in Chinatown regarding Yip On?" asked McCrossan. "Never a word," said Lew. He claimed to know only rumors about Yip. Lew explained that, after being threatened by both Chinese and Anglos for being a traitor, he had forgotten his sources. His entire report to O'Hara, Lew said, had come from a Chinese newspaper article.[225] McCrossan then read Lew's letters to Ottawa complaining of the extortion of legitimate Chinese merchants and a Liberal Party cover-up. "I do not care to withdraw anything," replied Lew. Ottawa, he said, should make Vancouver's officials more honest in their duties, as Victoria's interpreter, Lee Mongkow, claimed to be.[226]

> [S]aid Mr. Taylor [Yip On's lawyer], "why is the service at Victoria so much better than you say it is here? . . ." "Why," said Lew, "some people can ask questions for two hours and not get as much as others can get by asking just a few questions.""[227]

For Lew, retracting his letters would destroy his credibility, but testifying to their content could get him killed. He chose a middle course, and Yip's dismay was visible.[228]

Taylor, Yip On's attorney, then produced a letter from a fictitious author, "Len Kwong Quock," that accused Lew of conspiring with his Chinese merchant backers to seize the Vancouver interpreter post for himself. Len Kwong Quock claimed that Lew and his supporters had raised a fund of $6,000 for that purpose. Lew expressed indignation, and then lied, saying that he had no interest in the post.[229] His motive, he said, was the public good. The *Vancouver World* reported his less-than-truthful explanation:

> "I am," said Lew, leaning forward with great earnestness, "the only one in all of Chinatown who does not belong to any Tong or party." "Yes," said Mr. Taylor [Yip On's attorney]. "I am aware that you are an exceptional man."[230]

Although it is possible that Lew had the public good in mind, he did belong to a Chinese party, CERA, and to an informal association of Chinese from Panyu. Only Lee Saifan, from *Siyi*, conferred a broader mantle of legitimacy upon Lew's reform campaign.

However, Yip's reframing of the struggle as *Sanyi* versus *Siyi* made Lee's alliance with the *Sanyi* untenable. McCrossan had hoped that Lee's testimony would bury Yip On, but instead Lee praised him. Lee said that Chinese only complained about Yip On because he was "too strict" in enforcing the law. Everything else was "rumor."[231] Because they feared retaliation, most of Lew's Chinese witnesses testified against Yip through intermediaries and by affidavit. According to these men, Yip On's customers ended up in locations as diverse as Vancouver, Minneapolis–St. Paul, and New York City.[232] According to Canadian and U.S. diplomatic correspondence, the illegal immigrants' stories corroborated a pattern of illegal entry well known to officials in both countries.[233] However, neither country's officials disclosed this information at the Royal Commission's public hearings, so the corroborating witnesses appeared unconvincing. Yip On's side responded with hearsay witnesses who attacked Lew as a gambler and a thief.[234] Ultimately, the Royal Commission did not find documentary evidence for most of the accusations against Yip, Lew, and Vancouver's Liberal Party.

However, the commission did find Vancouver immigration procedures to be extremely lax.[235] Officials identified Chinese immigrants who had already paid the $500 head tax by written descriptions. The absence of photographic documentation encouraged fraud, especially because Yip made copies of the descriptions on file.[236] When Chinese immigrants arrived, Yip claimed to verify their identities. If mistakes were made, Yip felt that it was up to the Anglo officials to discover them.[237] The Royal Commission described the port guards, men hired from the Liberal Party list in Ottawa:

W. A. Kent, aged 48, given to drink and unreliable.
T. Physick, aged 63, physically unfit and service unsatisfactory.
H. H. Warburton, 50, cripple and unfit.
J. McPherson, given to drinking and unreliable.[238]

Even the immigration officials' measuring stick for height was discovered to be inaccurate, with one foot being only eleven inches.[239] Such shortcomings were apparently not unusual among patronage appointments.[240]

The Royal Commission's revelations also galvanized white Vancouver labor unions that were opposed to Chinese immigration. The Vancouver Trades and Labour Council (VTLC) donated funds to support legal representation for labor at the inquiry. Its representative, Gordon Grant, defended Lew while repeatedly raising questions about Yip On's ties to alleged Liberal graft.[241] Moreover, the VTLC hired an "army" of private detectives to scour the Chinese population in search of merchants whom Yip On had admitted. With Lew's help, the labor detectives captured two young Chinese workers at a Yip family business. Police rushed the surprised men to the Royal Commission.[242] One immigrant, Yong Jung Sum, had been in Vancouver for four years. He had never been a merchant, but he had come on a merchant passport arranged by Charlie Yip Yen, Yip On's brother in Hong Kong. The passport had the name "Lee Suo Wong." Once at Vancouver, Yip On had handled his immigration interview and loaned him gold "show money" to display to Canadian officials.[243] The testimony proved Yip's involvement in immigration frauds, though the question of Liberal Party involvement remained undocumented.

At the Royal Commission, dissident Liberal witnesses also condemned local Liberal leader Robert Kelly, striking blows to check the party's excesses without destroying the party itself. Kelly, a wholesale grocer and tea importer, had presided over Vancouver's Liberal Party executive since 1896.[244] Former provincial premier Joseph Martin, a member of Parliament in Great Britain, returned to Canada to denounce Kelly, stating, "I believe that there is graft in every department of this city. . . . No one can get a contract, an order or an appointment unless he buys it from Mr. Kelly. He is seemingly permitted—has been for nine years—to sell government places with the understanding that he finance campaigns at election time."[245] Harry Senkler, the Vancouver Liberal Party president in 1910, complained that he "didn't care a rap, personally, how many Chinamen got into the country illegally and without paying the poll tax, but that he did object to 'these fellows hogging it all,' but that if it went to the Liberal executive he did not care."[246] Ultimately, no Liberal Party witness offered any written proof, so the Kelly machine was spared criminal charges. Grant and Farris, as recent members of the Liberal executive, would have known more about the arrangements than they revealed. The Royal Commission helped to check Kelly's faction, while protecting patronage itself. According to historians of Canada's civil service, the Canadian public strongly favored patronage, though parties normally kept their dealings discreet to avoid embarrassment.[247]

## The Inquiry's Impact

The Royal Commission concluded that Yip On was dishonest. It could find no proof that Yip's defenders in the local party or in the cabinet had specific knowledge of his true character.[248] Because local Liberal Party leaders vetted all civil service appointments, this finding seems improbable. The commission also found Lew's behavior to be suspicious. It concluded that Lew's attempt to implicate Yip may have been a conspiracy to further his own interests, not a product of reforming zeal. The inquiry had no access to Lew's personal letters, but it was clear that his reputation as a Chinese broker on the edge of the law preceded him.[249]

In public, the Royal Commission strived to limit the damage to the Liberal Party. Somewhat disingenuously, the commission recommended raising Chinese interpreters' wages so that bilingual Anglo men from the British Empire's Far East could be recruited to manage Chinese immigration in Canada.[250] After all, Yip's part-time interpreter's salary of $960 per year already exceeded the Chinese immigration-related wages of the most senior Anglo official who supervised him.[251] Moreover, Yip's schemes relied on pliable Anglo customs officials, whom the Royal Commission publicly exonerated. Later, in May 1911, the Liberals quietly removed these Anglo officials from handling Chinese immigration when they moved the head tax administration to the Department of Immigration.[252]

Canada's federal government continued to turn a blind eye to illegal immigration. It continued to hire Chinese interpreters on a casual part-time basis.[253] It ignored the Royal Commission's recommendation to use fingerprints to prevent immigration fraud. Starting in October 1910, after David Lew's exposé, officials required Chinese to submit photos to obtain exit certificates.[254] In 1913, officials added photos to the entry records of new Chinese, but illegal immigration continued.[255] Japanese illegal immigration also followed a similar pattern.[256] Only in the 1930s, when the Great Depression caused nearly one-third of British Columbia's workers to lose their jobs, did Canada's immigration department stop turning a blind eye to Asian illegal immigration.[257]

Ultimately, David Lew's side won. His defeat of Yip On brought him great fame among both Chinese and Anglo Canadians. He made himself one of British Columbia's most dominant Chinese Canadian power brokers. He became a premier unofficial "Chinese lawyer" and a businessman with commercial interests in Vancouver, Victoria, and Nanaimo. As a household name, he titled his Chinese newspaper notices simply "An Announcement from David Lew."[258] He continued to lobby officials in Ottawa on Chinese Canadian matters. Officials treated his requests with great care, worrying about his reputation for politically dangerous "intrigue."[259] China's government also noticed Lew. By 1914, Lew was appointed China's assistant consul for western Canada.[260] In 1924, a Vancouver English newspaper deemed Lew "a prominent figure in the Oriental colonies throughout British Columbia."[261]

Lew's allies also benefited. In 1916, Tom McInnes realized his dream of a business in China, most likely due to the influence of Lew and his backers. He met with China's Dr. Sun Yat Sen, then won a concession to build Guangzhou's streetcar system. Between 1916 and 1924, McInnes lived in Guangzhou, supervising the demolition of the city's ancient walls and the construction of the streetcar lines.[262] In 1917, Lew's ally J. W. de B. Farris was elected to the provincial legislature and eventually served as the province's attorney general.[263] Yip On's side sustained the greater loss. Facing criminal charges, Yip fled to China, toppling from the peak of Chinese Canadian power into obscurity.[264] The Liberal Party cut off Kelly's political machine from patronage, ending its influence.[265]

Despite the setbacks, the Yip family continued to build a fortune through its brokerage talents. Yip Sang had established his Wing Sang Company as Chinese Canada's premier brokerage firm. His network of younger relatives and his twenty-three children ensured that members of the Yip family would have dominant broker roles. The Conservative victory in the 1911 election ended fifteen years of Liberal Party rule, but the Yips' influence persisted.[266] By 1916, Yip Sang's son Yip Kew Him had become Vancouver's Chinese immigration and CPR interpreter, a position he held until at least 1941, lasting through Conservative, Unionist, and Liberal governments. After Yip Sang passed away in 1927, his son Yip Kew Mow (*Ye Qiu Mao*) became the family patriarch. Yip Kew Mow continued the family's Liberal Party ties, attending a Vancouver Board of Trade dinner for Prime Minister William L. Mackenzie King in 1929.[267]

Yip On's fall rippled across the forty-ninth parallel: the United States quietly ended Vancouver's monopoly on issuing Chinese merchant certificates. From that point, Chinese Canadians could apply at Vancouver, Victoria, or Ottawa for documentation of their class-exempt status from the U.S. Chinese Exclusion Act.[268] But the connected Chinese population of Mexico continued to seek admission to the United States via similar "merchant certificates" and appeared to practice some parallel forms of political brokerage.[269] The preceding analysis of the Yip-Lew conflict thus suggests new ways of reading Chinese migrants' resistance and collaboration within the settlement nations of the Pacific world.

## Conclusions

The struggle between Yip and Lew shows that Canadian party machines had such an extensive role in local society that even members of disenfranchised groups found party ties to be indispensable.[270] Canada's first tentative steps toward restricting immigrant entry thus were taken with great ambivalence. The Chinese head tax system's restrictions, tracking mechanisms, and border controls set important precedents. They began Canada's turn away from a laissez-faire immigration policy toward a modern system of control, a change that eventually affected all immigrants. However, before World War I, neither Laurier's Liberals nor Prime Minister Robert Borden's Conservatives had much interest in taking strong measures to stop illegal Chinese immigration. Political brokerage by Chinese and Anglo leaders alike determined the politics of enforcement.[271]

David Lew won in the short term, but the Royal Commission's outcome also revealed the enduring power of the institutions. No real reform of the Chinese immigration system followed. Multinational corporations like the CPR continued to be influential; sometimes, their interests coincided with those of Chinese Canadians. Political parties continued to seek election funds and often preferred not to know their source. Chinese power brokers continued to build alliances that fused ethnic, mainstream, and transpacific ties. They traded dollars for modest influence, but they could not buy respect for their race.

We might consider the early history of Canada's immigration policy as analogous to bootlegging and gambling, illegal activities that enjoyed sufficient public support to deter effective law enforcement.[272] There were many individuals profiting from illegal migration, but for all parties in the exchange, local politics proved to be a competitive, unstable environment. The wealthiest Chinese Canadian merchants could at times buy influence by asking their Anglo business associates to lobby on their behalf.[273] Nevertheless, prejudice and the taint of illegality forced Chinese brokers to operate in covert, subordinate roles in which they depended heavily on Anglo intermediaries.

Future research might explore the connections between Chinese Canadian politics and the widely reported but understudied phenomenon of Chinese Americans' relations with political machines. Every component of Yip On's transnational Chinese Canadian political machine had U.S. ties: the Chinese Freemasons, the Chinese Empire Reform Association, and the Self-Governing Association. In the United States, mainstream parties also made bargains with Chinese who could not vote. In New York City, Chinese Americans openly supported the Tammany Hall machine, despite their lack of votes, and won patronage posts in return.[274] On the West Coast, Chinese could not operate so openly, though the press reported that they made unofficial campaign contributions at election time.[275] Mary Coolidge, a sociologist, in her 1909 book *Chinese Immigration*, also found that Chinese in San Francisco managed anti-Chinese laws at all levels through graft alliances with officials, police, and the political parties that appointed them.[276] Before 1910, U.S. Chinese immigration interpreters generally held political patronage appointments,[277] and civil service reforms did not erase these outside considerations. In 1916, a congressional commission found that many Anglo U.S. immigration officials acknowledged that they hired "dishonest" Chinese interpreters.[278] As in Vancouver, Chinese political brokerage for illegal immigration survived. Chinese immigration interpreter posts also continued to be highly politicized as U.S. officials often appointed well-connected Chinese American leaders despite policies to the contrary.[279]

These Chinese dealings suggest a need to revisit the political history of this era. On both sides of the forty-ninth parallel, local, national, and transnational politics contributed to the capture of posts. Official history records the victors, but it does not reveal the full story of how Chinese-Anglo alliances helped to influence Canadian and U.S. immigration. As in Vancouver, much of the unofficial story can be found only through sifting the evidence in the surviving Chinese-language sources.

TWO | **Arguing Cases**
*Legal Interpreters, Law, and Society*

IN 1924, DAVID LEW'S CHIEF profession as a legal broker made his murder fascinating and worrisome to British Columbians. Canadians prided themselves on a justice system based on British fair play, but the investigation cast an uncomfortable light on apparent contradictions between legal ideals and local practice. On the night of 24 September 1924, at the corner of East Pender and Carrall streets in Vancouver, a Chinese man dressed in black stepped from the shadows, shot Lew dead in the street, and then fled. Shortly after the killing, rumors started that a powerful Chinatown faction had ordered his death. Witnesses were afraid to speak with police. The sheer number of suspects produced months of coverage in Vancouver's Chinese- and English-language press. Lew's sudden end left many mysteries, but it also exposed evidence that highlights the controversial power he had accrued as a legal mediator between Chinese and Anglo Canadian society. As British Columbians discussed Lew's life, they interpreted him as a leader who had for decades wielded a partly hidden power that influenced both the Chinese and Anglo communities.[1]

The story of Lew's work as a legal broker contributes a new vision of Chinese initiative in Canadian and U.S. legal history. It extends Canadian legal history into new spaces of Chinese-Anglo relations and allows us to explore Chinese legal brokers' daily work and Chinese migrants' negotiations within the Pacific world. David Lew's case also represents an often overlooked part of legal personnel history: the ethnic and immigrant interpreters who acted as legal experts.[2] In British Columbia, Asians and First Nations people could neither become lawyers nor serve on juries.[3] The legal system was effectively "white." Like those in British Columbia, most law societies in Canada and the United States denied Chinese immigrants the right to become lawyers.[4] Nevertheless, Chinese Canadians often made the law their instrument through legal brokers. British Columbians often referred to men like Lew as "Chinese lawyers."[5] They were paralegals who served Chinese clients and sometimes other nonwhite groups, such as Japanese, First Nations people, and East Indians.[6] The brokerage relations of these Chinese lawyers also illuminate another less visible aspect of legal history: the profoundly integrated nature of Canadian justice. Ethnic dispute resolution processes continually interacted with the formal justice system. As legal historians have found elsewhere, formal police and court actions often happened after the resolution or failure of informal negotiations.[7] Chinese immigrants needed law for their society to function. On a daily basis, Chinese encountered police, filed legal complaints, and appealed to authorities to use their discretion on their behalf. In court, the weak often hoped to triumph over the strong.[8] Despite Chinese legal brokers' informal position, they helped to make the Canadian state a central institution among Chinese immigrants in British Columbia.

While the law was an instrument of exclusion, Chinese Canadians' popular use of British Canadian justice also made it into a structuring force that helped to regulate and sustain Chinese migration. Chinese Canadians perceived legal processes as aiding individuals and groups in several ways. Immigrants brought from China a custom of informal lawyers, who helped ordinary people navigate the legal system.[9] Chinese lawyers buffered Anglo discrimination, helped to resolve disputes, regulated economic relations, and at times checked abuses by the powerful. Like much legal practice, a good part of their brokerage did not enter the official records of the courts. Further, these negotiations took place in the shadow of anti-Chinese policies and their enforcement. Police disproportionately targeted Chinese for crimes such as gambling, prostitution, and drug use, while often showing more tolerance for comparable activities among middle-class whites.[10] Chinese legal power brokers backed by wealthy merchants also became influential forces within the larger legal culture. Their mitigation of anti-Chinese laws made Exclusion Era Chinese life both possible and tolerable. Lew's final act involved a legal contest between two factions of Chinese Canadian businesspeople: a small group from his ancestral county of Panyu in Guangdong China, and one of British Columbia's largest, most powerful Chinese associations, the Chinese Freemasons. Ultimately, the issues raised by Lew's murder would prompt public questioning about the morality of brokers' power over a dependent majority of

Chinese workers and merchants.[11] The wider social aspects of legal practice helped immigrants to fuse Canadian law with Chinese migrant society.

## A Community Made by Laws: The Daily Work of Chinese Lawyers

Lew's murder was an exceptional fate for a Chinese broker, but his efforts to secure dominance in legal brokerage reflected the position's prestige and profits. Chinese legal interpreters behaved much like lawyers, though they could not represent their clients in court. Brokers collected information, wrote briefs, made arrangements with Anglo attorneys, and interpreted for Chinese in court. Chinese newspaper reports of trials routinely named the interpreters, crediting them for their work.[12]

David Lew's letterbook from 1906 to 1909 illustrates a typical case. In 1908, a man called Lee Ghia (*Li Jia*) came to Lew in a state of great anxiety. He had been using another man's immigration papers. As a result, Canadian authorities had instituted court proceedings against him. Lew wrote, "Mr. Lee, you do not need to worry any more." An Anglo lawyer would present the case Lew had prepared, and Lew comforted Lee, "Trust me that everything has followed as planned, and all will be okay."[13] Chinese advertisements and immigration department records confirm that Chinese legal interpreters like Lew often successfully restored "lost" immigration documents.[14]

These legal negotiations suggest that men like Lew were more akin to lawyers than they were mere interpreters. Chinese treated legal brokerage as a different form of leadership than the power rooted in Chinese merchants' business or social movements or simple bilingualism. Chinese newspapers portrayed legal brokers as part of the institutions that governed both the ethnic community and the larger society. Foon Sien Wong's firm of legal interpreters, the Kwong Lee Tai Company, advertised its partnership with prominent Anglo barristers. It handled "all cases either civil or criminal, such as immigration, deportation, merchant certificates, contracts or leases with occidental people."[15] Won Alexander Cumyow (*Wen Jinyou*), a police court interpreter who had trained as a lawyer, also ran a private "negotiating firm" specializing in the resolution of immigration, commercial, financial, and property matters.[16]

From the mid-nineteenth to the mid-twentieth century, Chinese legal interpreters in Canada strived to compensate for the uneven nature of Chinese-Anglo relations within the law, especially Chinese Canadians' lack of equal access to legal counsel. In 1924, Joseph Ambrose Russell, an Anglo lawyer in Vancouver, termed his thirty-five years of work for Chinese clients as purely business. They were loyal customers who always paid well and on time. However, Russell's ties to Anglo society trumped his legal representation of Chinese clients. In one murder case, Russell chose not to present evidence that he believed would acquit his client, a Chinese boy, because it might embarrass an Anglo friend. The boy was convicted and sentenced to life in prison. Chinese merchants paid Russell to prevent the boy from being hanged, which he did, but their wealth could not buy a complete legal defense.[17] Chinese Canadians' decades of work with Russell suggest that more reliable legal counsel could not be found.[18] As evidenced by this example, the great differences in legal power between the Chinese minority and the Anglo majority often undercut Chinese Canadians' chances of due process.

Chinese legal interpreters helped to offset Anglo power in the legal system through paralegal help that increased their Chinese clients' chances of effective representation. Chinese legal interpreters helped Anglo law firms as cheap labor. They dealt with clients, gathered information, wrote briefs, and negotiated settlements. However, interpreters could not file proceedings nor speak in court as barristers. Anglo lawyers took credit for their cases and received most of the legal fees. Chinese Americans developed an institution of Chinese legal interpreting that paralleled Canadian practice.[19] In 1907, immigration interpreter Seid Gain Back Jr. of Portland, Oregon, became the first Chinese American lawyer to practice on the Pacific Coast. However, Chinese-Anglo relations continued to be uneven, so Back's law practice more resembled Chinese legal interpreters' informal power brokerage than a conventional Anglo legal career.[20] Perhaps because of these issues, few Chinese Americans became lawyers during the Exclusion Era.

Chinese legal interpreters often attempted to balance uneven Chinese-Anglo legal power through subterfuge: they often shaded their clients' testimony and used translation to slow down proceedings. In British Columbia, even English-speaking Chinese often used interpreters in court. For example, in 1917, Victoria's immigration interpreter Lee Mongkow, a fluent English-speaker, insisted on testifying in court through Chinese legal interpreter Harry Hastings.[21] Interpreting delays gave Chinese more time to compose their testimony. The prevalence of these subterfuges led to the practice of hiring extra "checking interpreters" to confirm translations in high-profile cases.[22] Often, legal interpreters located Chinese witnesses in advance and prepared them for their testimony, sometimes to the extent of guiding Chinese witnesses through subtle hand signals.[23] The exceptional skill and education required of early twentieth-century legal interpreters made them prized commodities for Chinese associations.

Like Lew, most interpreters belonged to Chinese associations that added to their negotiating heft. At the turn of the twentieth century, members of the Chinese political party, the Chinese Empire Reform Association (CERA), often distributed legal interpreting jobs among its members.[24] Chinese factions backed by wealthy merchants could also create alliances based on mutual profits from commercial businesses and illegal activities. In 1907, landlord Wong Lung came to Lew asking for advice about renting out cabins to Chinese prostitutes in Steveston, a practice made difficult by the Steveston city council's recent zeal for law enforcement. Within six days, Lew and Russell negotiated an agreement with the Steveston police that they would only arrest Chinese prostitutes once during the fish-canning season. Wong preferred to handle business matters in English, so he hired Lew primarily as a mediator, not as an interpreter.[25] Such ongoing business relations with Anglo officials, police, and lawyers sometimes gave Chinese more influence over the legal system. These informal ties, albeit bought and therefore precarious, gave a few legal brokers greater access to make their case. Indeed, Lew spent much time with Anglo lawyers.[26] This exceptional access sometimes earned Lew's clients a greater hearing within the justice system.[27] Interpreters' unofficial standing obscured their multifaceted roles in court records, but they played crucial roles in incorporating Chinese concerns into the justice system's operation.

As an institution, Chinese legal interpreting developed alongside the legal profession. By the early twentieth century, Chinese legal interpreting had become a profession in major urban centers of Chinese immigration. Besides training in law, legal brokerage required quick thinking, deft political skills, and fluent bilingualism. However, positions for Chinese court, police, and legal interpreters were few. Thus, legal brokerage often required political backing in both Chinese and Anglo society. In the frontier days of the mid-nineteenth century, pioneer Chinese merchants in Canada and the United States acted as jacks-of-all-trades mediators.[28] As British Columbia became an Anglo settler society, the legal profession as a whole became more educated. In the late nineteenth and early twentieth centuries, Chinese legal brokers began to clerk with law firms, the standard apprenticeship for lawyers which Canadians called "articling," though Chinese could not practice law due to their race.[29] By the 1920s, British Columbia's Law Society expected its new lawyers to be law school graduates.[30] These rising standards privileged Chinese legal brokers who had attended universities or law schools.[31] Immigrants also brought from China a tradition of informal litigators, unofficial lawyers who offered popular access to the law.[32] Legal brokers' business records show that Chinese of all classes frequently turned to the Canadian legal system. Through the law, they sought to resolve disputes, handle routine matters, and seek their own power.

Many Chinese immigrants valued legal brokers who could smooth over relations, resolve their legal problems, help to shape favorable responses to police questions, or, if necessary, offer bribes at the right moment. An account book kept by Won Alexander Cumyow shows that police and court interpreters during the early twentieth century received handsome wages of Can$2–$5 for each client's session in their private legal practice. In an hour, brokers could earn over twice as much as a Chinese laborer received for a day's work. Cumyow represented Chinese, First Nations, and East Indian clients. A typical session involved interpreting and legal advice in the event of an arrest, court hearing, or civil lawsuit.[33] Won Alexander Cumyow's son Gordon Cumyow was also an interpreter. Every day, he went to Vancouver's police court and found Chinese clients in need of assistance. He recalled, "Always something there, some kind of scrap or something. Or a white man beat a Chinese up or something like that. It was always busy."[34]

A considerable portion of Vancouver's legal brokers' handling of criminal matters concerned anti-Chinese patterns of law enforcement. These patterns extended to both Canada and the United States.[35] Mary Coolidge, author of a study of Chinese Americans in San Francisco published in 1909, termed most anti-Chinese policing as pretexts for extortion, blackmail that made Chinese appear to be an "exceptionally law-breaking population."[36] Vancouver's pattern was similar. City authorities appeared most concerned with anti-Chinese arrests as a source of revenue-producing fines; they wanted to "tax" rather than halt illegal activities.[37] Legal power brokers thus became daily negotiators in contests between Chinese and Anglo institutions over determining a tolerable level of anti-Chinese law enforcement.

Legal relations also included civil matters. Brokers' letters record the kinds of civil business they performed. A number of Chinese in Canada continued a common Chinese social practice of using multiple names, not realizing that discrepancies in naming could lead to legal and immigration troubles. Immigrants had difficulties figuring out how to apply for business and driver's licenses. They wanted help with collecting debts, figuring out Canadian insurance, and dealing with the consequences of automobile accidents. They also turned to the courts to handle family matters, such as the custody of the children of Chinese fathers and Anglo mothers who were not their wives. Immigrants frequently turned to Canadian courts to adjudicate disputes about breaches of contract, unpaid wages, and divisions of profit among business partners. Often, the involvement of a Chinese legal broker in disputes about debts, rents, or wages persuaded the opposing side to pay without any involvement of a more costly lawyer. Generally, Chinese could expect fair treatment in civil matters, so they made the Canadian legal system an important arbiter of social and economic relations related to their migration.[38]

## Legal Brokerage, Labor Contracting, and Class Relations

One of the most noted aspects of Chinese legal brokerage is its associations with the commerce of migration, above all, Chinese labor contractors' efforts to regulate, control, and protect Chinese migrant workers. During the late nineteenth and early twentieth centuries, the anti-Chinese movement often denounced Chinese merchants' role in legal brokerage relations as Oriental despotism. In 1902, American Federation of Labor (AFL) president Samuel Gompers and secretary Frank Morrison opened an anti-Chinese pamphlet by attacking Chinese merchants' "despotic sway" over Chinese workers. They quoted an 1876 U.S. legislative report that alleged that Chinese merchants "levy taxes, command masses of men, intimidate interpreters and witnesses, enforce perjury, regulate trade, punish the refractory."[39] In 1903, Canada's Parliament concurred and outlawed Chinese community "courts" and "tribunals."[40] Scholarship on Chinese American legal brokerage has built on the concept of merchant-interpreters' bilingual rule over a separate monolingual community.[41] Granted, Chinese merchants and interpreters exploited ordinary Chinese, but they also acted as leaders and as patrons of legal challenges to discrimination. Legal brokerage in class and race relations involved a deeper interweaving of Chinese and Anglo politics than is captured by most simple notions of merchant rule.

Legal work helped to structure Chinese labor contracting, a major basis of Chinese employment and Chinese merchant business. Chinese made extensive use of the U.S. and Canadian legal systems to regulate their financial dealings. Legal brokers drew up contracts with Anglo firms and suppliers and prepared contracts to be signed by individual migrant workers.[42] Cumyow's letters show that he arranged labor contracts for Chinese and European immigrants with Anglo employers, charging a small commission from each worker's monthly salary as a finder's fee.[43] David Lew arranged labor contracts as well, working for the large labor contracting firm Kwong and Company, which sent Chinese workers to make bricks at the Columbia Clay Company in 1909.[44] In exchange for the job, transportation, and a local Chinese foreman, workers typically agreed to purchase all of their housing and supplies from their contractor, who made the majority of his profits selling food, housing, alcohol, mail delivery, and remittance services. Chinese migrant laborers usually lived seasonally at their remote job sites, so labor contractors sometimes provided other forms of leisure, such as gambling, opium, and prostitution.[45] While this relationship was exploitive, it was for the most part mutually beneficial. When Kwong and Company's contract workers encountered problems, Lew became their legal defender.[46] This protective legal relationship between contractors and workers became one of the founding bargains that structured Chinese migration in the Exclusion Era.[47]

The entire system of Chinese migration depended on maintaining Chinese workers' confidence that immigration offered safe, profitable work.[48] When the Columbia Clay Company's kiln collapsed in 1909, killing two Chinese workers, Lew pressed the provincial police for an inquest into the accident on behalf of the Chinese subcontractor which had employed them.[49] Before the accident, a Chinese foreman had told his Anglo supervisor at the brick company that he thought the kiln roof looked dangerous. The supervisor told the Chinese that it seemed fine and that they should keep working. The workers obeyed. At the inquest, an Anglo judge ruled that the Chinese workers had knowingly risked their lives, so the brick company was not criminally responsible for their deaths.[50] To deter future negligence, Lew filed two $1,500 wrongful-death lawsuits against the brick company on behalf of the dead men's families. He also handled their probate cases so that their Canadian savings could be sent to their widows and children in Guangzhou.[51] In matters of industrial accidents and in the handling of estates, legal brokers represented Chinese Canadian interests which would otherwise likely not have been fully addressed by Anglo authorities.

Lew's legal work for Chinese labor contractors also adopted a protective role to deter labor unions. Contractors often used their control over workers' debts and their knowledge of workers' immigration status to pressure Chinese to renounce unionization efforts. Chinese labor contractors did so in Vancouver Island's coal-mining strike of 1912–1913, and frustrated white miners attacked the strikebreakers, including Chinese workers, destroying and looting their homes.[52] Six years later, in 1919, David Lew and other Chinese labor contractors were still pressing Canadian officials to compensate Chinese for this miners' "rebellion."[53] By that time, many Chinese workers had joined labor unions, which challenged Chinese labor contractors' claims to speak for all Chinese.[54] Lew's attempts to secure redress for white labor unions' past misdeeds helped with the argument that Chinese merchants would be better protectors.

As long as Canada and British Columbia had weak collective bargaining laws, labor contractors' claims to be collective legal protectors appeared to be somewhat persuasive. However, contrary to Anglo fears that Chinese practiced "yellow slavery," labor contractors could not fully control immigrant workers.[55] Indeed, they had to cultivate Chinese workers' confidence continually. Dissatisfied Chinese workers would stop work, throw down their tools, protest, and vote with their feet, taking their scarce labor to better-paid locales in the United States.[56] The Sam Kee Company (*Sanji Gongsi*), with which Lew was allied, found that in any given month, about half of its Chinese lumber workers left for other locations.[57] In 1908, the Vancouver General Hospital demanded that the Chinese Benevolent Association (CBA, *Zhonghua Huiguan*) pay all Chinese unpaid bills. However, most of the Chinese debtors could not be found, so Lew negotiated that their hospital debts be written off in exchange for an $800 goodwill donation from Chinese merchants. He asked that in the future the CBA be informed when Chinese entered the hospital so that they could be tracked before they left the city.[58] Legal brokers' work reveals a dynamic picture of Chinese Canadians' dealings with the law and governance of economic affairs, suggesting that popular uses of the law should be taken into account as fully as Chinese merchants' court challenges to discriminatory laws.

## *Canadian Courts, Community Dispute Resolution, and Intra-Chinese Conflicts*

Immigrants also saw Canadian courts as an effective means to compel the resolution of intra-Chinese conflicts. Chinese frequently turned to Canadian courts to adjudicate disputes.[59] Despite this, most scholars have interpreted Chinese organizations' exhortations to resolve disputes internally as evidence of an unassimilated immigrant population. The majority of Chinese in British Columbia belonged to community organizations, such as the Chinese Freemasons and local Chinese benevolent associations, whose charters emphasized that members should resolve intra-Chinese disputes internally.[60] For example, Victoria's Chinese Consolidated Benevolent Association (CCBA, *Zhonghua Huiguan*) claimed the authority to judge intra-Chinese disputes. It mandated that each side bring advocates and witnesses to an association hearing for judgment. The CCBA's 1884 charter stated that failure to abide by its rulings would lead to the expulsion of offenders, who would be "handed over to the police."[61] However, Chinese Canadians faced a situation in which all processes of dispute resolution had shortcomings. In principle, Vancouver's Chinese Benevolent Association (*Zhonghua Huiguan*) had a mandate to represent all Chinese. By 1924, though, the CBA had become a battleground for community control rather than an impartial mediator. Supporters of China's Nationalist Party competed with the Chinese Freemasons to control Vancouver's CBA. Canadian courts had disadvantages as well, but brokers' business records reveal that Chinese Canadians readily used the Canadian legal system to adjudicate disputes.[62]

Brokers mediated between the informal Chinese and the formal Canadian justice systems because immigrants often treated these two dispute resolution mechanisms as parts of a single continuum. Turning to Canadian courts was an implied critique of immigrant institutions that had failed to meet the need for impartial conflict resolution. The courts complemented Chinese community organizations, which often were unable to reach consensus when mediating disputes and which sometimes favored the strong. The following two cases show this blended process of dispute resolution.

According to *Da Han Gong Bao*, on 23 August 1924, police arrested a man called Chong Sing (*Zheng Sheng*), whom David Lew accused of assaulting and robbing two Chinese of $300. One of the robbed Chinese had to be treated at the hospital. At first, the victim felt that he could not testify in court against Chong, but with David Lew's help, the victim swore out a warrant against him. Lawyer friends of Lew reported that, afterward, Chong had the chance to go to "the association" to confess. *Da Han Gong Bao* does not specify which Chinese association, but it was probably the CBA. The association arranged to slow down the court case in the hope that a settlement could be negotiated.[63] After hearing the facts, the association offered to cancel the criminal charges if Chong paid $1,000 to the victims, but Chong's friends rejected this offer.[64] As a friend of the injured victim, Lew tried to use Canadian justice as a tool with which to pressure Chong to accept the Chinese community's sanctions for his alleged crime, although conflict-of-interest issues raised questions about the association's impartiality. The CBA officers were elected by the heads of all the major Chinese associations in Vancouver, but at the time of this dispute, Lew's brother dentist Yick Pang Lew (*Liao Ye Pang*) was serving as CBA president.[65] Further, if the Chinese robbery victims had to file charges with the Canadian police to get help from the Chinese associations, the internal dispute resolution mechanisms may have been weak indeed.[66]

The interplay between internal and external forms of conflict resolution was also evident in a 1933 dispute between Jang Jack and G. Yom over the ownership of a vegetable-peddling truck. The evidence here comes from the papers of Yip Quene, a Canadian-born Chinese interpreter, insurance agent, and all-around fixer who often handled Chinese immigrants' legal problems as part of his work for Vancouver's Wing Sang Company. When Jang Jack returned to China in 1930 to visit his family, he sold his truck and vegetable-peddling business to G. Yom for $400. As part of the sale, the two men agreed that Jang could buy back the business when he returned. To seal their verbal agreement, G. Yom announced it to members of the Chinese Peddlers' Association (*Caiye Gonghui*). As Yip noted in a brief prepared for Yom's lawyer, "It is the general custom of the Vancouver Chinese peddlers to sell and buy their trucks through verbal agreement. Generally all their transactions are based on trust and promise." After the sale, as was customary, Jang accompanied Yom along his vegetable-peddling route to show him the business and introduce him to his customers. Jang then left for China and did not return until 15 May 1933. He then asked to buy back the business from Yom for $400, but Yom insisted on $450, resulting in an impasse.[67]

In August 1933, Jang, with the help of Foon Sien Wong, charged Yom with the theft of his truck. The Vancouver police then arrested Yom and seized the disputed truck. Yom's arrest moved the Chinese community's process of dispute resolution into high gear. H. Y. (Hok Yat) Louie, a prominent Chinese merchant in the fruit and vegetable retail industry, vouched for Yom. He had heard that Jang sold his business to Yom, and based on their twenty years of acquaintance in Vancouver, Louie knew Yom to be an honest man. Louie put up $3,000 of his own money for Yom's bail. Louie's knowledge of the fruit and vegetable retail business carried much weight, especially because most vegetable peddlers came from Louie's ancestral county of Zhongshan. On the Sunday following Yom's arrest, Yip and members of the Chinese Peddlers' Association conducted an investigation. Jang's legal assistant, Wong, told Yip that Yom paid Jang in full for the truck in 1930. Meanwhile, several delegates of the Chinese Peddlers' Association interviewed Jang, but according to Yip, Jang denied that he had ever received payment in full from Yom. No witnesses or receipts could prove either man's account. In the end, Yom offered to resolve the conflict by either keeping the peddling truck and business or selling it back to Jang for $400. Ultimately, Jang appeared to get his wish, and here again, Chinese immigrants had used the Canadian legal system via brokers to force the resolution of an intra-Chinese dispute.[68] As in other legal practice, court action escalated the costs and risks of continuing the dispute, raising pressure on both sides to negotiate a resolution. Both of these cases suggest that the terrain of legal history should be extended to better encompass informal negotiations. When juxtaposed, ethnic and mainstream dispute resolution processes often appear inextricable, pointing scholars toward a broader conception of the legal history of Canada, one deeply embedded in multicultural negotiations.

## Chinese Legal Brokerage as Law Enforcement

Vancouver police did not hire Chinese directly, so they used men like Lew on the sly to do their detective work. For sleuthing, Lew charged $10 per day plus expenses for his wages and those of his Chinese helpers who collected information. The British Columbia provincial police hired a private detective agency that employed Chinese operatives. Brokers investigated Chinese business disputes and crimes such as auto accidents, assault, theft, and murder. They examined crime scenes, interviewed community members, sent agents to watch suspects, gathered physical evidence, and translated what they found for Anglo police and attorneys.[69] While police relied on Chinese brokers for a variety of services, it was difficult to assess the reliability of the Chinese who were hired to do detective work. Western Canadian cities at times turned to outsiders in the hope of finding impartial Chinese detectives. In 1909, Lew warned the Winnipeg police chief, J. C. McRae, that there was little chance of enforcing the law among Chinese because "[s]ome interpreter[s] may conceal from the police while pretending to assist them."[70] Chinese legal interpreters, however, often belonged to political networks which influenced their appointments within the judicial system.

Legal interpreters had multiple allegiances, and sometimes they aided extralegal actions that reflected their compromised position as brokers. Political appointments strongly influenced the personnel of British Columbia's justice system,[71] so Chinese Canadian legal interpreters often had political debts. In August 1924, British Columbia attorney general Alexander Manson appointed Foon Sien Wong as a court interpreter. The same month, Wong joined his employer and probable sponsor, the private detective firm Robinson-Mansfield, in the illegal kidnapping of a Chinese servant, Foon Sing Wong (*Huang Huan Sheng*). The provincial police suspected that Foon Sing might know about the shooting death earlier in the year of his coworker, white nursemaid Janet Smith. On their behalf, the private detectives kidnapped Foon Sing and savagely beat him, while Foon Sien translated Anglo detectives' questions.[72] Chinese and English debates over the interpreters' conflict of interest ensued.

At the time, many Anglos in the United States and Canada expected Chinese legal interpreters to be entangled in political dealings related to their appointments. These arrangements, which usually involved graft and political patronage, interacted at the same time with widespread Anglo and Chinese convictions that the courts should be just. The public debate over Chinese legal brokers' ethics appeared to recognize their difficult position in the political structure. The English press exposed Foon Sien as an employee of a detective agency that did "off the books" work for local police agencies. Foon Sien also had negotiated a written contract among himself, a Chinese drug dealer called Wong Ming Choo, and Oscar Robinson, a private detective involved in the kidnapping, to "deal in opium and other drugs." Yet, Foon Sien's actions were not unprecedented. Several other prominent Chinese legal power brokers had criminal convictions, so this revelation alone did not appear to tarnish his business.[73] However, Chinese and Anglo outrage at the kidnapping prompted unnamed "older Chinese merchants" to hire David Lew to draft an official complaint to the attorney general about Foon Sien's actions. Hundreds of ordinary Chinese and the *Vancouver Sun*, an Anglo newspaper, donated to Foon Sing's legal defense.[74] Foon Sien's subsequent actions seemed to indicate that he felt the Chinese community's pressure to treat Foon Sing better. When requested in court to ask Foon Sing whether he had loved Janet Smith, Foon Sien replied with a lie: he could not translate the question because "there was no word for 'love' in Chinese."[75] In actuality, Foon Sien was a Chinese matchmaker and published poet, so he spoke the language of love with both verse and verve.[76] Like Foon Sien Wong, Chinese legal brokers often became collaborators with the Anglo legal system to access influence, while also mitigating anti-Chinese measures. In doing so, brokers walked a political tightrope.

## *The Politics of Policing Chinese Gambling*

Scholars have used the historical term "tong war" to describe a range of political conflicts involving Chinese associations seeking to control and protect illegal activities. Most U.S. scholars interpret tong wars as organized crime.[77] David Lew's murder mystery underlines the different Chinese Canadian perspectives of the associations and their legal brokers. Chinese Canadians recognized their compromised nature, but they also respected that the associations met their members' needs for legal representation. Thousands of Chinese Canadians came out to honor Lew during his funeral procession. Men, women, and children dressed in their Sunday best packed more than seven blocks of Vancouver's streets to honor him as a legal hero. *Da Han Gong Bao* described Lew as an oppressor, but reported that even his Chinese enemies felt obligated to pay their respects. Today, Lew lies in an unmarked grave, remembered only briefly by historians as a murdered corrupt interpreter.[78]

In British Columbia, as in the United States, gambling's staggering profits united legal brokers, influential Chinese, and white law enforcement officials in exploiting a captive Chinese market for recreation. Liang Qichao, a political leader from China who visited in 1903, estimated that Chinese in Vancouver spent over $300,000 annually on gambling. In British Columbia as a whole, Chinese gambling was a million-dollar industry.[79] In 1924, Vancouver had twenty-six big gambling houses, where Chinese went to eat, drink, socialize, gamble, and smoke opium.[80] The clientele for Chinese gambling clubs in British Columbia also included white, Japanese, and black workers.[81] By the 1920s, Chinese gambling had become a popular pastime across racial, gender, and class lines. The *Vancouver Sun* published stories about English society matrons in Vancouver and Victoria holding mah jong parties, where they gambled with friends while dining on homemade Chinese dishes made from recipes published in the newspaper, such as egg foo young, almond chicken, and white chopped chicken.[82]

At the time, social gambling was popular among all classes, but British Columbia law allowed gambling only in private settings and at horse-racing tracks. Individuals could place wagers with each other, but public gaming was restricted to licensed private clubs. These private clubs were not permitted to profit from members' private games. Effectively, the law permitted middle-class whites to gamble while making most lower-class public gaming illegal.[83] The police especially targeted Chinese for gambling arrests.[84]

The political conflicts preceding Lew's murder began when his association of Chinese from Panyu, the Yue Shan Society (*Yushan Zongxinju*), joined China's Nationalist Party in challenging the Chinese Freemasons for dominance in legal brokerage over Chinese gambling.[85] By 1918, British Columbia's gambling policy had begun to change. Lew's lawyer ally J.W. de B. Farris had become attorney general of the province in 1917 (he would serve until 1922). Farris began to grant licenses to some Chinese gambling clubs.[86] Chinese Freemason complaints in *Da Han Gong Bao* suggest that the new licensing policy favored Lew's faction.[87] Gambling club licenses conferred great competitive advantage, the security of state sanction. Most Chinese clubs remained unlawful and were thus obliged to bribe police and officials lest their patrons become targets of the frequent anti-Chinese gambling raids of the era.[88]

For Chinese, the selective nature of police enforcement directed customers toward gambling houses owned by powerful people whose arrangements with the authorities could protect clients from arrest.[89] The police court often fined Chinese a month's wages for being "an inmate of a gambling house."[90] Business records show that many successful, legitimate Chinese entrepreneurs also ran gambling dens, including the Yips, Lee Saifan, Chang Toy, and Lee Mongkow.[91] Vancouver police cracked down sporadically, but made no sustained effort to root out Chinese gambling because the payoffs were so profitable.⁹² In his final days, Lew was planning to ask for a British Columbia provincial inquiry into Chinese gambling to override local corruption.⁹³ By appealing to a higher level of government, Lew sought advantage within a larger political arena that was less easily manipulated by local officials. Politically, he intended to destroy not only his Chinese opponents but their Anglo allies as well.⁹⁴

Transnational and domestic rivalries amplified Lew's British Columbia disputes over gambling into a wider struggle for legal brokerage power. During the early 1920s, China's Nationalists saw North America as a rich source of revolutionary funds. Along the Pacific Coast, from Mexico to Canada, the Nationalist Party and the Chinese Freemasons engaged in a bitter rivalry over the control of Chinese immigrant communities. At the same time, a tong war broke out in the United States between Hip Sing Tong (*Xie Bang Tang*) and On Leong Tong (*An Liang Tang*), both affiliates of the North American Chinese triad federation to which the Chinese Freemasons belonged. *Da Han Gong Bao* printed allegations that David Lew's brother, a Chinese interpreter at New York's port, had been involved in these U.S. tong conflicts.⁹⁵ However, despite the larger backdrops, Lew's struggle also continued an earlier competition among factions of Chinese businesspeople from his minority *Sanyi* and the majority *Siyi* regions of Guangdong. The other two dominant forces in Chinese legal brokerage over gambling, the Chinese Freemasons and the Chinese Nationalists, had stronger, broader memberships. Lew sought a middle position in the quarrels between these two larger associations, playing them against each other.⁹⁶ Thus, ongoing Pacific world ties and continuing Chinese-Anglo negotiations both shaped the exercise of legal brokerage power.

Initially, Lew's much smaller but wealthy faction held sway. Lew helped police to crack down on Chinese Freemasons' gambling businesses in Victoria, in Vancouver, and on Vancouver Island. *Da Han Gong Bao* alleged that his actions destroyed hundreds of thousands of dollars of gambling revenue.⁹⁷ Lew also targeted the Chinese Freemasons' illegal immigration, labor contracting, prostitution, and bootlegging businesses. In Vancouver, Lew acted as a powerful Chinese representative to city officials and police, relentlessly pressuring the Chinese Freemasons.⁹⁸

Strife between Chinese merchant factions in the Chinese Freemasons and the Yue Shan Society also led to clashes on Vancouver Island over business territories for the Chinese commerce of migration.⁹⁹ In 1920, Lew's Yue Shan Society had attempted to challenge the powerful Lun Yick Company (*Lianyi Gongsi*) of Nanaimo, which controlled much of the Chinese commerce in that city.¹⁰⁰ The Yips were part owners of the company and collected its rents.¹⁰¹

The company had built a gated Chinatown, and it exercised great control over Chinese jobs, housing, and gambling services.[102] Lew helped to establish a rival enterprise and used his own money to make loans for Chinese illegal immigrants' passage. The illegal immigrants worked for Lew's labor contracting firm, lived at his boardinghouse, gambled at his gambling club, and bought supplies at his company store until they paid off their debts. The Lun Yick Company did not want a rival, and it harassed Lew's firm. It built a house that blocked his front door until Lew persuaded the city of Nanaimo that his property was on a public road, which forced the house's removal. The Lun Yick Company had Lew arrested in 1922 on trumped-up charges that he had removed a surveyor's post.[103] Lew was acquitted in 1923 and countersued his opponents for false testimony and malicious prosecution. A jury awarded Lew an immense $10,000 settlement against Wing Lee (*Rong Li*), the Lun Yick Company's president. Canada's supreme court planned to hear the case only weeks before Lew's death. The chance that Wing might lose to Lew on appeal was one possible motive for the killing.[104]

By the summer of 1924, it appeared that Lew's probable alliance with the provincial Liberal government had ended. He hired a spy to infiltrate a Chinese Freemason bootlegging operation whose exposure would have damaged the ruling provincial Liberal Party. His espionage targeted an unnamed Chinese liquor store owner who was the powerful concubine of an unnamed wealthy Chinese Freemason leader. The *Vancouver Daily Province* described this leader as an "influential old tyee," a Chinook term which referred to a respected Chinese chief.[105] The infiltration of the Chinese woman's liquor business, which involved either false or stolen British Columbia Liquor Control Board seals on the bottles of alcohol, coincided with a wider public scandal over bootlegging.[106] This scandal involved allegations of patronage, corruption, and graft at the Liquor Control Board.[107] From mid-June 1924 through 20 September 1924, Lew and his allies taunted their opponents in a signed front-page *Da Han Gong Bao* advertisement stating that the city of Vancouver had snared the woman's Canadian Oriental Wine and Liquor Company for illegally selling alcohol without paying the proper taxes.[108] Vancouver city officials penalized the Chinese liquor store owner's business. However, she appeared to have powerful protectors; police declined to arrest her until four months later, on the night of Lew's death.[109] The contradictory pattern of events—official action but police delay—suggests there was a power struggle among Chinese for influence with Vancouver's authorities.

Chinese merchant factions in the Freemasons and Yue Shan also clashed over the control of illegal immigration to the United States. In 1920, *Sanyi* and *Siyi* competed for the CPR's favor, seeking to secure the lucrative position of Hong Kong ticket agent. The CPR awarded the position to *Sanyi* Lee Mongkow, taking it away from *Siyi* Yip family businesses. The Hong Kong ticket agent sold steamship and rail tickets to Chinese passengers traveling to Canada, the United States, and the rest of the Americas. By the interwar era, many settlement nations in the Americas had implemented anti-Chinese immigration policies, ranging from exclusion laws to informal deterrence. The global creation of barriers to Chinese migration meant that the CPR's continued profits increasingly depended on Chinese Pacific world political networks. The continuity of Chinese migration in the Exclusion Era involved more than economic or cultural factors. It depended on political initiatives by Chinese resident in the Americas. Their political alliances at ports and borders made Chinese migrations possible. Presumably, the CPR judged Lew's faction as being better able to deliver the political goods. Lee retired from his post as Victoria's official Chinese immigration interpreter, and he returned to Hong Kong to set up his CPR ticket agent business, which Chinese on both sides of the forty-ninth parallel regarded as a "most desirable commercial position."[110] Shortly afterward, David Lew began work as the official immigration interpreter at Victoria, screening Chinese entering Canada and the United States.

Given the unsettled situation for Chinese in Canada and abroad, Lew's faction moved quickly to consolidate its position as a premier legal broker. It targeted a faction of Chinese Canadian businesspeople within the Chinese Freemasons. While working as an immigration interpreter, Lew gathered evidence of a Chinese human-smuggling ring that made "huge profits" through the evasion of Canadian and U.S. immigration laws. Lew then revealed his findings to U.S. immigration authorities, enabling them to crack down on the ring in the United States. As a result, federal authorities arrested David C. Kerr, the U.S. vice consul in Vancouver, for accepting bribes from Chinese in Canada to evade the U.S. Chinese Exclusion Act through fraudulent entry as "students" and "merchants."[111] Lew also attempted to expose the smuggling ring's involvement in the Chinese "slave girl traffic." Lew claimed that a ring of Chinese businesspeople in larger Pacific Coast cities of both Canada and the United States had organized this illegal sex-trafficking scheme.[112] Lew told his Anglo lawyer friends that these businesspeople would kill him if he revealed his discoveries to the Canadian authorities.[113] If Lew's revelations about Chinese prostitution had become widely known, there would have been Anglo outrage, fueled as much by anti-Chinese sentiment as the truth about forced Chinese female immigration.[114] Such a public uproar might have forced authorities to back off from their protection of Lew's rivals.

Minutes before Lew was shot dead, he had arranged to speak with a *Vancouver Sun* reporter about prominent Chinese merchants' involvement in "female slavery."[115] Perhaps Lew's last act came from the heart rather than from his survival instinct. Maybe, like many Chinese, he disapproved of the abuse of these women.[116] Still, public scrutiny after Lew's death did not fundamentally change the institutions that backed Chinese political and legal brokerage. Given anti-Chinese laws, many immigrants believed that, despite being less than ideal, Chinese-Anglo alliances were necessary to sustain their way of life in both Canada and the larger Pacific world.

The political processes of legal brokerage survived Lew, despite a swift crackdown on all Chinese associations in British Columbia following his murder. In Vancouver, police raided gambling clubs, strictly enforced all health regulations, and warned that any Chinese restaurant which sold illegal alcohol would be shut down. Vancouver mayor William Owen attributed the murder to Chinese disputes over gambling. Most people at City Hall agreed, believing that an unnamed wealthy local Chinese association had hired an assassin to kill Lew.[117] The graft of both police and officials had long been an open secret in Vancouver, but Owen blamed the Chinese for their corrupting influence more so than the city authorities who had lined their own pockets. Meanwhile, the *Da Han Gong Bao* reported that the illegal alcohol trade in non-Chinese areas flourished unhindered. Within three years, the corruption of police and officials returned to business as usual.[118]

Chinese also continued to use the law as a tool to resolve internal disputes. On Vancouver Island, David Lew's attempt to force the Lun Yick Company to share power with other Chinese merchants ultimately worked. David Lew's brother Yick Pang Lew inherited the lawsuit against Wing Lee of the Lun Yick Company. The two Chinese merchant factions appealed it all the way to the British Empire's highest court, the Judicial Committee of the Privy Council in London. The law lords ruled that the case survived the death of Lew, but ordered that a new jury trial be held to set the award at a more appropriate level.[119] By the mid-1920s, other Chinese companies in Nanaimo had developed the area around Lew's former leasehold, creating an expanded Chinese district on Machleary Street.[120]

Lew's murder remains a mystery, though his Panyu friends believed that a Chinese Freemason assassin was responsible. Lew's friends found the man they believed to be the shooter, Chong Sing, in Victoria on 3 November 1924. Chong, they alleged, wanted revenge for Lew's involvement in bringing robbery charges against him.[121] In court, Chong seemed an improbable shooter because he was in his fifties and appeared "old and slow."[122] However, in 1924, *Da Han Gong Bao* reported that Chong had assaulted with a hammer two gamblers patronizing a rival establishment, putting one in the hospital.[123] The Chinese Freemasons hired a legal team to defend Chong and brought J. P. Sam, a Chinese Canadian legal interpreter, from Toronto to assist with the case.[124] Chong's lawyers claimed that he was a victim of a Yue Shan Society conspiracy to frame him for murder. The Vancouver police forgot to check for fingerprints on the assassin's revolver, so no physical evidence connected Chong to the crime.[125] At trial, eyewitnesses to the shooting appeared unconvincing, so an Anglo jury acquitted Chong on 24 April 1925.[126]

The surviving evidence does not clearly indicate the identity of David Lew's successor. Lew's death left a power vacuum among Vancouver's Chinese legal brokers. During 1925, Tom Whaun (*Huang Song Mao*), a court interpreter and a student at the University of British Columbia, clipped an English newspaper article that reported that two unnamed young Chinese men had engaged in a fierce rivalry to replace David Lew as "the gamblers' lawyer," though whether the article was referring to Whaun is unknown. Each man sought to demonstrate his legal virtuosity. The first young man intended to legalize Chinese gambling through court challenges. The second young man chose to demonstrate his skill through legal fights between Chinese associations.[127] The struggle to replace Lew underscored that legal brokerage relations involved more than structures and institutions. Brokers also relied heavily on their individual leadership, skills, and idiosyncratic improvisations on their informal "Chinese lawyer" role.

## *Conclusions*

Much like other forms of brokerage politics, legal brokerage relations became a structuring force for Chinese immigration during the Exclusion Era. Nevertheless, Chinese legal brokerage's frequent association with Chinese community power had an uneven effect. Chinese women and workers had lower positions in Chinese Canadian community hierarchies. In 1921, only one out of ten Chinese in Vancouver was female.[128] Consequently, when Chinese women engaged in disputes with Chinese men, they more readily turned to outsiders, such as European Christian missionaries, to act as their legal brokers.[129] Likewise, Chinese workers sometimes used labor unions as alternate legal advocates. Relations between these outsider and insider forms of dispute resolution merit future research.

The study of Chinese brokerage relations also suggests the promise of studying a multicultural legal culture that takes ethnic minorities' alternative public spheres and informal dispute resolution processes more fully into account. Chinese in British Columbia also had many legal dealings with non-European peoples, especially First Nations people and Japanese Canadians. A more complete legal history of British Columbia reflective of its population would require exploring brokerage in relation to other minority groups as well.

Last, Chinese legal brokerage should be studied more in its transnational contexts. The field of U.S. legal history suggests promising avenues. In Canada, neither Chinese immigration files nor Chinese civil law cases have been systematically studied, so much remains unknown. China's practices also inform much of Chinese Canadian legal interpreting as a profession. Future research in Canada and the United States may wish to explore how legal culture, institutions, and personnel emerged from a Pacific world context. Ultimately, Chinese-Anglo legal relations and the Pacific world could not often be separated.

THREE | Popularizing Politics
*The Anti-Segregation Movement as Social Revolution*

FOR ONE YEAR, FROM SEPTEMBER 1922 to September 1923, at least 3,000–4,000 Chinese in British Columbia joined an anti-segregation movement, defying both white authorities and powerful Chinese leaders to demand equal education in the public schools.[1] Through civil disobedience, protesters challenged pro-segregationists determined to separate Asian and white children. In Vancouver, organizer Joe Hope (*Liu Guangxu*) described the stakes to 500 Chinese attending an Anti-Segregation Association speech day. Without equal education, he said, "Our people's body could die. Our wealth could be stamped out. When our people's roots are cut off, we have no choice but to resist."[2] To Chinese, rising calls for their exclusion felt like a *fenghu*, a political movement as potent as the winds and tides.[3] In *Da Han Gong Bao*, Chinese declared that world history was on their side. Many protesters believed the Pacific world to be in the midst of egalitarian social revolutions, and these global events gave their cause a moral force more powerful than their white opponents' votes and laws.[4] Their opponents, who were both Anglo and Chinese, viewed these revolutionary trends as dangerous.[5] Thus, a protest that started with a school boycott grew into a greater struggle over defining the limits of popular democracy.

Historians have studied the anti-segregation movement mainly in terms of domestic race relations, seeing clashes between the "Chinese" and "white" sides. In their readings, school segregation policies expressed an overwhelming white supremacy that Chinese resistance could at times temper but not entirely halt.[6] This reading, while broadly correct, presumes a racial unity on both sides that Chinese news reports from the time do not support. According to Vancouver's *Da Han Gong Bao*, Chinatown's power brokers sharply differed in their opinions about how best to manage the school segregation problem. As collaborators with white power, and as leaders of resistance to it, many had been cautious about antagonizing their white allies. Most Chinese power brokers worked quietly to mitigate racial discrimination, fearing that public confrontation would only make things worse.[7] This time, several thousand ordinary Chinese, and a good many but not all brokers, would take a stand against social injustice.

Following the First World War, new popular social movements transformed brokerage relations across Canada's Pacific world. The entry of great numbers of ordinary people into politics had a profound impact.[8] As a result, brokers who derived their power from traditional entrepreneurial structures had to deal with a more restive, demanding populace. Many of these traditional brokers, including the anti-segregation movement's leaders, adapted to social movement politics. Social movement politics also expanded the personnel of brokerage relations. New groups of Chinese power brokers, such as students, intellectuals, workers, and women, also contended to manage race relations. These movements sparked a series of challenges that rapidly altered Chinese Canadian politics; they also started to transform race relations.

The challenges occurred during an era of intense Anglo racial prejudices toward Chinese Canadians. *Da Han Gong Bao* reported that a political movement of 1,000 European Canadians (*xiren*) had expanded the segregation of Chinese children at public schools in the nearby city of Victoria. The pro-segregation movement leaders then traveled to Vancouver. Only with the yellow and white races segregated, they argued, would they be able to prevent future Chinese and Japanese dominance in Canada's government and industries.[9] In response, school boards in North Vancouver and Vancouver started to investigate the issue. At a meeting of North Vancouver's school board in October 1922, European parents denounced the presence of older Chinese immigrants in elementary grades and demanded that they be segregated.[10] In Vancouver, Anglo demands for expanded public school segregation prompted the city's education department to revisit the idea of fully segregating Asian children.[11] The question had come up in 1920, but had been defeated when Vancouver's school principals refuted the accusation that Chinese pupils hindered their classmates' progress.[12] In 1922, the anti-segregation movement had greater Anglo support. A "political storm for segregation" had arisen, said *Da Han Gong Bao*, and its "drenching had not yet stopped."[13] Seeing Victoria as the thin edge of the wedge, Chinese Canadians organized an anti-segregation movement, bringing the Pacific world's pressures into their local struggle.

Between the late 1910s and the late 1930s, Canada's exclusionary policies peaked. Most scholars have viewed this era as a time of nativism, dominated by political movements to expel immigrants whom mainstream Canadians felt threatened the nation. Most West Coast historians have examined this struggle to halt the expansion of segregation by focusing on how a local-born "second generation" of Chinese engaged in the politics of defining the meaning of Canadian or American citizenship. They attempted to establish the principle that all citizens deserved equal rights to opportunity.[14] But another type of politics also became relevant to all sides of the school segregation struggle: the popular movements for anti-imperialist nationalism that were sweeping the Pacific world.

I argue that the social movements of the late 1910s and 1920s profoundly influenced Canada's race relations. In China, these movements included the May Fourth movement (1917–1925), the Nationalist revolution (1923–1928), and the founding of China's Communist Party (1921).[15] All three struggles mobilized ordinary workers to boycott and strike in protest against foreign domination. These struggles emerged as part of a global set of movements for anti-colonial nationalism after the First World War's victors did not fulfill their promise of liberation for colonized peoples.[16] Concurrently, the global rise of socialism inspired workers to organize themselves as political actors and to demand greater power in class relations. Moreover, new discourses of national identity in the United States and Canada began to imagine immigrants' place in more pluralistic terms. A growing Anglo receptivity to second-generation immigrant youth expressed a nascent cultural pluralism in social understandings of citizenship. Collectively, all three movements helped to popularize politics. In doing so, they diversified brokerage authority and expanded routes to political integration.

This chapter explores the Chinese anti–school segregation movement from transnational and regional perspectives in order to balance the existing scholarship's focus on school boycott activities in Victoria. Particularly, this account of the anti-segregation movement challenges a view about Chinese in Canada and the United States that sees protests for equal rights as an outcome of assimilation, rather than as a product of Pacific world experience, when often it was both.[17] Moreover, this literature has often missed the ways that global anti-colonial nationalist protests affected immigrants and race relations after the First World War.

Copious documentary evidence situates the anti-segregation movement in relation to Canadian encounters with Pacific world events. In the years shortly after the First World War, the pages of *Da Han Gong Bao* demonstrated a pattern of expansive hopes about the social revolutions coursing through China and Canada, followed by defensive retreat.[18] Most historians' retrospective analysis views the postwar period as one in which social justice movements were defeated by counterrevolutionary forces. Many Canadian historians see the period through the white labor movement's apparent failure to embrace a working-class solidarity that transcended racial divisions and its expression of anti-immigrant nativism.[19] An examination of the school boycott in the context of social movements helps to reconstruct the political contingencies of the moment. Inside this political maelstrom, a third generation of Chinese brokers in Vancouver and Victoria came of age. Many of these social movement leaders were merchants and interpreters who transformed their leadership of traditional institutions like Chinese benevolent associations[20] to meet changing Chinese Canadian public expectations. However, Chinese brokers in British Columbia divided on questions about the proper extent of popularizing politics. In China, Nationalist Party and Communist Party members often led the anti-colonial protests and boycotts that mobilized ordinary people, making some established Chinese merchants wary of the anti-segregation movement's leadership. Chinese political brokers had built their power through managing Chinese relations with Anglo institutions. Mass politics threatened to redraw those borders, reshaping the territory for leaders who collaborated across them. Local politics were forged within the dueling forces of global revolution and counterrevolution.

## *Contexts of Anti-Segregation Protest: Canada, the United States, China, and the British Empire*

The anti-segregation movement of 1922–1923 began when Chinese in Victoria boycotted public schools to protest against the expansion of racial segregation, but over the course of the year, it grew into a regional protest movement for equality. It was a response to Anglo pro-segregation pressures across the West Coast in the 1920s for more complete separation of the Chinese and white races in public schools.[21] At the time, Vancouver and Victoria practiced partial segregation by separating Chinese children from white children in the lower grades and by separating the "over-age" immigrants whose English was behind their grade level. San Francisco and Oakland, California, did likewise.[22] However, pro-segregation activists wanted to extend segregation to the few Chinese students who reached higher grades in both British Columbia and California.[23] In 1922, Victoria's school board expanded Chinese segregation to the first seven grades, drastically reducing Chinese children's opportunity to interact with English-speaking children.[24] Other immigrants, including Japanese, did not attend segregated schools. The majority of Chinese left school to work at age fourteen, so the new policy effectively excluded them from mingling with other Canadian children.[25] Enraged, Chinese Canadian parents organized a boycott of the Victoria public schools, creating a political crisis that neither side could easily resolve.

On 6 September 1922, the *Victoria Daily Times* reported that Chinese had "rebelled" over attending segregated public schools. At the Boys' Central School, Principal Cunningham ordered Chinese children out of their regular classrooms. As he started to lead the Chinese students away, a Chinese boy called out "in the Oriental lingo" and, in a flash, all of the Chinese students suddenly dispersed on cue, starting a citywide "school strike."[26] During 1922, over 125 similar politically motivated school strikes occurred in China. Three institutions organized the boycott: the Chinese Consolidated Benevolent Association (CCBA), the Chinese Chamber of Commerce, and the Chinese Canadian Club (CCC).[27]

Public pressure, boycott organizers hoped, would force the school segregation conflict into more favorable arenas than municipal politics. Chinese Canadians in Victoria raised money throughout British Columbia and Canada to support the boycott and to fund a court challenge. Simultaneously, they appealed to their Anglo allies in Canada. To Victoria's school board, Chinese boycott organizers submitted a petition with "the strongest possible objections to segregation."[28] As disenfranchised residents, they were legally powerless, so they appealed on moral and diplomatic grounds. "We are bitterly conscious of our helplessness so far as legal and constitutional redress are concerned, and we can only invoke the world reputation earned by the British Empire for justice and 'fair play' and the close friendship which has existed for many years between the British Empire and China."[29] The letter encapsulated the organizers' transpacific strategy, creating public pressure not only in Canada but also in China and the United States.

Locally raised Chinese youth in Victoria's Chinese Canadian Club (also known as the Chinese Canadian Citizens' Alliance and, in Chinese, as the *Tongyuanhui*, or Common Origins Association) also exerted public pressure on sympathetic Canadians.[30] In the *Victoria Daily Colonist*, Hope asked, "What can be the purpose behind this movement [for segregation]?" "Can it be the intention to prevent us securing an English education so that our children can be permanently ignorant, so that they must remain laborers to be exploited?"[31] His strategy tapped into a larger shift in public discourse about immigrant youth in U.S.–Canadian culture: the second-generation narrative.

By the 1920s, the second generation had become a popular phenomenon, a stage of assimilation and estrangement that was explored in fiction, films, popular songs, and social science.[32]

In Canada, second-generation immigrant youth groups emerged with the recent social invention of adolescence as a life stage.[33] To Anglos, members presented themselves as assimilated young Canadians and representatives of China. According to the *Da Han Gong Bao*, locally born Chinese (*tusheng*) in Victoria founded the Chinese Canadian Club in 1914 "to fight discrimination through dialogue with Western people."[34] In spirit, the club followed its probable American template, which shared the same Chinese name, *Tongyuanhui*, the Chinese American Citizens Alliance (CACA), also known in San Francisco as the Native Sons of the Golden State.[35] In Vancouver, the Chinese Students Alliance (CSA) performed a similar function, and memberships in CCC and CSA often overlapped. Like the CCC, the CSA also had strong ties to its counterparts in the United States.[36]

Protesters intended the boycott to press for recognition of youths' status as Chinese Canadians. Boycott spokesmen felt that their Canadian and U.S. educations showed that other Chinese also deserved the opportunity. Chinese Canadian Club president Joe Hope had graduated from a Victoria high school. Steering committee member Cecil Lee was a graduate of an American university. In 1924, the CCC had about thirty male and female members who had attended Canadian high schools. They were both immigrants and Canadian-born.[37] Members combined publicity with private persuasion, enlisting support from Canadian schoolteachers and education associations against segregation.[38] Boycott organizers also sent cables appealing for help to the Beijing government and to the British imperial government in London. They contacted workers' groups, student organizations, business associations, and newspapers in Shanghai, Guangzhou, and Hong Kong. Further, they mailed circulars asking for help from Chinese organizations across Canada.[39] In the spirit of the natural laws of equality, they asked their Chinese compatriots to boycott Canadian goods and to use public pressure to end Victoria's "crime" against the Chinese people.[40]

Chinese from Canada, the United States, and China responded with support. Chinese Canadians from across the country raised funds. Sailors from China on CPR ships sent donations. *Da Han Gong Bao*'s accounts of political repression in China reminded immigrants of their freedom in Canada, which gave Chinese Canadians a duty to become the educated leaders of a future modern China.[41] Vancouver's CSA wrote a front-page editorial, urging Chinese Canadians to stand steadfast and stick to the boycott despite fears of backlash: "Too many sides of our movement do not dare speak out.... Though the struggle for equality will not be quick, dare to act with determination."[42] Chinese students also offered their help, coming from as far as McGill and Columbia universities to advise the boycott organizers.[43] Chinese students at the University of Chicago wrote letters to the Victoria school board, the chamber of commerce, politicians, teachers, and citizens, asking them to reverse school segregation in the name of international friendship.[44]

As residents of the British Empire, the protesters' tactics also borrowed directly from Mohandas Gandhi's noncooperation movement, a peaceful challenge to British rule in India much scorned and feared in British Columbia's English press.[45] The Anglo newspaper the *Victoria Daily Times* saw a striking similarity between the Chinese strategy and the mass protests recently quashed in British India, noting, "No purchases of Canadian goods and no patronage of educational institutions fostered by the Canadian authorities is the plan favored by some of the more radical elements in Chinatown. In fact the plan is identical with that adopted by Gandhi and his followers in Indian to hamper British rule in that country."[46] Noncooperation also evoked the recent popular Chinese resistance to British imperialism, particularly the Hong Kong seamen's strike of 1922. In Hong Kong and Guangdong, 120,000 workers had blocked trade at the ports until Chinese seamen won more equitable pay compared with white seamen and the right to unionize.[47] China's Nationalist Party activists targeted race, class, and imperial relations that subordinated Chinese in British East Asia; by extension, noncooperation with segregated public schools in Canada suggested a parallel challenge to British dominance.

The Chinese protesters' name for their boycott, the school strike, also evoked recent labor militancy in British Columbia that had emboldened Asians to join with Anglo workers to challenge their subordination. Some Chinese in Vancouver had joined sympathy strikes during the Winnipeg general strike of 1919, which historian J. M. Bumstead called "one of the best-known events in modern Canadian history."[48] A great many others had followed the general strike in *Da Han Gong Bao*, which covered the events in Vancouver and Winnipeg in great detail.[49] Although large, the literature on the strike has not yet inquired into its effects on nonwhite workers, who were often the most subordinated members of the labor force.[50] As Canada confronted the prospect of a socialist workers' revolt, unions provided the first serious alternative to Chinese labor contractors' brokerage.[51] While the general strike did not succeed, Chinese workers attempted to unionize and strike frequently between 1916 and the early 1920s. Influenced by other events in Canada, China, and the United States, these workers asserted the power of noncooperation to claim an independent voice for ordinary Chinese.[52] For example, in 1919, over 1,000 Chinese shingle workers went on strike with European and Japanese workers. Their actions shocked Chinese labor contractors, who saw unions as a betrayal of trust. The unions forced the labor contractors to rescind wage cuts and restore the jobs of striking Chinese workers. The labor contractors also agreed to work together with Chinese unions to negotiate with mainstream employers.[53] The resulting hybrid system increased workers' power but did not displace the labor contracting system as the dominant means of hiring nonwhite migrant labor. Workers did not always win, but successful strikes suggested that people power might be able to challenge Chinese worker-master relations with the British Empire in both Canada and China.[54]

## *Setbacks and Leadership Splits: Brokerage Rivalries and Popular Protests*

Mass protest as an instrument of brokerage politics was a confrontation in which each side hoped to outlast the other, forcing its opponent to blink. Keeping the school protest together became more challenging when it became clear that the boycott would not immediately succeed. The boycott started in high spirits, but one month into the protest, the Chinese protesters' court challenge failed, establishing the legality of school segregation.[55] Negotiations stalled, but Victoria's school board compromised, allowing a few Chinese to return to integrated classes. The school board announced that five Chinese students had passed an English-language test, qualifying them to be admitted to regular, integrated classes. All five were children of wealthy Chinese merchants. For all other Chinese students, there were two options: attend segregated schools or attend no classes at all. They could be declared truants and have no public schooling for the rest of the semester. George Deane, a school board member, insisted that a lack of English-language ability was the reason for Chinese segregation. However, Victoria schools tested only Chinese Canadian children for English-language proficiency. Other immigrant children continued to attend regular, integrated classes.[56] Meanwhile, Chinese picketers intimidated the boycott-breakers. In October 1922, police had to protect the handful of Chinese children still attending public school classes. After three weeks of harassment, the Chinese boycott-breakers gave in and stopped attending public schools. The school board then canceled all Chinese classes.[57]

On 28 October 1922, the Anti-Segregation Association established an alternative community school in Victoria's Chinatown, where boycotting students received education in English and Chinese. Two Chinese students who had graduated from U.S. universities and returned to China, Huang Zhuo Tang and Huang Xia Sheng, came to Victoria to teach in the Chinese resistance school and to aid the protest.[58] The two returned students symbolically linked Victoria's struggles with China's student movement for anti-colonial nationalism. One European female teacher also taught the English language to the Chinese students attending the resistance school so that their Canadian schooling would not be interrupted.[59]

Sustained mass protest also created dilemmas for political entrepreneurs striving to make themselves into bridges between British and subaltern populations. In October 1922, *Da Han Gong Bao* recorded mounting political divisions among Chinese. Organizers' tones shifted from confidence to defensiveness.[60] This shift, which historians have overlooked, undermines interpretations of the boycott as an expression of Chinese racial unity. Granted, Chinese statements to Victorian authorities and the English-language press almost always claimed unity for strategic reasons. However, internal community debates contained more variation. *Da Han Gong Bao* printed only stories friendly to the boycott, but even within its partisan pages, boycott organizers increased their pleas for solidarity. The Victoria CCBA called for a unified strategy to fight for equal education that would involve all Chinese workers and merchants in Victoria and beyond. "If we can unite our hearts, we can join our powers into one resistance struggle," wrote Joe Hope to Vancouver Chinese. "If we give an inch, they will take a mile."[61] As powerful Chinese brokers divided over the wisdom of continued mass protest, Hope implored Vancouver Chinese for support in *Da Han Gong Bao*. "Stopping the boycott now would be a one hundred percent loss. We would step backward and see intellectuals' progress dissipate."[62] However, Chinese depended on Anglo goodwill for their prosperity in Canada. They wondered whether they could afford to offend their hosts.[63]

The fissures among Chinese leaders reflected intense competition over political power within Chinese migrant communities. The *Da Han Gong Bao* never revealed the names of the wealthy Chinese leaders whom it alleged opposed the boycott. Like ordinary Chinese, the newspaper feared leaders with influential brokerage ties to Canadian government and business institutions. To combat these brokers' power, boycott organizers turned to the egalitarian language of mass politics. "For the future equality of all people," wrote Hope, "do not follow a policy of yielding because stopping in the middle when we are very close to reaching success humbles the hopes of every sacrifice and the currying of every favor except wealth."[64] These appeals to popular power and critiques of wealthy, self-interested community leaders soon injected new life into the movement. Leaders had already framed the movement as a clash between global revolution and counterrevolution. They now presented the rivalries among Chinese leaders as similar battles.

A stunning betrayal within Victoria's Anti-Segregation Association provoked Hope to reframe the movement in even more revolutionary terms. The *Da Han Gong Bao* described the event in a story titled "Because of the Reckless Rash Actions of an Overseas Chinese Corrupt Leader." Negotiations between the Anti-Segregation Association and the Victoria school district had been on the verge of success when an unspecified Chinese leader betrayed the resistance. Boycott leaders felt that "attaining justice would come from discussions, negotiations, legal challenges, organizing associations, and asking for help. Each would add to the weight of the resistance's hand."[65] Rival brokers, identified in *Da Han Gong Bao* only as wealthy merchants, viewed the school protest leaders as dangerous radicals. In October 1922, Vancouver's *Da Han Gong Bao* claimed that a "cunning, adulterous criminal" had envied resistance leaders' success so much that he had spied for Victoria's government. This Chinese leader had many friends in Victoria's governing party. Secretly, he met with them to "destroy our overseas Chinese plan to resist segregation."[66] The paper did not disclose exactly how this leader allegedly betrayed the boycott movement's negotiations. This leader may have been Harry Hastings, a Chinese British legal interpreter who had been hired to represent the boycotters in negotiations with the Victoria school board. In 1924, Hastings told Winifred Raushenbush, an interviewer for the Survey of Race Relations, that he had curbed the school boycott's radicalism. His public admission suggested that he believed that his actions needed no defense. Hastings had advised a British Canadian politician friend not to give in so that Chinese protesters "would not feel their power." He claimed to have stopped Chinese "hotheads" from bringing the radical politics of the Hong Kong seamen's strike to the school protest. He especially discouraged noncooperation, dissuading Chinese workers who wanted to punish segregation supporters through labor strikes.[67] Whether it was Hastings or not, the unnamed informer's actions immediately led to a sterner school board position, possibly because the informer revealed the Chinese community's strike fund. After the betrayal, the Chinese and English press dropped all mention of noncooperation except for the school boycott itself.

Further, this rival Chinese broker informed his white friends that the school board should win. The boycott, this leader claimed, did not spring from the "public will" but from agitators who stirred up ignorant Chinese to revolution (*qiao qi fenghu*). To crush the school boycott, he advised, the board had to become sterner. It had not used terror, and it had to cause more fear to bring Chinese to heel. "Among Victoria's Chinese, promised this 'headman' and also among Canada's Chinese, there existed the utmost degree of loyalty and obedience to white people,"[68] wrote *Da Han Gong Bao*. He implied that the character of Chinese abroad (*qiaobao*) made them easy to manipulate and, in any case, they had little influence within Canada's political system. The Anti-Segregation Association's noncooperation plans only would anger Canadian businesses and employers. For the sake of the Chinese themselves, he advised, Victoria's politicians had to stand firm on school segregation and crush Chinese resistance.[69]

The fragmentary Chinese newspaper record cannot independently confirm this account of betrayal. To many Chinese Canadian readers, however, it appeared plausible. Many Chinese power brokers routinely collaborated with white political and economic elites through backroom brokerage. For Chinese merchants who acted as economic middlemen, an indefinite boycott with prospects for noncooperation through Chinese strikes and boycotting Anglo businesses would have strained their relations with their Anglo patrons. The boycott organizers, however, also would have had a motive to deflect attention away from their protest's lack of success. Regardless, the betrayal accounts brought new energy to the boycott, making it a struggle over egalitarianism both within and beyond the Chinese population.

## *Revolutionary Politics*

To fight fear, Hope and a young Vancouver leader, Foon Sien Wong, appealed to the exuberant mass politics of the age in the indelible language of revolutions. Young Chinese boycott leaders rallied their Vancouver followers with calls for national awakening that echoed both China's revolutions and Canada's class politics. Hope appealed to Gold Mountain sojourners' (*jinshanke*) manly responsibilities for their families and their nations in *Da Han Gong Bao*:

> If this policy is implemented, our people will have no room to move here, so our strong resistance is just. . . . We act, legally, not with any ill intentions, nor do we evade danger. We do this to show our country's struggle and to show the character of overseas Chinese.[70]

Hope urged Chinese to conquer fear by standing up for themselves. If Chinese continued to defer to Europeans and to Chinese leaders allied with them, Chinese "without money" would have no future in Canada. Only protest would reveal their hidden strength: "Like an underground spring, whose deep waters only bubble up on the surface, I call on you to flow forth boldly."

With mass protests, "we will become the River Han," the birthplace of Chinese civilization.[71] China's Nationalist Party revolutionaries frequently made similar allusions.[72] To his audience, Hope's equation of the masses with Chinese political and cultural authority evoked a revolutionary populism.

From a Chinese newspaper's perspective, the school strike protests took place on greater global stages than did domestic relations, yet these interactions gave regional Chinese politics their distinctive shape. The prospect of longer-term struggle and a divided Chinese leadership in Victoria prompted Hope to request help from Vancouver Chinese. On 2 November 1922, he appealed for support in *Da Han Gong Bao*: "In the past, Chinese coming here had this fate: we were swept into a corner. However, we slowly crept in, extending our community across the entire country. In this situation, in this place, we therefore stand determined to defend our territory."[73] This movement for equality mobilized the Chinese population of both greater Vancouver and Victoria on a mass scale. As the strike dragged on into November 1922, Chinese in Victoria held a community speech day to protest school segregation. *Da Han Gong Bao* reported that over 2,500 Chinese braved drenching rain to gather in a white-owned theater to hear speeches protesting school segregation.[74] In the past, Chinese meetings usually had been held in Chinese theaters. White theaters usually segregated Chinese, so the meeting site itself symbolized Chinese claims to Canada. Men, women, and children packed the theater. Speakers included Joe Hope, Vancouver's Seto Ying Shek (Seto More, Situ Mao), and a woman named Li Yun He. After hearing speeches, the assembled Chinese decided to petition as a group for help from the government. They sang Chinese and Western patriotic songs. A Chinese resistance school choir of boys and girls then performed the songs "National Shame" and "Citizens Come Together."[75] *Da Han Gong Bao* described the meeting's stirring conclusion:

> When the meeting came to a close, all of the Chinese seated at the meeting rose to their feet. In unison, the great sea of Chinese shouted that they pledged their lives to resisting until the Anti-Segregation Association had won victory. Then they shouted three times: "Long live China's great Republic!"[76]

The movement had started with a school boycott, but it had become greater than a stand against British Columbia's anti-Asian movement. Their pledge to resist to the death was more than rhetorical. In China during this era, boycotts to protest against repressive governments had led to the jailing and injury of activists.[77] In Canada, too, Chinese had experienced violence when they attempted to move beyond the margins. In addition to Vancouver's two anti-Asian riots, violence often happened between Chinese and white individuals, even among children in the public schools.[78]

Chinese Canadians in Vancouver also mobilized to support the anti-segregation movement through the popular culture of China's anti-colonial nationalism. In February 1923, Chinese students in Vancouver performed a fundraising play written in *baihua*, vernacular spoken Chinese. The students titled their play *Virtuous Women Avenge a Grievance (Lie Nu Bao Jiao Chou)*.[79] Other Vancouver Chinese groups also performed plays to support the boycott. In March 1923, *Da Han Gong Bao* reviewed one fundraising theater performance, a new Chinese drama to help education in the "new world society" of the homeland. This "great" play, wrote the paper, told the story of a young concubine's son in love.[80] Vancouver Chinese-language school students also performed a fundraising *baihua* play, *Man in Black (Hei Yi Ren)* in Cantonese.[81] At the performance, over 200 Chinese households and firms donated funds to fight school segregation.[82]

At a second Victoria mass meeting at a white people's theater in November 1922, school boycott organizers again framed the school protest as a vital struggle against a rising anti-Asian movement in Canada. Meeting chair Ma Yu Ru addressed an audience of thousands. If Chinese permitted school segregation to be expanded, "every class of overseas Chinese" would face diminished future opportunity. The public schools produced most brokers and community leaders. He urged Chinese to defend their freedoms in Canada and to resist segregation in the name of China's national honor. Joe Hope pleaded for unity, claiming that only a show of strength would force Victoria's school board to back down.[83] A white lawyer informed the crowd that Canada's Parliament was considering a proposal to end Chinese immigration.[84] The anti-segregation movement brought together international ideas about revolution with the local politics of school protest, so ties to the Pacific world added more than diplomatic pressure; they also contributed to the anti-segregation movement's ideas.

## *The Anti-Segregation Movement Spreads to Vancouver: Brokerage Politics in Regional and International Perspective*

Vancouver Chinese power brokers formed the Anti-Segregation Support Association, led by Chinese Benevolent Association (CBA) leaders who had halted Vancouver's earlier attempt to expand school segregation.[85] On

5 November 1922, the Vancouver Anti-Segregation Association and local Chinese merchants sponsored a speech day at Chinatown's 500-seat theater. Joe Hope explained that Europeans feared Chinese as economic competitors, so they treated Chinese like "criminals."[86] After the speech day, interpreter Lambert Sung (*Song Lang Bi*) wrote about the anti-segregation movement's importance in a front-page editorial in *Da Han Gong Bao*. Chinese must "stamp out" the anti-Asian movement, Sung warned, because it threatened Chinese Canadians' future. "We need unity that puts public interests above personal interest because it will affect every family and every person," he wrote, alluding to Chinese merchants who had collaborated with Victoria's school board against the boycott.[87] Chinese Canadians also had to strengthen China, because its chaos led other nations to disrespect Chinese immigrants. Sung described the work of the Vancouver Anti-Segregation Support Association leaders as negotiation and education. Its leaders included the famed legal interpreter Won Alexander Cumyow, the scholarly travel agent Seto Ying Shek, and dentist Yick Pang Lew. Swiftly, these Chinese leaders lobbied sympathetic European contacts in Vancouver.[88] They also wrote to English newspapers and to papers in China. Further, they requested that China's government send a representative to negotiate the issue.[89] Perhaps as a result, *Da Han Gong Bao* reported no further action by Vancouver's school board. Still, Chinese consul Lin warned Chinese children to behave. They should avoid fighting with European children because disputes would fuel calls for segregation.[90] Ultimately, the threatened European boycott of Vancouver's public schools to force full Chinese segregation never materialized.

In Vancouver, as in Victoria, the school protest provided a platform for new, populist political brokerage relations against the backdrop of divides in both the Chinese and Anglo populations. University student Foon Sien Wong helped to organize a new Vancouver Chinese Students Alliance (CSA, *Zhongguo Liuyun Xuesheng Hui*), based on May Fourth movement models, to deal with the school segregation issue.[91] Given divisions within the Chinese population, Wong's new CSA appeared to be a temporary off-shoot of the larger, older Chinese Students Alliance. The original CSA had included those with high school educations and those with college educations in Vancouver and Victoria since at least 1916.[92] As Victoria's school board mused about a law that would force Chinese boycotters back to school, the CSA quickly organized a mass speech day in Vancouver. The Chinese students explained the boycott movement to readers of Vancouver's Chinese newspaper, *Da Han Gong Bao*: "We know that this policy's goal is to separate Chinese, first employing measures to separate Chinese children and then the rest of the overseas Chinese. Malice lies in its heart.... Only united together will we be strong. Fight for justice."[93]

Besides rallying support within the Chinese population, CSA members planned a campaign of personal diplomacy. They met with individual Anglos, such as high school principals.[94] Local merchants sponsored Chinese banquets at which CSA members mingled with Anglo politicians, including the mayor, other officials, and police.[95] The CSA also sent a delegation to Victoria. Speakers at a CSA speech day included Consul Lin Bao Heng and representatives from the leftist Chinese Workers' Party (*Zhonghua Gongdang*), which was affiliated with China's Nationalist Party, the Vancouver Anti-Segregation Support Association, the Guangzhi school, and the Xian Xiang Theatrical Society. The groups also sent a joint request to China's government asking for its assistance in the resolution of the issue.[96]

Within days of the CSA petition, China's consul general, Zhou Qi Lian, arrived in British Columbia to negotiate with Victoria's school board. The Beijing government only controlled the northern part of China, so Zhou threatened Canada with both an official economic boycott and a popular boycott by China's citizens, which together would cut off Canadian business relations with China.[97] But Zhou's negotiations proved fruitless.[98] The paucity of scholarship on early China-Canada relations makes it difficult to determine the immediate impact of Zhou's boycott threat. Canada's officials sent an emissary to check with ruling warlords in Beijing, Shanghai, and Guangzhou about whether an economic boycott might result if Canada's Parliament cut off Chinese immigration. The warlords reassured the emissary that no boycott would happen; they could contain China's Nationalist Party.[99] However, the Nationalist revolution caught the warlords by surprise. In 1925, the Nationalists in China rose to power on a wave of anti-colonial nationalism. Chinese in China boycotted Canadian and British goods. With help from Chinese Canadian funds, the Nationalists also organized strikes to impede all economic relations with Canada and Great Britain, which greatly harmed trade.[100]

In the spring of 1923, a more dire threat emerged: a proposed national law to end Chinese Canadian immigration. Besides barring future Chinese entry, the bill would deport all Chinese who were unable to speak English and all illegal immigrants. Further, the law required all Chinese to register with the immigration department and to carry special photo identity papers. Even naturalized and Canadian-born Chinese had to register.[101] Previously in Canada, only African slaves and First Nations people had been subject to this kind of "pass system."[102] Zhu Bo Ran advised the readers of *Da Han Gong Bao* that "personal friendship diplomacy by individual citizens" would be necessary to combat the new Chinese Immigration Act. Chinese who were fluent in English should lobby the major party leaders, the legislators, the white business community, and newspapers across Canada. Labor leaders, too, should be lobbied, wrote Zhu, because organized labor was the main opponent of Chinese immigration. Chinese in Canada wrote to allies in Shanghai and Guangzhou for help. They appealed to Chinese workers, businesses, and student groups. However, China had no effective national government so international pressure had little influence. Newspapers in China also published Chinese Canadian letters urging boycotts of Canadian goods.[103]

As Parliament debated the anti-Chinese bill in 1923, Chinese Canadians were isolated from the mainstream political system. Power brokers could at times make backroom arrangements to mitigate anti-Chinese immigration laws, but they had little influence over the formal legislative process. By the 1920s, many Anglo and French Canadians believed Chinese to be not assimilable based on an ambiguous set of ideas about supposed racial, cultural, and national differences that suggested incompatibility with the "white Canada" ideal. Many white Canadians also opposed Chinese as economic competitors, while China's political instability reduced the value of Chinese Canadians' Pacific world ties.[104] Hoping to stop the bill, British Columbia Chinese sent two representatives to Ottawa, Joe Hope and Seto Ying Shek. They lobbied legislators for several days, handing out eighteen-page briefs, which the MPs did not read.[105] Canada's elected House of Commons passed the bill with a requirement to deport all Chinese who could not pass an English test, which Canada's unelected Senate later removed.[106] Hope and Seto returned to British Columbia, disappointed that the anti-segregation movement could not prevail on the national stage.

The anti-segregation movement had more impact in British Columbia, where most Chinese Canadians lived. After one year, Chinese protest in the Vancouver-Victoria region stopped school segregation's advance. On 4 September 1923, the *Da Han Gong Bao* announced that "Resistance to School Segregation Achieves Victory." All Chinese students in Victoria returned to regular classes in their neighborhood schools except for seventeen students who did not know English. However, the school board insisted on returning to the pre-boycott segregation policy. Chinese children living in the North Ward District would have to attend a separate segregated school for the first four years of their elementary education. The board also renewed its offer that Chinese children who succeeded in rapidly learning English could be promoted earlier to integrated schools at the discretion of the teachers and principals. When the boycott had started in September 1922, the school board had insisted on increasing Chinese school segregation to grade seven. Given the unfavorable political climate, returning segregation to just the first four elementary grades was remarkable. At a Chinese community meeting to discuss whether to accept the school board's offer, resistance leaders explained that a compromise without any school segregation was unacceptable to the school board, so parents voted that Chinese children would return to the public schools.[107] Partial Chinese school segregation in Victoria continued until after the Second World War; in Vancouver, it lasted until 1936.[108]

## Conclusions

Scholars of Canada have often debated whether the brief egalitarian moment after the First World War had any lasting impact. Most of these discussions stress Canada's domestic labor movement.[109] Despite the fact that many non-British immigrants participated in this radical moment, scholars have overlooked its racial/ethnic dimensions. Like Yip On in the generation before them, these new brokers constructed political strategies that built on larger social movements, both local and global. Thus, a Chinese minority amplified its claims to more inclusive visions of immigrant nation-building. New brokers also tapped into larger unease about tensions between British imperialism and democracy. They desired an expansion of Chinese rights in Canada, but they also spoke as part of the anti-imperialist movements for self-determination that were challenging the British Empire in Asia.

Political responses to Canada's diversifying population included more than Anglo nativism. Granted, shortly after the First World War, anti-Asian movements triumphed in their quest to restrict immigration, and the Ku Klux Klan established itself in Canada's West.[110] Still, a nascent Canadian liberal, pluralist ideology of society had a measurable influence on the school segregation debates in both the English and Chinese press. When the boycott began, Victoria's *Daily Colonist* first took a neutral position, but it also gave Chinese Canadians an unusual opportunity to reach the English public on its letters page.[111] In April 1923, the *Colonist*'s editors denounced discrimination in the public schools as "narrow-minded visions which sowed the seeds of international strife."[112] Chinese-language newspapers also reported that European Canadian allies' quiet support helped to stem the tide of school segregation.[113] The steadfast conviction behind Chinese protests and their ultimate victory showed that a deep well of sympathy existed.

The new populist political brokers of the 1920s had seized initiative just as Chinese immigration exclusion altered brokerage's political context. In 1923, *Da Han Gong Bao* offered the following "plain talk about overseas Chinese resistance to harsh immigration regulations": Chinese needed to develop more extensive political alliances in Canada.[114] Still, Canadian-raised brokers who projected second-generation immigrant identities operated within both transnational and local contexts. Their calls for the oppressed Chinese masses "to flow forth like the River Han" resonated with the age's revolutionary spirit.[115] Canadian-raised Chinese leaders also readily forged social ties with Anglo Canadians, but like their elders, their efforts to position themselves as crucial links between ordinary Chinese and the greater powers required constant maneuvering. The second generation's political power still depended largely on the first generation's goodwill. To lead, the younger generation had to mobilize both Chinese immigrant followers and capital. Second-generation Chinese political brokerage thus remained rooted in Chinese diaspora, Canadian, and U.S. identities.

The outcome of British Columbia's anti-segregation struggle paralleled events on the U.S. West Coast. In 1926, Chinese Americans in San Francisco also stopped an expansion of partial school segregation. Scholars interpret their struggle as a product of second-generation leadership.[116] From the fragmentary surviving Chinese American newspapers, researchers believe that more populist aspects of China's May Fourth movement and Nationalist revolution did not have great force in the United States.[117] Since West Coast Chinese communities shared newspaper content, Vancouver's complementary set of surviving Chinese immigrant newspapers suggests a more profound shift and split in the political landscape. New social movements helped to popularize political power, altering relations among immigrants and in the larger society. Future research may expand the implications of this global and local moment for evolving senses of immigrant nationhood in Canada and the United States.

The political organization of Chinese Canadian intellectuals also marked a turning point in Vancouver's history. For many years, merchants and interpreters with entrepreneurial motives had dominated Chinese community life. Their economic alliances with mainstream society, however, proved vulnerable to changing business conditions. By 1926, British Columbia's slackening economy and a minimum wage law made many Chinese workers more disposable, weakening Chinese unions.[118] Chinese workers also lost the support of China's Nationalist Party, which purged leftist members.[119] Meanwhile, the Canadian Parliament's ban on Chinese entry and China's boycotts imperiled merchant brokerage that depended on the commerce of migration.

Nevertheless, revolutions in China and exclusion in Canada had begun to change the terms of political leadership. The injection of mass politics into immigrant communities shifted power relations between ordinary people and their leaders. Educated youth and the labor union organizers of social movements added new alternatives to the dominance of wealth. Further, debates over China's future brought new urgency to intellectuals' public service within emigrant communities.

By June 1924, Vancouver Chinese leaders had exhausted every legal and political strategy to overturn the Chinese Immigration Act of 1923, which they called the "forty-three harsh regulations" and the "exclusion act." Zhou Chi Zhu wrote in *Da Han Gong Bao*: "Canadians should ask in their hearts, would it not be more virtuous to treat overseas Chinese kindly? The forty-three harsh regulations' passage oppressed us overseas Chinese, humiliated our entire country, destroyed our way of life, and took away our freedom."[120] In the aftermath of the passage of Canada's Chinese exclusion law, Chinese Canadian intellectuals decided to take another page from the strategy of China's May Fourth movement. In China, reformers had decided that the nation needed to change its social relations by fundamentally altering its way of thinking.[121] Chinese Canadian intellectuals regularly debated the merits of particular incidents of discrimination in letters to the editor in English newspapers. Perhaps, if they could change the premises of knowledge about Chinese immigrants, they could alter the terms of the debate in their favor. As we shall see in the next chapter, their actions would influence future scholarly perceptions of immigrant brokers for longer than they ever imagined.

FOUR | # Fixing Knowledge
*Pacific Coast Chinese Leaders' Management of the Chicago School of Sociology*

IN 1924, ROBERT PARK, A sociologist from the University of Chicago, directed a study that asked: are Asians more like blacks or whites?[1] To find the answer, Anglo American researchers interviewed Chinese from British Columbia to California, starting with Vancouver, Canada.[2] West Coast Chinese felt that Park's answer could not be left to chance, so they mobilized the Chinese community to steer the researchers in a specific direction. Chinese leaders hoped to win white scholars' sympathy and turn the power of social science against anti-Chinese policies. Chinese regarded the study as a battle of wits, a battle that the researchers did not know they were fighting.[3] This meeting of community activists and scholars would help to shape a pivotal set of ideas about immigration and race that would become known as the Chicago School of Sociology.[4]

During the early twentieth century, sociologists often depended on local ethnic leaders for access to foreign-language research data.[5] Studies of the Chicago School do not completely take into account these collaborations. They favor the perspectives of the researchers but do not fully consider the possibility that their subjects could also be creators of expert knowledge. While researchers often imagined interviews as transactions between individuals, their nonwhite immigrant subjects often approached them as political exchanges between two groups.[6] Ethnic leaders' mediating role in community-academic relations made them the unsung coauthors of some of the twentieth century's most influential ideas about human migration.

I explore these collaborations in intellectual history through a new interpretation of a foundational study about Asians in Canada and the United States, the Survey of Race Relations. Most scholars treat the survey as a uniquely rich archive of early Chinese and Japanese life on the West Coast.[7] However, the survey can also be read as an exceptional record of brokered knowledge between Chinese and Anglo elites.[8] Henry Yu argues that white American scholars' Orientalism, beliefs that cast Asian Americans as exotic informants, defined this meeting.[9] The racial dynamics within the ivory tower, however, had different valences out in the field. The survey's researchers could not speak or read Chinese, so they needed ethnic leaders' help.[10] In West Coast Chinese communities, Anglo researchers were the outsiders. Chinese newspapers reveal what interview subjects chose to say—and what they left out. The personal papers of some Chinese further illuminate the men and women who spoke with the survey as part of the community plan. In British Columbia, where the survey began, two-thirds of Chinese Canadian interview subjects were brokers.[11] These brokers hoped to "fix knowledge" by shading the data that researchers would find.

In 1924, Vancouver's *Da Han Gong Bao* told its readers about a community-wide plan to manage visiting American researchers conducting the Survey of Race Relations. "This matter involves every Chinese person's future," wrote the paper.[12] Most Chinese leaders knew it would be dangerous for the survey to discover the "truth": the majority of the city's Chinese residents were temporary workers who intended to return to China or move to the United States.[13] If the researchers saw Chinese as temporary migrant workers, then Canada's anti-Chinese movement might be strengthened.

At the time, most white West Coast residents assumed Asians to be undesirable strangers. *British Columbia Magazine* described the "Oriental" character: "Racially he is opposite to the Anglo-Saxon in life, thought, religion, temperament, taste, morals, and modes, as ice is to fire."[14] Many Canadians believed racial differences to be immutable, even biological, so even a small number of Asians posed a threat to maintaining a "white Canada." Following this logic, British Columbia denied all Asians voting rights regardless of their citizenship. In 1924, racial conflicts over Asians' alleged inability to assimilate had reached a fever pitch as Canada and the United States took further steps to exclude new Asian immigrants. Now, leading American scholars within the new field of immigration studies planned a scientific study of Asian immigrants' capacity to assimilate.[15]

In response, the Chinese Benevolent Association (CBA) organized a public meeting to discuss how to respond to the researchers. The CBA president, Yick Pang Lew, presided. Two co-chairs, the interpreters Seto Ying Shek and Lambert Sung, helped to organize the strategy.[16] Many of the power brokers attending the meeting guided and guarded the junctures between societies.[17] They included Chinatown's most politically skilled leaders, scholars, legal assistants, interpreters, professionals, businesspeople, and clergy. According to the *Da Han Gong Bao*, all Chinese questioned by the researchers were to emphasize their assimilation in Canada. Any contrary evidence should be explained as a result of racial discrimination.[18] Chinese leaders also controlled the researchers' access to interview subjects. Their influence ensured that ordinary Chinese would comply.[19] According to the *Da Han Gong Bao* and survey records, Chinese management of the researchers extended beyond Vancouver to Chinese community power brokers in Victoria, Seattle, and San Francisco. Brokers believed that, by controlling the premises of knowledge about Chinese immigrants, they could alter the terms of West Coast racial politics in their favor.[20]

## *Surveying the "Oriental Problem"*

The survey's efforts to find the truth about the "Oriental problem" unfolded against the backdrop of a growing public faith in science as a nation-building guide.[21] It was the first major social science study of Asians in Canada and the United States.[22] Though much ink had been spilled about West Coast racial conflicts, few scholars had included Asians' viewpoints in their research prior to 1924. Chinese Canadians felt even higher stakes: no scholarly book about them ever had been published. Given Park's stature, *Da Han Gong Bao* expected that his planned book about East Asian immigrants would be used by educational institutions across the United States and Canada.[23]

At the time, most scholars viewed Asian immigration as an issue that affected the United States and Canada jointly.[24] Canada thus provided a means to test the global relevance of the researchers' approaches to immigration. The survey's ultimate goal was to compile a hemispheric account of race relations on the Pacific frontier from Canada to Mexico. In this grand project, the survey's interviews with East Asians in Canada and the United States served as the first stage.[25]

As planning for the survey began in 1923, the researchers found broad support in British Columbia. At the time, Canada offered little funding for social science research. The University of British Columbia, a survey cosponsor, had been open only since 1915. It operated out of church basements, makeshift shacks, and tents in downtown Vancouver because the provincial legislature had never fully funded its construction.[26] The survey was sponsored by a New York–based foundation, the Institute of Social and Religious Research, adding to its prestige. *Da Han Gong Bao* reported that the survey had a budget of US$25,000 to $30,000, an astounding amount from a Canadian perspective.[27] In British Columbia, the survey recruited Anglo supporters among both friends and foes of Asian Canadians, including organized labor and middle-class reform groups. Mainstream corporations like the Hudson's Bay Company donated funds. Institutions as diverse as the Catholic Church, the *Vancouver Sun*, and the Asiatic Exclusion League all endorsed the research.[28] The survey appointed John Nelson, a journalist and political leader in British Columbia's Provincial Party, as its British Columbia regional director.

Nelson was one of Canada's most influential opinion shapers on Asian immigration issues. In 1921, he wrote in *Maclean's*, English Canada's national news magazine, that Asians showed little sign of being able to fully assimilate to Canada's European "national type" and heritage. Therefore, he advised denying Asians the franchise and restricting their numbers, lest their race supplant Europeans and "occupy Canada's one strip of Pacific littoral."[29] His new Provincial Party (1922–1924) and another new organization dedicated to political reform, Vancouver's Ku Klux Klan (1924–1925), targeted party machines' corruption.[30] The English press often linked Chinese to this political graft, portraying brokers as a corrupting force.[31] However, Nelson could contribute only modest time to supervising the survey's research. His other work as an editor of the Provincial Party organ, the *Searchlight*, and of the farm journal *United Farmer* came first.[32] The survey needed an early success to ensure future fundraising, so Park sent a trusted doctoral student, Winifred Raushenbush, to British Columbia for six months to conduct the survey's Chinese field research.[33]

Vancouver's Chinese brokers felt that Raushenbush's inquiry required careful management. She had a sharp intellect and tongue, along with cutting-edge research experience in the new science of sociology. She had assisted some of the United States' most brilliant scholars of immigration and race relations. In 1919, she had worked with William I. Thomas on *The Polish Peasant in Europe and America*, a groundbreaking study of ethnic consciousness that drew heavily on personal letters and life histories. Raushenbush also had worked with immigrant leaders across the United States on Park's 1922 book, *The Immigrant Press and Its Control*.[34] During the first six months of 1924, she conducted the survey's British Columbia field research. She also planned to write a dissertation about Chinese Canadians.[35] In the battle of wits, Chinese Canadians quickly found that she was no fool and a far more prepared researcher than they had anticipated.

Like many of their Anglo counterparts, Chicago sociologists presumed racial difference, though they often appeared somewhat agnostic about its source. Robert Park's early research had focused on the "Negro problem" in the United States. Before coming to Chicago, he had worked with Booker T. Washington at the Tuskegee Normal and Industrial Institute. In the southern United States, Park puzzled over the seeming inability of African Americans to assimilate to white cultural norms. He also wondered about the causes of their subordinate status in U.S. society. Park's scholarly articles suggested a combination of social, historical, and cultural causes for Africans' apparent slowness in becoming part of the mainstream. In Park's time, his belief that racial differences might be socially constructed was relatively progressive, though he did not expect white and nonwhite to become equal.[36]

The effort to steer the survey counted on three Chinese organizations to produce interview subjects. Each group had a roster of experienced cultural brokers. They included CBA regulars, a stable of men and women who represented traditional Chinese Canadian power in the business, legal, and professional realms. (The CBA did not invite Chinese workers' groups to participate; at the time, Canada was deporting leftist European immigrant leaders.)[37] They also included two new youth groups that had proved effective in the anti-segregation struggle, the Chinese Students Alliance (CSA) and the Chinese Canadian Club (CCC). The CSA and CCC represented themselves to the survey as the first fruits of their people's future destiny as assimilated settler-citizens. In Chinese Canadians' alternate public sphere, these youth groups appeared to be as transnational as their elders, but to Anglo Canadians, their Canadian education opened doors.[38] The CSA lodges extended across the United States and Canada, and members were represented as survey subjects on both sides of the border.[39] The CCC appeared to share a strategy with its U.S. counterpart, the Chinese American Citizens Alliance (CACA).[40] These brokers made themselves the medium for their message: the assimilation of Chinese leaders and youth justified their presence in the Pacific Coast's maturing white society.

Collectively, Chinese brokers attempted to control the survey's access to information, while persuading the researchers that their personal lives served as compelling evidence of racial injustice. The survey's desire to collect Chinese Canadian life histories required Raushenbush to build relations of trust and reciprocity with her subjects. But Chinese Canadians brought mixed motives to the exchange. Brokers attempted to convince Raushenbush that their partial performance conveyed the most important part of the Chinese Canadian story and that their loyalty to the Chinese plan did not diminish their sincere affinities with their Anglo peers.

The researchers knew that collaboration involved conflicts of interest. They did not trust Chinese to collect objective information. Anglo researchers always asked the questions, even when a Chinese interpreter was present. Park and Raushenbush recognized that Chinese Canadians saw the survey's field research as an opportunity for public relations. However, as social scientists, they felt confident that they were more sophisticated than their subjects.[41] Together, American researchers and Chinese Canadian subjects would determine which of their particular ambitions would triumph. As the survey's first major community study site, British Columbia set the precedent. Later, when the survey moved on to U.S. cities, Chinese and Japanese brokers continued efforts to manipulate its findings. Indeed, over nine-tenths of the survey's Chinese American interview subjects would be brokers.[42]

## East as West

For Chinese Canadian leaders, the first challenge was to decide what "truth" Raushenbush should discover. On 13 February 1924, Vancouver's Chinese Benevolent Association held a large Chinese public meeting to discuss what to do about the American researchers. The meeting co-chairs, Y. P. Lew, Seto, and Sung, translated the survey's English-language circulars.[43] The researchers were asking for Chinese life histories from all classes.[44] Ordinary Canadians viewed Chinese as inscrutable strangers, wrote Winifred Raushenbush. The survey hoped that life histories such as "the struggle to make a living, adventure, hardship, romance" would make Chinese intelligible to white society. The researchers strived to find the truth about Chinese assimilation, Anglo anti-Chinese prejudices, economic competition, tongs, female slavery, intermarriage, human smuggling, drugs, and gambling. Only the best Chinese life histories would be printed in the survey's forthcoming book.[45]

Brokers knew that it would be impossible to conceal all negative information. Much of it was public knowledge. Further, the researchers had been consulting with white Christian missionaries, wildcards beyond Chinese community control, especially in Vancouver where less than 5 percent of the Chinese population was Christian.[46] The CBA would host welcome dinners for Raushenbush and Park, introducing them to articulate interview subjects who could craft vivid, quotable self-narratives. No Chinese would approach the survey independently.[47]

Originally, the survey planned a detailed study of Chinese male sojourners, but the self-selection meant that the more eloquent Chinese brokers captured the lion's share of Raushenbush and Park's attention. Poorer Chinese generally spoke less English, limiting the subject pool to the strongly acculturated portion of the population who self-selected into the project. Raushenbush felt sympathy for workers' tales of toil and separation from families in China, but she did not find them very interesting. Most workers possessed only a few grades of Chinese education, so they had difficulty establishing a rapport with Raushenbush.[49] In contrast, Chinese brokers dedicated a great amount of time to cultivating her sense of affinity and friendship with them.[50]

The Chinese brokers' strategy involved two discursive performances.[51] Both argued for Chinese capacities to assimilate. Brokers presented themselves as natural counterparts of their white, middle-class, educated peers. Through social affinities, brokers hoped to demonstrate their loyalties to Canada and the British Empire. They reframed their community's transnational ties. Brokers also spoke of China as a nation becoming Western, with democratic, educated, modern, and free characteristics. This imagined transference of the modern goods of Canada to the homeland framed Chinese leaders in the West as China's vanguard.

Their East-as-West performances also countered white fears that Chinese could not assimilate with evidence of Canada's transformative power. Brokers presented themselves as passive, receptive, and reactive subjects molded by British Canada. They acted as enlightened leaders whom ordinary Chinese gladly followed. They argued that Chinese leaders were not the Oriental tong despots of pulp fiction and films.[52] They were not engaged in "yellow slavery" of Chinese workers, as white unions often feared.[53] Leaders projected a simple, even naïve, faith in Canada. They were not foreigners who threatened British democracy, but Chinese who had become Canadian at heart.

The Chinese Benevolent Association secured the backing of powerful merchants, such as Yip Mow, Yip Sang's eldest son and the chief manager for the Yip family firms, to direct all Chinese Canadians to perform according to the plan's script.[54] *Da Han Gong Bao* printed the official position. Brokers acknowledged white objections to Chinese immigrants, and then attempted to explain away each concern. They could not deny, for example, that most Chinese workers had not fully assimilated.[55] In reply, Chinese intellectuals presented themselves as evidence of their race's adaptability "in society, customs, and lifestyle." With education, they argued, Chinese everywhere would embrace modernity.[56] As for social problems like gambling, opium use, and prostitution, brokers blamed racial exclusion. Lonely immigrant men engaged in "bitter pleasures" because they were unable to bring wives and children to

Canada.[57] These "improper" activities developed in Canada, not China. As for interracial marriage, Chinese argued that it was not a social problem but a matter of personal choice.[58]

Defusing Anglo fears of Chinese economic competitiveness was a greater challenge. Racial discrimination in the job market could explain why Chinese workers competed through accepting low wages,[59] but the rising success of Chinese entrepreneurs cut both ways. Most Canadians respected business success, regardless of color.[60] British Columbia's English newspapers often printed respectful coverage of West Coast Chinese millionaires, such as Yip Sang and Chin Gee Hing.[61] However, white farmers and small retailers frequently complained about Chinese competition, though Chinese firms had no shortage of white customers.[62] Brokers thus would hedge their responses to white fears of Chinese economic competition. They proudly asserted Chinese entrepreneurial drive, while lamenting that their assimilating children had lost their Chinese work ethic.[63] As for the nature of race itself, many Chinese believed that race was biological,[64] but the official position would claim race to be a cultural construct. Vancouver Chinese would conceal all other potentially damaging information, including the Chinese population's spiritual beliefs, the community's transnational outlook, anti-British aspects of Chinese nationalism, and illegal immigration.

To the survey's researchers, the brokers often claimed to be "entirely British" or "completely Canadian," but Chinese sources show that many pursued careers as transnational power brokers. Tom Whaun said that he had nothing to do with Chinese affairs until Canada blocked Chinese immigration in 1923.[65] Actually, he had come to Canada to "save China" by getting a modern education.[66] Further, Whaun had been a Vancouver Chinatown leader since at least 1916.[67] In 1918, he joined Chinatown power struggles during which supporters of China's Nationalist Party called for a Vancouver police crackdown on their political rivals' gambling operations. Whaun also had won a Canadian political patronage appointment as a court interpreter.[68] Most brokers shared this pattern: evident assimilation and deep ties to Canadian society, but also enduring ties to the Pacific world.

Survey interview subjects claimed that Chinese Canadian leaders had become essentially British while they attempted to explain away inconvenient facts. Canada's recent discovery of 10,000 Chinese illegal immigrants, interpreter Ko Wing Kan argued, resulted from corrupt officials who absconded with immigrants' papers, not Chinese evasion of immigration laws.[69] The inability of many Chinese to speak English came from a lack of education, not a disinclination to learn.[70] Moreover, brokers argued that Chinese experiences of Canadian rejection had provoked their Chinese revolutionary politics. Their anti-imperialism was not really anti-British. Chinese revolutionaries, they said, wanted to make China like Canada.[71] Leaders also did not mention Chinese beliefs about their own racial and cultural superiority.[72] Interview subjects emphasized Chinese as settlers in Canada, but in Chinese-language settings, even the Canadian-born leaders celebrated by the survey never referred to Chinese as immigrants (*yimin*).[73] Chinese felt deeply connected to Canadian society as long-term migrants, but they deemed these views as too perilous to share. If they exposed their transnational world, they might be forever excluded from Canada.

At first, Raushenbush responded with skepticism to Chinese Canadian brokers' performances. In a typical British Columbia interview, Tom Whaun described his vision of identity as beyond racial and ethnic categories: "Among my friends, and I think the same way myself, we do not care about nationality. That is all old stuff. We think of ourselves as citizens of the world. 'A man's a man,' that's what we believe."[74] Raushenbush responded with incredulity. Why did Whaun not adopt a more realistic strategy? He must know that most Canadians did not see beyond his nationality. Surely, the Japanese

FIGURE 4.1. Thomas Moore Whaun. Photo from *Totem*, 1927. Reproduced courtesy of the Alma Mater Society Archives, University of British Columbia.

immigrant strategy of claiming social privilege on the basis of nationality made more sense than naïve appeals to universalism?[75] However, Whaun, a member of the University of British Columbia's Social Science Club,[76] had chosen the strategy intentionally.

Brokers intuited that participating in a shared culture with elite Anglos created more constructive engagement than did confrontation. Indeed, Raushenbush was initially surprised that many of the Chinese young men she met were angry and "sullen" over how the Chinese in Canada were treated. Almost all young Chinese carried a notebook that documented grievances that they wished to address.[77] Their direct approach alienated Raushenbush.[78] She did not record many of these conversations in her research reports.

Socializing and conversing about a wide variety of topics served as a less threatening way to imply injustices done to the Chinese. Whaun elaborated:

> The other day I was riding in a street car with a professor from the university. We were talking Epictetus, Marcus Antonius, and all our favorites, especially Marcus Antonius.[79] I told him I liked Emerson very much. He was so delighted, he said: "I must have a talk with you. Come to my office to-morrow. Do you know this opera they are giving, Il Trovatore? My daughter is playing a leading role." When people have the same ideas, that binds them together.[80]

When asked about his cultural stance, Whaun said that other Chinese thought that he was pro-British.[81] Personally, he believed that many Chinese were rapidly assimilating. Countering the popular European belief that Chinese preferred to live in Chinatowns, he explained that he had never lived in Chinatown.[82] Like Whaun, other brokers who spoke with Raushenbush presented an image of cultural blending in their social lives. Ko Wing Kan, a ginseng merchant, drank cream with his tea in the English fashion.[83] Cecil Lee and his wife entertained Raushenbush in an English style.[84] Chinese youth participated in sports, dances, and socializing like their British peers.[85] Raushenbush was also impressed with the conformity of young Chinese to Anglo Canadian fashions and etiquette.[86]

Still, the high number of brokers among her interviewees in Vancouver and Victoria made Raushenbush question their claims. "I wonder," she wrote, "how many professional trouble-straighteners this town of ten thousand can really support."[87] She confronted Chinese diplomat Herbert Wang with rumors that Chinese newspapers had organized a cover-up during her visit.

Wang, who had helped to plan the survey management strategy, appealed to Raushenbush's elitism to soothe her worries. Her interviewees had the education to appreciate science, but most Chinese did not.[88] He admitted that Chinese had organized a community meeting to discuss the Survey of Race Relations, and afterward Chinese newspapers "wrote that everyone must be on the defensive and protect themselves because you were going to find out everything. But I told them this was to be a scientific study, and that they should give Dr. Park a chance to understand." Wang dismissed Chinese fears as ignorance, saying "They have no ideas." However, he claimed that the tradition-bound nature of ordinary Chinese had an advantage; they often followed more educated modern men like him.[89] By that time, Raushenbush had been interviewing Chinese in British Columbia for three months. She noted Wang's explanation in her report and then tested his claims about Chinese workers. With the help of an Anglo missionary, she interviewed retired Chinese workers at a nursing home. In broken English, two older workers described their lives of toil. Raushenbush found them baffling, writing of one, "I do not understand what he got out of life."[90] She chose to believe Wang.

Brokers made themselves the proof of their message: educated Chinese had the same aspirations as their Anglo peers. Lew Shong Kow, a former president of the Chinese Empire Reform Association's Vancouver branch, granted that most Chinese workers sojourned, but he predicted major changes within twenty to forty years. "I think the Chinese think by that time everything will have changed. Like the Russian revolution. Or like the Alliance between Japan and England. . . . The Chinese and Canadians will be all mixed up."[91] Already, said Herbert Wang, "everybody in China is Europeanized now, everybody. Only the very lowest class they do not change. They are very conservative. I suppose it is the same class you have in this country."[92] Cecil Lee, a banker, attributed white anti-Chinese prejudice to Chinese lower classes. "I do not think that there is any real prejudice against the Chinese," he said. "There would not be if the Canadians knew them."[93] These brokers claimed to lead the Chinese workers, so their assimilation represented the future of Chinese in Canada.

Throughout the Pacific Coast, survey researchers would find hints of transnational complexity, but brokers' testimony would lead them to conclude that Chinese conformed to a natural pattern of immigrant assimilation. Chinese in Vancouver, Victoria, Seattle, and San Francisco similarly directed survey researchers to educated, assimilated, and successful Chinese. Over 90 percent of Chinese interview subjects in Seattle were brokers, and nearly half were also native-born U.S. citizens. In San Francisco, all interviewees were college-educated, American-born Chinese.[94] As in Canada, almost all ordinary Chinese Americans refused to speak with the survey researchers.

Both Chinese Canadians' and Chinese Americans' testimony steered researchers away from the open-ended world of Chinese Diaspora migrations. Rather than the back and forth of global migrations, brokers argued that their lives demonstrated a propensity toward settlement in their new nations. In actuality, Chinese of all generations had transnational ties. Chinese interviewees attributed their persistent homeland ties to the distorting effects of white prejudice, declining to disclose fully their generations of transnational family life. Seattle businessman Pany Lowe described himself as a spurned second-generation Chinese American. "Me being citizen I vote in all election. Sure I vote every time I get chance. When I young fellow I felt that I American. I no Chinaman. Now I get more sense. I know I never be American, always Chinaman. I no care now anymore."[95] Lowe's personal loss of faith in America added credibility to his claims that white prejudice caused Chinese tongs and illegal immigration. Rather than seeing an international migrant group with a flexible sense of national destiny, which would have described more than a third of all Canadian residents, the survey researchers saw Chinese in terms that did not fundamentally question the permanent-settlement ideal.[96]

## Performing Political Power

Brokers had much to gain by disavowing foreign ties, especially in British Columbia. There, the survey's Anglo supporters added an extra question to the study: they wanted to know Chinese Canadians' fitness for democracy.[97] Canadian voters had long regarded Chinese political participation as undesirable, so judges routinely restricted Chinese access to naturalization.[98] Canada's Parliament reaffirmed in 1919 that British Columbia could continue to disenfranchise Asian Canadians, a category that included the Canadian-born, naturalized immigrants and British subjects from elsewhere in the Empire.[99] The 1923 act harshly restricted Chinese immigrants' political freedoms: involvement in China's revolutionary politics would lead to deportation.[100]

At the time, Chinese Canadians of all generations had relatives in China, so most felt homeland politics to be a right and a duty. Beijing did not control Guangdong province, where Dr. Sun Yat Sen was raising a revolutionary army to restore his shattered country.[101] However, to many British Canadians, China's revolutionary politics, from Nationalism to Communism, sounded subversive, especially as the politics of Sun's Nationalist revolution directly challenged the British Empire's interests in China.[102]

To the survey researchers, Chinese Canadians described themselves as passive recipients of Canadian influence rather than as active shapers of Canada's and China's destiny. Tom Whaun's comments exemplified the strategy. He defended China's people power as Chinese Canadians' only means of leveling the political playing field. The 1923 Chinese Immigration Act's denial of British freedoms provoked Whaun to mount a national letter-writing campaign.[103] On 23 June 1923, the *Vancouver Sun* and the *Daily Province* printed Whaun's warning:

> If we cannot stop your discriminative and anti-racial laws against us here, we can retaliate in many ways. The consequences of your unjust treatment will reverberate throughout China in the form of boycott against British and Canadian goods.[104]

Whaun also privately urged Lord Byng, the governor general of Canada, to modify the act.[105] To the survey's researchers, Whaun defended his politics by claiming that Canada's racial injustice jarred him out of his natural Britishness.[106] In contrast, to Chinese Canadian audiences, Whaun stated that he emigrated to Canada to acquire a modern education, "determined to do or die for New China that would again command respect from all."[107] He said to Raushenbush:

> I never belonged to any Chinese organizations until recently. But when this bill appeared I wrote a letter about it that was translated in all the Chinese papers. . . .
> This is too much. What can they do? They can't put us all on a boat and dump us into the ocean.[108]

His direct appeal to the Canadian public failed, leaving him angry and disillusioned, but China's support provided a ray of hope. Newspapers in China printed his letter and encouraged Chinese citizens to boycott Canadian goods.[109] Whaun warned that China's people could compel the respect that was their due:

> We'll have armies and navies too, if we have to, and we'll take what is ours. Do they think they can take all the land of the earth? I guess we can take it too. And we will. Why half of the Chinese here have got a picture of Jack Dempsey on their walls, and we're ready to show them.[110]

However, he hoped that the British Empire would choose voluntarily to right its wrongs, rather than being forced to do so by a Chinese revolution. He then alluded to the Hong Kong seamen's strike of 1922. "Mr. Whaun was wistful about this," Raushenbush wrote. "He did not like to think of China sovietized, he said, and thought the Western world might have the shrewdness enough to realize how much they would lose if they did not make capitalism conform to the Chinese idea of justice."[111] By portraying Chinese indignation as a reaction to being excluded from the West's superior way of life, Whaun tried to tamp down British unease about anti-imperialist protests in China.

By framing his Chinese politics as Western, Whaun also attempted to defend his work for a revolutionary Nationalist newspaper, *Jianada Chen Bao* (*Canada Morning Post*). To Raushenbush, Whaun did not mention its open advocacy of Communist revolution, which was illegal in Canada regardless of one's ethnic origin.[112] A surviving issue of *Jianada Chen Bao* from 1927 shows that one of the largest Chinese clan associations in Vancouver, the Wong Kung Har Tong (*Huang Jiangxia Tang*), to which Whaun belonged, allowed its Chinese-language school, the Mon Keang school (*Wenjiang Xuexiao*) to sponsor a Communist speech day, during which Chinese Canadian children spoke eloquently about the need for a workers' revolution.[113] To Raushenbush, Whaun described *Jianada Chen Bao* as catering to Chinese readers' Canadian interests. He described its goals: "Disseminate among the Chinese in Canada the principles of democratic and constitutional government, the liberalism and democracy as already established in the west."[114] He did not mention that the paper's editors actually came from the Nationalist Party's left wing in China.[115] Instead, Whaun stressed his own British influence. He claimed to have added new features to North America's Chinese newspaper world, such as police court news and a pictorial section. Vancouver's other Chinese newspaper, *Da Han Gong Bao*, already had these features,[116] so Whaun's claim that this was new in *Jianada Chen Bao* was exaggerated. Since she could not read Chinese, Raushenbush could not verify these claims.

Midway through Raushenbush's research, she discovered that Whaun and many other Vancouver interviewees came from the Chinese Students Alliance. Hilda Hellaby, a white Anglican missionary, informed Raushenbush that the CSA was a pro-Chinese, nationalist, anti-white organization. The accusation imperiled the Vancouver Chinese community plan. Hellaby described Vancouver's CSA:

> The younger generation have what they call a students club. I don't know why they call it that [since] most of them are not students. The

native born Chinese and the white women who are married to Chinese belong. They are anti-foreign, anti-missionary, and [against] the government . . . generally.[117]

Members of the CSA included Whaun and about twenty to thirty other Chinese who had at one point studied in public high schools, universities, or normal schools in Canada.[118] Earlier, the membership numbers had been higher, but quite a few men had departed for education in California and on the East Coast of the United States. Most of the remaining members no longer attended school.[119] In reply, Whaun claimed that his "Chinese student" politics strived to create a world where British Chinese could belong. By saving China and raising its stature, students hoped to save Canada. Whaun quoted from a friend's letter:

> Across the ocean 3,000,000 Chinese students, intellectual pure souls, are ready to sacrifice—to die if need be—in order to save China from being dismembered.[120]

"Yes," said Whaun to Raushenbush, "the man who wrote that is going back to China. I am going back. We all are." But he had become too British to return. "But what are we compared with the Chinese scholars, we with our Western education?" In China, "we are nothing." White missionaries often promoted a return to China to resolve the problem of Chinese Canadian "youth without a country."[121] The implied injustice of having no better recourse made a strong impression on Raushenbush's sympathies.

Perhaps because Raushenbush had heard about the CSA's militancy, Chinese brokers in Victoria afterward performed an even more assimilated version of leadership. Their performance showcased a British Chinese legal interpreter and merchant, Harry Hastings, and the young, educated Chinese of Victoria's Chinese Canadian Club. Hastings reportedly attended Oxford University, and Victoria's English press frequently printed his letters about British Columbia politics.[122] In 1922 and 1923, the CCC had helped to lead a Chinese Canadian public school boycott against segregation. To Raushenbush, the members described the CCC as a social club. They proudly displayed the club's reading room and she noted that it had a complete collection of Jane Austen's books.[123] However, *Da Han Gong Bao* reported in 1923 that the CCC had been founded for a political purpose. In 1914, this group of local-born Chinese (*tusheng*) had organized to fight discrimination.[124]

The CCC members and Harry Hastings portrayed Chinese Canadian protest as nonthreatening. Hastings termed the recent year-long public school boycott as Chinese Canadian children's spontaneous act.[125] Yet, in actuality, the largely immigrant leaders of Victoria's Chinese Benevolent Association and Chinese Chamber of Commerce had planned the school boycott in advance, along with CCC leaders and Hastings.[126] Survey interviewees also separated the school boycott from the anti-colonial protest movements in British Asia that had helped to inspire it.[127] Interviewees' accounts of the boycott balanced assimilation to British democracy with patient acquiescence to white supremacy. Hastings said that, as soon as children walked out of their classes, he took charge, and all Chinese parents obeyed him without question. His enlightened control prevented Chinese from making the boycott into a radical challenge like the Hong Kong seamen's strike. Further, Hastings claimed that his loyalties toward British society came first; he had advised British politicians in Victoria not to give in so that ordinary Chinese "would not feel their power."[128] *Da Han Gong Bao* portrayed events differently: an unnamed leader, probably Hastings, had betrayed the Chinese anti-segregation movement.[129] The CCC leaders had been bitterly unhappy about the betrayal, but they said nothing about it to Raushenbush. They claimed not to seek confrontation with white society, but professed a patient faith in Canada's democratic future. Cecil Lee said, "I think if I had ability enough there would be no position in Canada that would not be open to me. You know how the Canadians feel about the French Canadian, and yet Sir Wilfred [sic] Laurier is Premier of Canada."[130] Overall, Hastings and the CCC leaders presented themselves as examples of a model minority: patient, assimilating, nonthreatening, and in control of Chinatown.[131]

The British Columbian example set a pattern that other West Coast Chinese brokers would follow. To an extent, Chinese Canadians shared their alternate public sphere with Chinese Americans. Chinese associations in Seattle and San Francisco often subscribed to Chinese Canadian newspapers, and the Chinese immigrant press often covered both countries.[132] In the United States, the CCC's sister organization, the Chinese American Citizens Alliance, set the survey strategy.[133] At the survey's only other major Chinese fieldwork site, Seattle, educated brokers monopolized interviews. Asian immigrants in the United States were ineligible to become naturalized citizens, but in 1898, the U.S. Supreme Court confirmed that U.S.-born Chinese were citizens, which included voting rights. Seattle interviewees stressed that U.S.-born Chinese Americans were good citizens, voters, and businesspeople who benefited the United States, offering themselves as proof of anti-Chinese laws' injustice.[134]

The Chinese were not the only group who attempted to manage the Survey of Race Relations. Most Japanese presented shaded testimony to the survey that downplayed the transnational outlooks prevalent among all generations of Japanese Americans during the 1920s.[135] Chinese Canadian sources do not mention any formal relationship between Chinese and Japanese efforts, but the groups' alternate public spheres overlapped. Highly educated Chinese and Japanese often read both languages.[136] Indeed, Vancouver Chinese organized to meet the survey right after Park told a Japanese-language newspaper in California that he saw Asians as more black than white.[137] Chuichi Ohashi of the Japanese consulate responded to Park's comments in a letter to the survey, arguing that Japanese should be compared with European immigrants. He wrote, "Superiority over the Negro does not amount to anything."[138] Ohashi claimed that racial discrimination blocked the assimilation of Japanese, a tragic situation for youth who had become Americans in every way except color. Events in Japan, he said, also showed "Japanese' real ability as a race." For the sake of good trade relations, he hoped that the ignorant classes of anti-Japanese agitators would not be heeded.[139] At Raushenbush's fieldwork in California, Japanese American community leaders pointed her toward Americanized youth, while downplaying the actual extent of their community's dual Japanese and American national identities.[140] Survey researchers could not read Japanese-language newspapers, and Raushenbush noted that Japanese American leaders treated the survey interviews as "public relations."[141] A more complete exploration of Japanese American approaches to the survey would require research with Japanese-language sources. In any case, Chinese brokers' efforts to "fix" knowledge had a profound impact.

## Brokering Knowledge

In the short term, during the 1920s and 1930s, the researchers' findings did not convince policy makers to improve the status of Chinese. Park never wrote his promised book, and in 1925, the Institute of Social and Religious Research did not renew the survey's research grant.[142] Still, the survey changed the minds of some influential Canadians, creating avenues for continuing conversation. In 1926, Theodore Boggs, a University of British Columbia economist involved in the survey, lobbied for Asians already in British Columbia to be given voting rights. "Injustice leads to disharmony," he wrote, and a "democratic country cannot be stratified either socially or racially." Still, Boggs opposed Asian immigration. He felt that Asians' inability to intermarry made them Canada's "Negro problem."[143] But Raushenbush's data left him with an abiding curiosity; Boggs became a fixture at Chinese Canadian community events.[144] John Nelson had a similar awakening. Before the survey, he had written many articles condemning Asian immigrants. Raushenbush's interviews transformed his thinking about Chinese, inspiring him to join American survey researchers in founding the Institute of Pacific Relations (IPR) in 1925. That year, Chinese in China boycotted Canadian and British Empire goods. In the IPR, Canada worked as a partner with Japan and China to improve international relations. Other member countries included the United States, Russia, and Australia.[145] In 1928, Nelson wrote about the survey's findings in *Maclean's*, a national Canadian magazine: ". . . for the first time, a real exploration was made into the human factors and emotions that were involved, the investigators soon became conscious of a great undertow of racial resentment and prejudice, difficult to fathom and impossible to explain." He noted that his past approach to the "Oriental problem," treating Chinese as a menace, was wrong. Only "racial accommodation" would enable the peoples of the Pacific world "to live together in peace." Canada must deal with Chinese as human beings.[146] Canada's future trade prospects depended on understanding China and Chinese Canadians. The IPR debated these issues, and Nelson also worked with leading Canadians to press for improved knowledge of Asia.[147] At the time, few Canadians had expertise about China. One of Tom Moore Whaun's University of British Columbia classmates wrote in his yearbook, "Thoroughly versed in Chinese affairs, Moore may often be found explaining the situation in the Far East to a group of interested students. We are truly indebted to him for a broader and truer understanding of China."[148] British Columbia's universities did not offer any courses in Asian studies until after 1945, so Chinese Canadian brokers often served as de facto experts on China.

Chinese Canadian brokers shared the Chicago scholars' belief in the transforming power of interpersonal relations. Tom Moore Whaun crusaded for Chinese Canadian justice throughout the 1920s by speaking to white labor, leftist, and student groups.[149] For men like Whaun, this brokerage was both personal and political. Years later, in the 1960s, he recalled Raushenbush as a kindred spirit, and he wrote a letter asking what had happened to her planned dissertation on Chinese in British Columbia. Raushenbush had married and did not complete her doctoral studies. The two rekindled their friendship, but Whaun never told her about the community plan.[150] Chinese Canadians' influence on the Chicago School's data has remained hidden until now.

## Conclusion: Finding the "Real" Chinatown

In 1924, Raushenbush's findings in British Columbia set the stage for the survey's future research on Chinese and Japanese immigration. White researchers felt confident in their sociological ability to "know the whole people" through English-speaking mediators.[151] From that point on, they would focus more on brokers and the native-born than on the majority of Asian North Americans, immigrant workers. Above all, the American researchers felt pleased that their data had affirmed their hypotheses about the national environment's power to reshape immigrant culture.[152] When Raushenbush returned to the survey's head office in San Francisco, she continued with Chinese and Japanese field research. Park also assigned her the task of classifying the survey's entire data pool. The survey would distribute only items that she deemed important. Before survey researchers drew their conclusions, Raushenbush's choices helped to determine what data they would consult.[153]

Chinese and Japanese immigrants managed the survey researchers so effectively that its final data set leaned toward a progressive narrative that flattened immigrants' complexity. The data set's vast size reflected the magnitude of this accomplishment. When the Survey of Race Relations finished its field research in December 1924, writes historian Eckard Toy, its scholars had collected 640 life histories and nearly 6,000 pages of data about assimilation and race relations.[154] The survey copied major portions of the documents to associated scholars across the West Coast.[155] The resulting archives became a unique repository of interview data from early twentieth-century Asian Americans and Asian Canadians. In 1926, the survey published a journal issue dedicated to its findings.[156] The survey data would inform many of the most influential ideas about immigration. Further, the researchers' peers would label them the "Chicago School of Sociology" because of these ideas' profound influence on American social science, popular culture, and history.[157]

Raushenbush's findings, published in the journal *Survey Graphic* in 1926, concluded that youth represented the leading edge of inevitable West Coast Chinese assimilation. Older Chinese workers remained "remote" from Europeans, but the second generation would determine the community's future. In between, she wrote, stood a young Chinese-born generation that identified with China's revolution. These "wildly discontented" would-be modernizers disavowed nationalism, but they needed a strong China to be respected in North America. In contrast, the "native born," she wrote, "know little about the old China or the new; England, especially Victorian England, seems closer to them than the aphorisms of Confucius or the dreams of Sun Yat Sen." In Canada, she argued, second-generation rule was so effective that British Columbia did not have American-style tong wars over trafficking in illegal immigrants, gambling, and opium.[158] To the *Survey Graphic*'s U.S.–Canadian audience of social scientists, social workers, policy makers, and missionaries, Raushenbush predicted that West Coast Chinese problems would fade as youth took the helm. Her article ended with a quote from a second-generation San Francisco Chinese leader, "Just wait until the native-born ride into power here . . . and you will see a different Chinatown."[159]

The survey's evidence strongly supported Chicago sociologists' theories about migration and human cultural transformation. Their earlier studies of European immigrants had viewed migration as a universal process of uprooting and transplantation, culminating in adaptation to the new environment. Much like biologists who study the natural world, they desired to chart individual sites of assimilation and conflict as distinct local ecologies. The visible persistence of homeland ties, Chicago scholars argued, was often a temporary reaction to the new land's challenges. Ultimately, they believed, assimilation would triumph, and new groups would reach some sort of accommodation with established residents.[160] Much subsequent research would explore race relations using plant metaphors from the natural world.

For more than eighty years, the survey's conception of early Asian immigrants as tragically thwarted Canadians and Americans has strongly influenced social sciences and humanities research.[161] The survey's data appeared in over forty monographs. Its concepts and its data continue to be cited by sociologists and historians. The survey's ideas are also taught in American and Canadian classrooms to the present.[162] The Chicago School's intellectual history, however, cannot be complete without more scrutiny of its collaborations with local ethnic leaders.

Evidence of immigrants' malleability helped Chicago scholars to forcefully argue for North America's absorptive capacity, while it undercut the biological premises of more pessimistic "sciences," such as eugenics and Social Darwinism.[163] The Chinese brokers' victory, however, came at a price. They had presented their Chinese ties as so limited that Raushenbush concluded that their culture had no substance. In Chinese culture, she found "none of the philosophic aura of Hindu mysticism, none of the human and moving loyalty of the Japanese patriot. The Chinese are realists."[164] Brokers also downplayed North American Chinese connections to China to the extent that their transpacific lives became less visible.

Brokers chose to steer the researchers away from their transnational world, precluding discussion of their political power. They spoke most freely about their conflicts of consciousness between the two cultures, while saying far less about their political brokerage as an integrating force. Following the Chicago School, generations of ethnic studies scholars have explored discourses of identity.[165] However, interviews about personal identity are often manipulated, especially if researchers do not know the subjects' language and community. Despite their history of political initiative, Chinese brokers portrayed themselves as passive, reactive, and patient; these images contributed to the later popular myth that Asians were a model minority.[166]

The Chicago School concluded that assimilation was a natural process akin to plant ecology, a conception that gave little attention to ethnic leaders, political power, or mediators as parts of stratified immigrant communities.[167] Like flora replanted in a new environment, immigrants adjusted to their new culture and affected its ecology. The researchers believed that consciousness foreshadowed later social change. They privileged the subjective question of identity, seeing leaders as assimilation's leading edge, as "marginal men," a term Park coined in 1928.[168] The researchers concluded that immigrants' cultural change is an ecological process dependent on the host society. Park also conceived of race relations as a cycle of conflict with newcomers. The survey's interviews with Chinese suggested that Asians would adjust and, perhaps, be accepted in the distant future. The Chicago School's ecological conception of assimilation suggested a natural progression, which removed any necessity for understanding the political aspects of social change, such as brokers' mediating roles. Even today, ethnic leadership continues to be a neglected topic in immigration studies.[169] Chinatown's power brokers, the most visible members of their communities, became relegated to scholarly obscurity.

Restoring power brokers to their rightful prominence suggests new ways of thinking about immigrant history. Many popular, mainstream histories celebrate individual initiative. Ethnic historians, however, have emphasized collective experiences, such as community and race. This preference for writing history "from the bottom up" obscures the role of brokers as creative individuals. Brokers strived daily to shape the spaces between societies. From the start, Chinese influenced the affairs of their locality, of Canada, of the United States, and of China. A West Coast Chinese history with brokerage at its center can no longer be conceived of as a separate, specialized topic. Brokerage also matters because scholars of political incorporation have focused on immigrants who acted as citizens.[170] However, the political integration of newcomers did not always start or end with citizenship rights. To disenfranchised immigrants, leaders' brokerage took on outsized importance. For nearly a century, Chinatown leaders' brokerage profoundly shaped ties between Chinese and their North American neighbors.[171]

The development of a model minority myth was perhaps the most influential outcome of the survey. During the 1920s, West Coast Chinese helped to write Chinese agency out of their own—and all of our—history. Brokers constructed a story of assimilation that built upon popular ideas about the contrasts between China and the West. They often explained their own transformation in terms of Western popular thought. This thought often presumed that the West had history, reason, and change, while the East had culture, despotism, and tradition.[172] Chicago scholars thus saw most Chinese brokers as between East and West, between tradition and modernity. They often elided class, educational, and political divisions within Chinese communities. The resulting model minority myth still survives throughout the United States and Canada. Scholars have believed the myth to be a product of the United States during the 1950s and 1960s,[173] but it has much earlier origins. Its narrative of Asian immigrants as achievement-oriented, hardworking, and deferential to authority plays a large role in both U.S. and global studies. Presently, over a thousand books and nearly as many articles discuss the model minority concept.[174] But Chinese brokers' interactions with the Chicago scholars tell a different story about the interracial politics of creating immigrant myths.

FIVE | Transforming Democracy
*Brokerage Politics and the Exclusion Era's Denouement*

BY THE END OF THE Second World War, Chinese power brokers' efforts to construct a model minority myth had directly contributed to the Exclusion Era's denouement. The myth's ideas greatly influenced changes in policy making, and the war was a watershed moment for Chinese-Anglo relations in Canada and in the United States. However, popular interpretations of the Second World War as a "good war" that brought about a "triumph of citizenship" for patient Chinese minorities tell only part of the political story.[1] Chinese Canadian mass protests also helped to transform Canada's democracy. Wartime crises forced political brokerage to extreme limits, suspended the usual rules, and forced sudden social change. Canada's war policies singled out Chinese Canadians for inequitable treatment, inciting persistent resistance. Traditional brokers failed to secure adjustments, so many Chinese turned to wider labor and anti-conscription movements. Together, mass protests and model minority rhetoric influenced the repeal of anti-Chinese policies, building a foundation for a new politics of minority human rights and equality.[2]

This chapter explores how Canada's wartime policies led to Chinese Canadian protests that interacted with wider national struggles over redefining the rights of Canadians. It traces Chinese Canadian calls for "taxpayers' rights," "workers' rights," and "soldiers' rights" as part of greater social movements for minority rights. Energized by the labor movement and its affiliated political parties, these global and local politics challenged Canada to adjust its British imperial identity. During the Second World War, this nascent rights culture created openings for both minorities and workers to push for a more egalitarian vision of Canadian citizenship.

When Canada declared war on Germany in 1939, most Chinese Canadians did not foresee great changes. The late 1920s and 1930s had been hard. Anti-Chinese laws drove the Chinese population into the shadows. Canada's exclusion law barred new Chinese immigrants, tripling the cost of fraudulent entry.[3] Chinese economic prospects also collapsed during the decade. The Great Depression (1929–1939) brought Chinese Canadian unemployment as high as 80 percent in greater Vancouver, over twice British Columbia's general jobless rate of 28 percent.[4] Without Chinese customers, the businesses of Chinese merchants and legal interpreters fell precipitously.[5] The overwhelmed Chinese and Anglo charities left hundreds of hungry, ragged Chinese homeless during the winter. Government relief programs could not adequately meet the needs of the destitute.[6] Vancouver city agencies provided Chinese with a lower level of daily food relief than Anglos received.[7] Without cash, Chinatown's traditional power brokers' influence diminished. Authorities cracked down on Chinese gambling and illegal immigration.[8] Return to China provided no escape; the global economic collapse had encompassed their ancestral homes.[9] Japan's invasion of China also caused Chinese Canadians great anxiety.[10] Further, Canada's war policies restricted the sending of relief remittances to relatives in China. The trials and tribulations of the 1930s caused growing numbers of Vancouver Chinese to conclude that the traditional power brokers had failed.[11] This crisis of traditional brokerage—and rivals' struggles to replace it—strongly influenced Chinese Canadian participation in the wartime struggles to reshape race and class relations.

Chinese Canadian workers, a group historically excluded from traditional brokerage, organized some of the war's most effective protests against racial discrimination.[12] In greater Vancouver, over 5,000 Chinese workers participated in mass protests.[13] Similar worker protests occurred throughout British Columbia's lower mainland and on Vancouver Island.[14] Chinese Canadian men also rebelled against military service, with thousands refusing to enlist unless Canada granted them equal rights.[15] These popular revolts belie English media images of obedient, loyal, allied Chinese. The smiling faces of Chinese Canadian soldiers in the English wartime press suggested that political brokers had become unnecessary.[16] In contrast, *Da Han Gong Bao* argued in a series of front-page editorials that Canada's war policies had to be changed to save Chinese Canadians' families.[17]

For most Chinese Canadians, the daily drumbeat of war news about bombings, destruction, refugees, and hunger in Guangdong provoked profound anxiety and grief. When Chinese Canadians read about dying children and elders collapsed by the sides of roads, too weak to walk, they wondered, could those be their children or their parents? As they joined their fellow Vancouver residents in practice blackouts and air raid drills, they could not help but think of cities in Guangdong, such as Guangzhou, Taicheng, and Foshan, where homes had been bombed, looted, and consumed by fire. They could only imagine the terror and the suffering of their loved ones, and most would have done anything to save their families in China. They believed that their families' lives depended on their aid and that, without urgent help, they might soon die.[18] For many Chinese Canadians, efforts to change war policies related to race, class, and the regulation of transnational immigrants became a sacred responsibility.[19]

In Canada's ethnic history, the Second World War often appears as the end of an old era of British imperialism and the start of a new era of pluralistic Canadian citizenship. Retrospective knowledge of subsequent events has inspired scholars to seek the causes of these changes in wartime events. Most present this postwar turn toward multiculturalism and human rights as resulting from enlightened Anglo attitudes. Some scholarship sees the process of change as a product of three wartime trends toward consensus: international alliances, racial harmony, and working-class solidarity. These accounts portray Chinese Canadians mainly as petitioners and responders to a more receptive mainstream. For most historians, the task has been to identify which moment crystallized Anglo society's cultural turning point.[20] However, all three consensus views seriously underestimate Chinese Canadians themselves as a political force for change.

The international alliance interpretation of the Exclusion Era's waning captures part of the change, but misses some of the continuities in Chinese-Anglo negotiations and in Chinese Canadians' ongoing ties to the Pacific world. Historians have emphasized that, in World War II, Canada and China fought on the same side, leading to policies that treated Chinese Canadians as "allies."[21] Granted, both Canada's war department and Chinese Canadian leaders encouraged the Anglo press to celebrate Chinese Canadians as valiant defenders of their homeland, China, against the common Japanese menace.[22] However, the war also led to an expansion of policies that treated all Chinese Canadians, regardless of citizenship, as foreigners. The federal government's strategic concern to support China's ruling Nationalist Party as an anti-Communist bulwark led the two states to cooperate in unprecedented interventions in Chinese Canadians' private affairs.[23] International alliances brought a degree of acceptance but also the state sanction of extraterritorial rule over Chinese Canadians by a foreign government.

The ties between the United States and Canada also helped to shape events. Chinese Canadians and Chinese Americans kept a close watch on each other in the Chinese-language press.[24] As one *Da Han Gong Bao* front-page editorial put it, Vancouver's protests belonged to the larger Chinese search for effective means of attaining equality in North America.[25] Canadians noticed that the United States made goodwill gestures toward its ally, China. To counter Japanese propaganda, the United States repealed its Chinese Exclusion Act in 1943. It also lifted bars to U.S. citizenship for Chinese immigrants and regularized the status of illegal immigrants who served in the military.[26] Chinese Canadians received none of these benefits. The Chinese press, more free of the censor's watch than the Anglo press, reported a mood of uncertainty among Chinese in Canada rather than a triumphant march to citizenship.[27]

While the international alliance interpretation offers some explanation for the collapse of the Exclusion Era, the racial harmony interpretation, which sees change as a process of consensus, has become the most popular explanation. This view comes mainly from English-language sources which celebrate Chinese Canadians' integration into the war effort as a heroic quest to earn equal citizenship rights. Television programs, films, newspapers, books, and government websites have depicted Chinese Canadians' military service and, to a lesser extent, war work as a test of loyalty passed with flying colors and leading to postwar voting rights.[28] Histories of Chinese American inclusion during the war often present similar narratives of patient model citizens.[29] These war hero stories have universal appeal across party lines, ideology, and ethnic groups, but they do not tell the full story.

An examination of Chinese Canadians' political brokerage reveals a new side of Second World War history, fraught with conflict but also empowered by new social movements. Granted, the war brought unprecedented opportunities for Chinese Canadians to integrate. Scholars argue that mainstream labor unions in war industries welcomed Chinese, overcoming the labor movement's historic antipathy to cheap Asian labor.[30] However, the Chinese press reported that the process of integration was neither smooth nor easy. Chinese workers in British Columbia organized to fight for equal pay within the labor union movement.[31] Chinese Canadians also confronted the wartime expansion of income taxes to low-wage workers, which affected policy debates over defining taxpayer rights for immigrants beyond the settler-citizen ideal.[32] While some Chinese served in the military, others joined a national anti-conscription movement of nonwhite Canadians. Scholarship on Canada's home front during the Second World War generally has been so fragmented as to preclude definitive synthesis, and discussions of race are even more incomplete.[33] Much about immigrants' views of the process of change remains to be explored, as do their roles in making it happen. This chapter only begins to fill these gaps, and it cannot make up for the limited historical studies on China-Canada relations.[34] Still, the Chinese Canadian case points toward political reconfigurations which were especially relevant to the one-fifth of Canadians who had transnational ties beyond the British Empire and to the 2 percent of Canada's residents who were nonwhite.[35]

## *Regulating Remittances: Nationalizing the Mechanism for Immigrants' Support of Relatives Outside of Canada*

For nearly a century, Chinese Canadians treated their migration, their families, and their economic dealings as mostly private affairs. However, Canada's war policies extended China's authority over Chinese Canadians. Together, the two states seized control over Chinese Canadians' private family remittances to China. Many Chinese Canadians challenged the legitimacy of these exactions and the trustworthiness of the collectors.

On 15 September 1939, Canada announced that all individual immigrant remittances and donations sent abroad during the war would require permits from the newly formed Foreign Exchange Control Board (FECB). Funds would henceforth only be sent abroad through authorized agencies at rates set by the government. The FECB would also regulate the maximum amount of Canadian cash that individuals could remit to family members in particular countries, and it set the family remittance limit for China to a US$25 purchase of Chinese *yuan* per month. The FECB set the limit in U.S. dollars because Canada required Chinese Canadians to send money through the Bank of China in New York. Any greater amount required a petition for an exemption. Immigrant groups seeking to send collective donations also had to apply for permission to send funds abroad, and every international business transaction required a permit.[36] To protect the value of the Canadian dollar, the FECB limited large purchases of foreign currencies.[37] Canada's population had extensive foreign ties, especially to the United States, so the FECB had a tremendous impact on domestic society.[38] The act inserted government control and surveillance into every non-British foreign financial transaction. Further, it authorized remittances only via Canadian chartered banks, displacing immigrant firms that had handled remittances for most Asian, Southern European, and Eastern European immigrants.[39]

The FECB constituted one of the earliest, most drastic interventions into domestic wartime society. Canada's federal cabinet used its emergency powers under the War Measures Act to create the FECB only five days after declaring war.[40] Nevertheless, even within Canadian economic scholarship, it is obscure. Generally, scholars have seen the FECB as the war propaganda described it: a measure to stabilize Canada's national finances.[41] A social history analysis, however, reveals a more sweeping personal and political impact. The FECB had an immediate effect upon Chinese Canadian communities.[42] It dealt a severe blow to Chinese immigration firms (*jinshanzhuang*) whose business capitalization depended heavily on selling remittance services.[43] The Yip family's Wing Sang Company's records show that the Yips conducted an extensive remittance business.[44] The loss of this business due to the FECB harmed a company already weakened by the Great Depression and the Sino-Japanese War's interruption of Pacific trade. After the Second World War, the Yips would never recover their former status. The FECB accelerated the decline of merchant brokers based in the immigration business, creating a power vacuum that rival brokers attempted to fill.

Further, the FECB outsourced the evaluation of Chinese Canadians' petitions for remittances to China's Nationalist Party government.[45] According to the records of China's consulate general in Ottawa, Chinese Canadians inundated the consulate with FECB petitions. Many Chinese Canadians believed that money could mean the difference between life and death for their family members in China.[46] One man asked to send money because his family's home had been destroyed. Another man asked to pay for his son's law school tuition. A third petitioned to send money to his elderly mother.[47] Li Donghai, author of *Jianada Huaqiao Shi* and an early Victoria community member, estimated that most Chinese remitted about a third of their income to China.[48] The war situation, however, made many Chinese anxious to remit larger sums, especially because the Second World War created full employment after ten years of economic hardship.[49] Applying for a one-time exemption to remit more than $25 to relatives in China required an explanatory petition and documentation of past remittances.[50] However, many Chinese did not have documentation.[51] By taking over the remittance functions, China's consulates exercised new political power over Chinese Canadians.

China's consulates found that controlling remittances also helped to extend their reach over assimilating Chinese Canadians. In March 1940, Vancouver's consulate announced that all Chinese had to register their name, profession, and salary in order to be taxed by China.[52] Thirty thousand Chinese in British Columbia registered; many were illegal immigrants or Canadian-born. Canada's Census, taken one year later, in 1941, counted only 18,619 Chinese in British Columbia.[53] China's government also used the FECB to quash rival brokers seeking to raise war relief funds for China independently of Nationalist Party control.[54] Besides the official resistance, Vancouver had five other major Chinese groups that raised humanitarian funds to aid war refugees in China.[55] Across western Canada, Chinese relief aid groups not controlled by China's ruling Nationalist Party found that China's consulate frequently denied their FECB requests.[56]

Foon Sien Wong, an officer of Vancouver's Chinese Benevolent Association in charge of "foreign relations" with Anglos and a censor of the Chinese press and mails for Canada's war department, pleaded with Canada's federal government to adjust FECB policy.[57] Letters smuggled out of Guangdong reported that family members of Chinese Canadians needed at least several thousand *yuan* per month to sustain life, far more than the FECB permitted.[58] *Da Han Gong Bao* reported that a million persons in the Chinese Canadians' principal region of origin, Siyi, were at risk for death from hunger.[59] In 1943, San Francisco Chinese Li Dao Wei received a letter that claimed that some residents of Siyi's Taishan County had turned to cannibalism. By 1944, a New York Chinese got a letter stating that 600,000 Chinese had starved to death in Siyi.[60] In addition to Canada's regulations, the Bank of China charged commissions on remittances, and it set its U.S. dollar–to–Chinese *yuan* exchange rates at one-fifth the going market rate.[61] Further, the FECB's required channel for approved relief remittances, the Bank of China in New York, appeared corrupt.[62] Chinese Canadians increasingly suspected that relief remittances never reached their intended recipients, but the FECB policy remained restrictive.[63]

Stymied, Wong began aligning with a new political force, the industrial union movement, which had become a powerful representative for unskilled workers in Canada's political economy in the 1930s and 1940s.[64] Unionized Chinese workers would score the first Chinese collective victories in wartime struggles for racial equality. They also directly challenged Chinatown's traditional brokers for the right to represent Chinese workers in the political and economic realms. Through civil disobedience, Chinese intended to force their unions, employers, and governments to curtail material forms of discrimination.

## *The Chinese Workers' Movement: Taxpayers' Rights, Workers' Rights, and Minority Rights in Canadian Organized Labor*

Brokers had always handled issues of material importance, but the war raised the stakes because families in China needed more exactly at the moment when families in Canada could provide less. This crisis provoked two mass protests against Canada's war policies and established community leaders. Neither mass protest movement has been fully explored in the existing scholarship because they were reported at length only in the Chinese-language press.[65] Both protests helped to establish new forms of brokerage, leading to power sharing and bringing Chinese Canadians more deeply into mainstream Canadian political life.

The Chinese workers' movement began on 7 July 1943, when over 5,000 Chinese Canadian war industry workers walked off the job, "desolating" local shingle mills and disrupting shipyard production.[66] Chinese had seen the effectiveness of sudden, sharp job actions within British Columbia's labor movement, so they hoped to press their employers, their unions, and China's consulate to lobby on their behalf.[67] The strikers demanded the right to income tax deductions for their dependents in China.[68] Since the spring of 1943, Canada's tax office had treated many Chinese workers as though they had no families.[69] Given high wartime income taxes, the new policy made a major difference in their paychecks. Before the change, a Chinese shipyard worker had $2.35 withheld from his paycheck for taxes, but afterward $11 was withheld, leaving him "very little."[70] For Chinese who supported family members in China, the loss of dependent deductions created a dire financial crisis,[71] and they turned to radical action to assert their rights as workers and taxpayers.

Politically, difficult documentation problems lay at the heart of the dispute. *Da Han Gong Bao*, Chinese consulate archives, and Canadian tax office records outline the background of the crisis. Before the war, according to *Da Han Gong Bao*, most Chinese earned wages too low to pay income taxes.[72] Beginning in 1941, when rising wages first started to bring tens of thousands of Chinese workers to the attention of the tax collectors, Chinese had sought tax deductions for their dependents in China.[73] It took until March 1942 for Canada's government to make Chinese workers' dependents in China eligible for deductions.[74] At that time, the deductions relieved most Chinese from income tax.[75] However, in 1943, Canadian tax officials cracked down on perceived fraud among foreign sojourners who claimed to support dependents outside Canada.[76] The tax office rejected most Chinese workers' claims as unverifiable. Their employers then withheld much higher taxes from their paychecks. Canadian tax officials promised to refund any erroneous withholdings after reviewing the documentation of each Chinese case. However, due to illegal immigration and language difficulties, Chinese Canadians had never been a well-documented people in the federal government's records.[77] Further, even Chinese who submitted acceptable documents could expect to pay the much higher taxes for five or six months before their appeals were processed.⁷⁸ The low wages of Chinese Canadian workers made higher taxation a hardship. Roy Mah (*Ma Guo Guan*), a union organizer, recalled in 1943 that Chinese laborers earned less than half of white workers' wages. For example, Chinese lumber workers earned twenty-five to forty cents per hour, while white workers earned seventy-five cents to a dollar per hour.⁷⁹ Chinese protested because they believed that many of Canada's other sojourners (*waiqiao*), Europeans and East Indians, received deductions for dependents living outside of Canada.⁸⁰ After China's diplomats failed to bring effective tax equity, Chinese workers, the most "bitterly" affected taxpayers, sought the help of the Canadian labor movement.⁸¹

The income tax issue arose in the midst of greater class conflicts over the representation of Chinese workers to Anglo institutions. Though Foon Sien Wong had never done manual labor, he reinvented himself as a champion of the Chinese proletariat. His shift began as early as 1942, when he voiced popular frustrations with the government-appointed rice agency. Many Chinese Canadians could not afford to eat a Chinese diet because of the high prices of imported American rice, soy sauce, bean curd, and salted fish.⁸² Before the war, rice cost $1.65 for a forty-four-pound sack, but by 1942, rice cost between $7 and $9.⁸³ In *Xin Minguo Bao*, Wong complained that Chinese Canadian rice merchants holding the rice monopoly demanded excessive tributes from "proletarians" like himself.⁸⁴ His work as a legal broker also changed. He chose to live in poverty, offering his legal skills without requiring payment. His Anglo wife, Joan, worked in a munitions plant and provided the sole support for their family.⁸⁵ Roy Mah felt "a little bit scared" of the labor contractors who competed for the loyalty of Chinese workers.⁸⁶ Established wealthy merchants and the traditional brokers had the most access to larger political power. The organizers of industrial unions—and their Chinese members—argued that conditions should change: the Allied struggle for democracy should include more worker concerns.

Labor historians have focused on unions as workers' voices in industry, but workers also sought power as political brokers. The "full glass of beer" protest of 1943 shows unions' growing influence as representatives of workers and consumers. *Da Han Gong Bao* reported that Vancouver workers complained to their unions that bar owners often shortchanged customers' glasses of beer by filling large portions of their cups with empty suds. The city's labor unions then requested a meeting with the bar owners association. On behalf of their members, the unions negotiated a guarantee that every worker would receive the full glass of beer for which he or she paid.⁸⁷ At the time, most Canadians purchased beer by the glass, so keeping drinking affordable protected a cherished form of social relaxation. Through experiences like the "full glass of beer" protest, Chinese Canadians found unions to be effective political brokers beyond the shop floor, and they pressed their locals to lobby on the tax issue.

The war gave unprecedented numbers of Chinese Canadians the chance to join industrial unions. As Anglo men departed for the front, Vancouver's booming war industries faced shortages of male workers. Lumber mills, shipyards, aircraft factories, munitions plants, and ports boomed. The British war effort in Asia required supplies, and Vancouver became an industrial center overnight.[88] Chinese Canadians especially benefited because Canada's federal government barred Chinese from military service to prevent them from demanding voting rights in British Columbia.[89] For the first time since Canada built the Canadian Pacific Railway, young, able-bodied Chinese men held an advantageous position in British Columbia's labor market. Herbert Lim remembered that the war opened up shipyard work to Chinese. The "men shortage" also allowed Chinese to jump from job to job, seeking the best wages and work conditions.[90] Bing Wong, a plate fitter, worked in Burrard Shipyard alongside European women.[91] Joe Sam recalled camaraderie in Victoria shipyards. Things were "improving every day," he recalled.[92] No one knew, however, if wartime changes would last. Full employment also added to workers' leverage just as Canada's federal government assumed extraordinary powers to manage the wartime economy.[93]

Controversies over Chinese workers' taxation were closely linked to general resentment against perceived inequalities in income tax policies. Canada's need to finance the war disproportionately affected low-wage workers. Public opinion polls found that over 40 percent of working-class Canadians opposed higher income taxes.[94] By 1942, Canada's war department mounted national propaganda campaigns to quell dissent over rising taxes. Jeffrey Keshen, the author of a study of Canada's home front, noted that a typical ad linked civilian "gripes" about taxes with a list of Canada's dead soldiers at Dieppe. The ads, like kindred campaigns denouncing strikes as "selfish," portrayed dissent against Canada's war policies as unpatriotic.[95]

British Columbia's labor movement found the Chinese income tax question "vexatious," and for several months, unions debated the issue.[96] *Da Han Gong Bao* reported that many Canadians questioned the merits of the Chinese workers' case. Jealousy, along with the long-standing taints of illegal immigration and sojourning, made granting tax deductions to Chinese controversial. The deduction question also sparked mainstream debate about what level of taxation an alien people deserved.[97] Anglos often resented that Chinese workers appeared to "unfairly" profit from Anglo men's military service. War worker Herb Lim recalled "a lot of resentment" against Chinese. Lim enrolled in the Canadian Officers' Training Corps but could not serve due to his race. Many Anglos refused to believe the racial bar existed. "How come you were not in the army?" they asked him constantly.[98] Further, *Da Han Gong Bao* noted that many Canadians did not sympathize with Chinese workers because they believed that their families in China did not really exist. They accused Chinese of evading income taxes. *Da Han Gong Bao* granted that a few fraudulent cases had happened, but Vancouver Chinese knew that nearly all family support claims were legitimate.[99] Because of popular resentment, Chinese workers judged that reversing the tax policy would require more potent brokers than Chinatown's merchant elite or China's consul.

The income tax question created a political dilemma for Chinese workers and their Canadian unions. In their wartime rhetoric, British Columbia's industrial unions proclaimed the racial solidarity of workers. They welcomed Asians as union members under the rubric of "equal pay for equal work."[100] However, the weakness of the unions in this era before the existence of strong collective bargaining laws meant that racial equality was not always a priority. The Chinese workers' protest compelled unions to act because of its timing in the midst of union drives for recognition. In June 1943, Nigel Morgan, head of the International Woodworkers of America (IWA) in British Columbia, testified to the National War Labor Board that his union had 9,000–10,000 members. Over one-tenth of IWA members were Chinese, numbering more than 1,500 workers. The IWA was negotiating at "29 different operations" in British Columbia. However, the union won only one contract due to "employers' refusal to sign."[101] The limited power of the unions made it difficult for them to risk their own political capital for an unpopular matter. Wartime opinion polls reported that most Canadians believed that strikes during the war were "unpatriotic" and "selfish."[102] Finally, the Chinese forced the issue by announcing their intention to hold an illegal strike. They would embarrass the unions, their employers, and the Canadian government unless their demands were met. They wanted tax deductions for their dependent family members because every other ethnic group received them. The threat to disrupt war production resulted in a conflict that appeared to be resolved in a single day.[103]

The Chinese Canadian workers' strike pressed their employers and their unions to advocate on their behalf, but at some political cost. Shingle mill owners quickly arranged to settle the matter. They brought together Vancouver's tax office, Vancouver mayor Jack Cornett, the Chinese consul, and Vancouver Centre MP Ian McKenzie. Within one day, the Vancouver tax office quickly agreed to rescind the restriction on Chinese deductions, but the Chinese workers' illegal strike incurred much criticism.[104] The IWA and the

Dock and Shipyard Workers' Union (DSWU) decried the racial strike as harmful both to the war effort and the unions' cause. Unions, they claimed, had no division by race or religion. Strikes also hurt Allied troops. For the sake of collective bargaining, the IWA asked Chinese workers not to undercut their union. "Every worker should return to his or her workplace," stated the unions. "We pledge our support for Chinese workers."[105] Meanwhile, Vancouver's Chinese consul scolded workers that the illegal strike had hurt China-Canada relations. They should return to work, follow orders, and unite for Allied victory. China's diplomats would take care of "miscellaneous" overseas Chinese rights.[106]

*Da Han Gong Bao* called the strike a victory for all sojourners in Canada, but a defeat for Chinese because Ottawa's tax office disallowed the Vancouver settlement. Chinese could deduct dependents in China, but the tax office wanted proof of their existence. The tax office required that all Chinese applications for dependent deductions include their immigration entry paper numbers and documentation of remittances. These regulations posed dilemmas for the great many Chinese who were illegal immigrants. Since Canada did not allow their families to come, many Chinese had not declared their real families to Canadian immigration.[107] Jin She, a Chinese striker, defended the illegal protest on the front page of *Da Han Gong Bao*. Canada's entry restrictions "force immigrants to become makers of change." The strike won government recognition of Chinese families in tax policy, perhaps a precedent for future changes in immigration law, but the "peril to overseas Chinese" continued.[108]

Jin wrote that Ottawa's response created a dilemma because Canada's authorities did not appear to know about the extent of Chinese illegal immigration. If Chinese declared their true dependents, would they be charged as criminals, or would they be seen as obstructing the war effort? A good number of Chinese had used "paper names" to enter Canada by reusing others' papers or through other fraudulent means. Many Chinese had entered Canada secretly, so they did not have any immigration entry papers. These illegal immigrants wanted to save their families in China, so many prepared to rush to Canadian authorities and confess their real identities. Further, regardless of their immigration status, many Chinese had no remittance documentation that Canada's government would accept. One-third of Chinese were illiterate so they had sent money to family members through Chinese remittance shops, relatives, and friends. As a result, Chinese claims for deductions often seemed so contradictory that Canadian tax officials believed most of them to be fraudulent.[109]

The strike's efficacy made organized labor appear like a broker that could deliver. One week after the strike, on 18 July, over 2,000 Chinese met in

Chinatown to create a new regional workers' organization that would coordinate their negotiating position. Chinese workers filled the Columbia Street Theatre to the rafters. Outside, Chinese workers crowded the sidewalks on both sides of the street, eagerly waiting for news.[110] *Da Han Gong Bao* reported that Canada's tax office had informed employers to calculate Chinese employees' income tax withholding to give lower than ordinary dependent deductions for workers' wives and children in China. This new order appeared to erase the strikers' past progress.[111] The Chinese workers at the meeting resolved to meet with every employer to discuss tax and wage issues.[112] The workers contributed $48.61 in donations, a paltry sum compared with past Chinese Canadian antidiscrimination campaigns, which had been backed by wealthy merchants.[113]

The Chinese workers' organization meeting, which the English press described only as a "protest," raised the specter of a racial split in the labor movement. A reporter from the *Vancouver News Herald* asked C. T. Lee, a worker spokesman, if Chinese workers intended to "menace" trade union unity by forming a separate union. Lee said that Chinese believed that "existing unions are powerful enough and conscious enough of the situation to get justice for their Chinese members."[114] Canadian unions moved quickly to mend the rift. Charles Saunders, chair of the Dock and Shipyard Workers Union, commented, "If an Axis agent were working to invite disaffection, he could not do it more effectively than the department of finance managed by such ineptitude as this."[115] After the Chinese mass meeting, the DSWU organized a meeting of its shop stewards to discuss the tax issue. The International Woodworkers of America attempted to quiet Chinese unrest by sending a brief to Ottawa regarding the tax matter.[116] However, the unions' help did not persuade Canada's tax office to relax its requirements for proof of dependents' existence.

At the time, workers were largely excluded from political leadership both in Chinatown and in Canada's labor union movement.[117] Roy Mah, a restaurant cook, university student, and IWA organizer, recalled that, during the war, young Chinese men from wealthier families looked down on him as a "working stiff" despite the fact that Mah's bilingual skills were superior to theirs.[118] War industries relegated most Chinese to unskilled labor, regardless of their past experience.[119] Chinese workers' ranks included a fair number of educated, bilingual persons like Mah, who served as shop stewards, foremen, union organizers, and ad hoc interpreters.[120] In Vancouver's shipyards, educated, bilingual Chinese often served as foremen for Chinese crews.[121] Chinese workers recognized their own lack of prestige. When they first organized their strike, Vancouver's Chinese consul spoke for them.[122] Workers also used other intermediaries for communications during the first three weeks of their protest. *Da Han Gong Bao* did not name these "intermediaries," perhaps because the Chinese workers' strike was illegal, but they probably came from Vancouver's pool of educated, middle-class brokers friendly to labor causes, such as Foon Sien Wong and Tom Moore Whaun.[123]

After three weeks, Chinese workers created a more democratic and inclusive political institution: an ethnic labor union within the larger Canadian labor movement. On 1 August 1943, Chinese workers in the greater Vancouver region organized a new central coordinating body, the Overseas Chinese Workers' Friendship Union (OCWFU).[124] The union allowed every Chinese to vote and run for office.[125] Now, worker-brokers had their own organization, ideology, and channels into Canada's political economy. Chinese workers in the OCWFU dealt directly with employers, unions, and the government. Chinese Canadian shipyard, lumber, laundry, restaurant, and farm workers joined to support the common cause of defending workers' interests, saving China, and raising Chinese workers' status. Members came from both mainstream and ethnic Chinese workplaces and included men and women, immigrants and the Canadian-born.

Chinese workers alone did not have the cash resources for a strike fund, so they invited allies from the wider Chinese community, including some "capitalists," to their founding meeting.[126] Tom Moore Whaun, a long-time supporter of the Left, a legal interpreter, and an advertising manager for *Xin Minguo Bao*, appears to have attended.[127] Union members resolved to plan more illegal strikes and job actions, to inform the Chinese consul of their position, and to conduct direct negotiations with Vancouver's federal tax office.[128] The Chinese workers' union brought greater democracy and inclusion both to the larger labor movement and to Chinese Canadian community leadership.

For seven months, Chinese workers in British Columbia protested against the income tax regulations, joining the wider patterns of labor militancy during the war.[129] Chinese wildcat strikes were one of many abrupt job actions that jolted Canada's war effort during 1943.[130] Chinese shingle mill workers across British Columbia protested against the income tax policies with illegal strikes, shutting down two mills and "drastically reducing efficiency" throughout the industry. They also demanded equal pay to that of white workers.[131] Further, Chinese workers forced greater Vancouver's shipyards into a tax strike. The shipyards defied Ottawa, refusing to enforce the new deduction regulations. The shipyards insisted that Chinese Canadian families in China be officially recognized, so they stopped complying with the tax office's orders and returned to withholding income taxes from Chinese

Canadian paychecks at the lower rates that applied to workers who supported dependents living in Canada.[132] Besides employers, the woodworkers and the shipyard unions also lobbied on behalf of Chinese Canadians.[133] Throughout the dispute, Chinese workers negotiated with the unions, the employers, the tax office, and China's consulate.[134] The Chinese strikers, wrote Jin She, experimented with a new strategy for achieving fairness for all of North America.[135] The efforts of Chinese workers to steer the rising power of their industrial unions resulted in their tax protest being supported by the protests of increasingly potent allies.

By showing their mettle as workers, Chinese immigrants demonstrated their commitment to organized labor principles. They helped to turn labor groups, which had historically opposed Asian immigration, into allies.[136] Canadian public attitudes toward unions also shifted from a grudging toleration to a widespread belief that unions should be major players in public policy.[137] By the end of February 1944, after Canada passed comprehensive collective bargaining regulations, the Chinese workers celebrated progress on the income tax deduction issue.[138] Through their protest, Chinese sojourners had joined Canada's union movement to achieve that most desired goal of labor, a family wage. After this victory, the union movement embraced the Chinese protest organization as a formal part of the labor community.[139] The IWA also hired its first paid Chinese organizer, Roy Mah of Vancouver.[140] The Chinese workers' tax protest garnered support from East Indian workers, who also saw the principle of deductions for family members as a priority.[141] Many East Indian workers also sojourned in Canada, remitting funds to their families in the Punjab; but their smaller numbers gave them less leverage for race-based protest on the job.[142] On May Day, Chinese workers proudly marched with European and East Indian trade unionists in the city's labor parade.[143] In April 1945, F. S. Wong helped to lead a Chinese and East Indian Canadian delegation that appealed to British Columbia's parliament for voting rights. "Every union," reported the *Xin Minguo Bao*, "supported the cause."[144] Although the provincial parliament deferred Chinese Canadians' request for voting rights until the postwar era, it granted a small but important concession: it enfranchised Second World War military veterans of Chinese, East Indian, and First Nations descent.[145]

It is possible to draw a direct line between the involvement of Chinese Canadian workers in these early coalitions and the labor movement's postwar campaigns for human rights in British Columbia.[146] Indeed, the rising political power of unions during 1943–1944 has often been seen as a defining moment in Canadian labor history.[147] To date, though, labor studies of conditions during the Second World War have not delved deeply into race relations.

Further research into diverse workers' interactions may reveal a more nuanced tale of the rights revolution's origins.[148]

## Chinese Canadian Mass Resistance to Military Service

Every Canadian textbook discusses the military "conscription crisis" as a signature conflict of the Second World War, as French-British differences over conscription provoked a political crisis that threatened to sunder Canada.[149] However, the majority of Asians and First Nations people also refused military service in protest against racial inequities. The Chinese Canadian case shows that the conscription crisis involved race as centrally as it did French-English divides.[150] The almost total disenfranchisement of Asian and First Nations people gave them no recourse at the polls comparable to Quebec's French Canadian population. Nevertheless, their protests presented a compelling challenge: reconciling a war for democracy abroad with racial injustice at home.

The race question had special salience for British Columbia because one-twelfth of the population was either Asian or First Nations.[151] Chinese Canadian histories have generally remembered the conscription question as specific to their group alone. Some retrospective interviews with surviving Chinese Canadian veterans also stressed those who chose to serve, while leaving the number who refused ambiguous.[152] Chinese newspapers from the time break this silence. Combined with information from military archives, they confirm that the majority of eligible Chinese Canadian men refused to serve. They also reveal connections among Chinese Canadian, First Nations, and East Indian Canadian protests. Thus, Chinese Canadians' resistance to military service confronted their fellow Canadians with broader questions of racial justice.

In 1944, the Canadian military reversed its policy of barring all Chinese Canadians from enlisting in the military.[153] The military ordered young Chinese Canadian men to enlist. It also allowed Chinese immigrants and Chinese Canadian women to volunteer. The tardy call-up created an immediate political crisis, because many Chinese Canadians who had wanted to volunteer had previously been turned away by recruiters.[154] The secret policy of denying Chinese the right to serve in the military had been designed to preclude future requests for voting rights.[155] To Chinese Canadians, conscription required very different handling than past problems. It was a public demand that required a clear reply. It could not be finessed in backrooms or negotiated away. Suddenly, young people faced decisions that might determine the community's future. Most Chinese men of military age refused to enlist. *Da Han Gong Bao* reported that British Columbia had between 3,500 and 4,000 Chinese men who were eligible to serve, but only about 400 enlisted.[156] The unilateral action set a collision course between the new Chinese Canadian politics of protest and more conciliatory traditional brokerage.

Many Chinese questioned Canada's and Britain's motives.[157] The swift imposition of the military draft followed two months of harsh, prejudiced, ill-informed criticism of Chinese on the *Vancouver Sun*'s letters page. Much of the backlash was related to Chinese workers' gains. Anglo critics decried Chinese war workers' pursuit of higher wages while Canadians died in battle. Letter writers accused Chinese workers of profiteering, not paying income taxes, and evading military service, and they had little sympathy with Chinese who insisted that they would not enlist unless British Columbia gave them voting rights. They accused Chinese of no longer keeping in their place, suggesting that their "newly independent attitude" made them "cheeky" toward Anglos.[158] Many Chinese Canadian letters rebutted accusations of their disloyalty and selfishness. Foon Sien Wong's letter pointed out that Chinese had registered for the draft despite their unequal treatment, but Canada had not wanted them as soldiers.[159] The *Sun*'s editorial board also denounced prejudice against Chinese Canadians as ill informed.[160]

Many Chinese Canadians also suspected that Britain, not Canada, had instigated the change in conscription policy. In the spring of 1944, British brigadier F. W. Kendall visited Vancouver to recruit civilian Chinese Canadians for secret British special operations executive (SOE) missions behind enemy lines in Southeast Asia. The secrecy denied Chinese Canadians who served public recognition of their service. Without recognition, their community would not benefit. Not surprisingly, Kendall failed to recruit sufficient Chinese for his purposes. Shortly afterward, Canada decided to conscript Chinese. Military archives show that Britain pushed for the change.[161] As Chinese began to receive draft notices, Kendall returned to Chinatown to persuade them to enlist. He promised that Chinese Canadians would receive voting rights if they served in the military and volunteered to fight overseas, even though Britain had no constitutional power to fulfill the SOE officer's promise.[162] Canada's voting rights were a purely domestic affair.

Conscription most affected young Chinese Canadian men, but it created a political crisis for the entire community. To many Chinese, the request appeared to arise more from expediency than principle. Outrage followed, and the Chinese Canadian population split on the issue.[163] *Da Han Gong Bao* refused to endorse military conscription, while the *Xin Minguo Bao* printed the traditional brokers' position: to keep good relations with Canada's government and to get the franchise, Chinese men should serve.[164] Young Chinese draftees in Vancouver quickly organized a protest rally in Chinatown on 23 August to declare their "noncooperation."[165] Canadian-born Chinese Bevan Jangze described his feelings, "I didn't have any rights, so why should I fight for a country that I didn't have any rights in. . . . We all decided we weren't going to join."[166] After the meeting, Vancouver's Chinese Youth Association (CYA, *Huaqiao Qingnian Hui*) published a call for Chinese to boycott military service until their demands for equal treatment were met. In *Da Han Gong Bao*, Chinese Canadian young men stated that "we will not cooperate with this public injustice."[167] Ann Lee recalled that most Chinese Canadians supported the resisters.[168] Though both men and women could volunteer, less than 2 percent of the 30,000 Chinese in British Columbia served in the Canadian military.[169]

Collectively, Chinese, East Indian, and First Nations protests against military service formed a noncooperation movement that highlighted the injustice of racism across every region of Canada.[170] Chinese in British Columbia shared economic niches with First Nations and East Indian peoples, so they knew about these groups' parallel protests. The CYA manifesto framed the conflict as part of Canada's national conscription crisis. It called on all Chinese to boycott military service until Chinese received "Canadian rights." Across Canada, Chinese declared to military officials that they would not serve.[171] Some, like T. S. Wong of Toronto, had previously volunteered and been rejected due to their race.[172] In British Columbia, military figures show that only 273 of 1,061 Chinese Canadian men who received orders to report for military service complied. Authorities deemed 128 of these men physically fit for service, with 19 pending. Presumably, the rest of British Columbia's Chinese enlistees, roughly 130 men and women, volunteered.[173]

In Vancouver's English newspapers, Chinese Canadian letters declared the injustice of military service without equal rights.[174] Fred Chun expressed a typical opinion, "Once again, may I say, that if the Chinese hold franchise in B.C. they will volunteer including myself."[175] Ann Lee recalled that most Chinese felt that only "suckers" enlisted. They believed that Chinese would be cannon fodder. Given the abuses that Chinese in Canada had suffered in the past, how could the military and government be trusted to treat them fairly?[176] Even Chinese Canadian soldiers joked with each other about the foolishness of volunteering to fight abroad.[177]

The Chinese Canadian debate over military service came to a head at a public meeting sponsored jointly by the CYA and CBA on 27 August 1944 at the Chinese United Church, a Protestant church where many Vancouver Chinese youths had attended English-language kindergarten.[178] Since the

Canadian government effectively barred most Chinese immigrants' access to naturalization, almost all the conscripted men were Canadian-born or illegal immigrants who had entered using "borrowed" Canadian birth certificates. At the meeting, around 400 attendees protested against conscription, declaring, "No vote, no fight!" They decided to obtain legal counsel and "forward a vigorous protest to Ottawa." Around 100 young men proudly stated that they would enlist, so the boycotters had the clear majority.[179]

Historians have recounted this debate as between the "No vote, no fight!" and the "Serve first, demand rights after!" factions, but this interpretation minimizes the two sides' goals. The CYA's demands focused on attaining both political and social equality for all Canadians whom Anglos treated like "foreigners." Besides the franchise, the CYA demanded five social rights. Its young members wanted equal treatment under the law, which would reverse anti-Chinese immigration, education, and business policies. They also claimed equal rights as soldiers, learning from the experience of First Nations people in military service.[180] If Canada treated Chinese soldiers similarly to First Nations soldiers, their sacrifices would have lesser value. When First Nations soldiers were killed or disabled, Canada gave their families much less assistance than the families of white soldiers received. They also received lesser veterans' benefits. The CYA thus demanded equal benefits and family support payments comparable to other Canadian soldiers.[181] The CYA also wanted Canada to guarantee equal treatment of Chinese Canadians in post-war social welfare, labor, and industrial relations policies, so that union members could retain wartime gains.[182] In contrast, the pro-conscription side led by Roy Mah argued that the Chinese minority was too small to make demands. Fighting in the war, he said, would give the most "solid credentials" in order to "demand rights." The debate lasted a number of hours, and neither side could persuade the other to change its position.[183]

Given the Chinese community's divisions, representatives chose to acknowledge both sides. Foon Sien Wong participated in the debate, and decades later, he still recalled the community's "intense anger" at the call-up.[184] Local leaders from China's Nationalist Party attended, as did China's consul, leaders of clan and district associations (the *huiguan*), the United Chinese Workers' Union (i.e., the renamed OCWFU), and a women's group. Yip Sang's son Yip Quene also attended. The representatives chose to ask for voting rights on the grounds that Chinese Canadians were serving. They also decided to take advantage of the boycott to challenge in the courts the legality of conscripting Canadians who could not vote.[185] No Chinese Canadian court challenge to conscription had yet been mounted, though a First Nations challenge had failed. Chinese Canadians' protest created enough sympathy that war officials did not force most boycotters to serve, evading a costly legal test case.[186] Further, Chinese Canadian soldiers received pay and veterans' benefits equal to those of Anglo Canadian soldiers.[187]

After the war, the presence of Chinese Canadian veterans became a standard feature of Chinese Canadians' successful requests for federal, provincial, and municipal voting rights.[188] As a matter of war policy, the English press portrayed Chinese Canadians as model, loyal, patriotic, un-protesting citizens.[189] However, the model minority rhetoric of Chinese Canadians lobbying for voting rights coincided with mass protests for social justice. Petitioning and protest thus reinforced each other.

Ultimately, Chinese-language sources suggest that much of Canada's Second World War history of race relations remains to be told. Collectively, disenfranchised Chinese, First Nations, and East Indian peoples contributed to a nationwide wartime protest movement for equal rights. Historically, most Anglo Canadians had viewed Asian and First Nations people as "aliens," so they had paid very little attention to minorities' concerns. Scholarship has often duplicated this omission. Frank Wong recalled that, when he served in the Canadian military, Anglo soldiers were surprised to hear that Chinese in British Columbia could not vote.[190] Change was neither automatic nor caused solely by external forces. Chinese Canadians themselves provoked changes in race relations.

Canada's wartime turn toward human rights politics was especially important to Chinese Canadians. In 1947, Chinese won the right to vote in British Columbia. That year, Canada's federal government also repealed the Chinese Immigration Act, permitting Chinese Canadians to legally sponsor the entry of foreign spouses and minor children. War heroes may have won the accolades, but mass protests helped to decouple whiteness from the popular ideals of Canadian citizenship.

# Conclusion

THE POLITICAL HISTORY OF THE Exclusion Era was far more integrated than scholars presume. Chinese immigrant power brokers mitigated even the most direct processes of exclusion. Interpreters collaborated with ruling party machines to foil anti-Chinese laws. Chinese Canadians embraced Canada's legal system, seeing its rule of law as crucial to defending their interests in both internal and external conflicts. Their informal advocates, Chinese legal interpreters, gave the larger legal culture an unofficial, and often recognized, multicultural dimension. In addition to the legal experts, thousands of ordinary Chinese Canadians sought political power in Canada through modern social movements. Their boycott of the public schools to protest segregation built on Pacific world protests against the British Empire's colonialism, while also advancing an emergent Canadian–U.S. discourse of cultural pluralism more accepting of non-Anglo immigrants. In these ways, Chinese Canadians helped to create their own myths. The selective story that brokers gave to the Survey of Race Relations in 1924 later became popularized in U.S. and Canadian culture as the natural, inevitable trajectory of all immigrant groups. Thus, Chinese brokers helped to shape the myth of Asians as a model minority, a popular concept that continues to have great influence in Canada and the United States today.

Canada's official ideal of immigration—assimilation and settlement—coexisted awkwardly with Chinese Canadians' transnational way of life. During the Second World War, Canadian war policies forced Chinese workers, whether legal or illegal, to confront the state's unease with their transnational existence. The successful public stand of the Chinese marked a new epoch in their relations with their neighbors. By mobilizing as an ethnic bloc within the labor and anti-conscription movements, Chinese workers strived to expand Canadian rights politics. The ability of Chinese Canadians to garner support suggested a growing sympathy for a redefined national identity that would include all Canadian residents, even those with transnational ties. By the mid-1940s, many British Columbians saw sojourners and illegal immigrants as deserving members of the national polity. These findings underscore the need to conceive a more integrated history of Canada, the United States, and the Pacific world during the Exclusion Era.

A conception of politics which includes Chinese Canadians' alternative public sphere contributes to a more complete model of immigrants in political history. Because a lack of voting rights limited Chinese Canadians' formal access to political power, brokers' resistance to exclusion often took indirect forms. A brokerage relations approach complements the existing literature's stress on direct Chinese responses to Anglo discrimination in English-language contexts.[1] While Chinese were less effective when directly challenging mainstream power, they were influential when working through under-the-radar brokerage. Historians' emphasis on white practices of racial exclusion has thus led to a problem: the belief that Chinese Canadian history is so estranged from the rest of Canada that it is a separate, specialized topic is a profound erasure.[2] Brokers' work reveals the human connections and shared institutions that helped to cement Canada's mosaic into a single whole. When leaders' brokerage is restored to history, Chinatowns will no longer be seen as ethnic islands. Chinese Canadians were significant actors in their locality, in Canada, in China, and in the United States.

The lens of immigrant leaders' brokerage relations holds great promise to mend divides between domestic political history and its outlier, the transnational turn which is transforming global migration and exclusion studies.[3] One of this book's most intriguing findings is that a transnational perspective of a global, mobile immigrant group rooted in the Pacific world further integrates rather than fragments Canada's national narrative. Even without voting rights, Chinese Canadians in British Columbia became deeply involved in Canada's political and legal institutions. A focus on brokers' dealings points toward a more complete national narrative, one that more accurately takes into account both immigrants' assimilation and their continued ties across borders. Many of Canada's immigrants led transnational lives.[4] During the Exclusion Era, one-third of the total Canadian-born population moved to the United States.[5] Thus, a transnational life is typically Canadian, which underlines the importance of brokers and brokerage as a model for connecting together the many facets of Canada's immigrant narrative.

Brokerage was inescapably a story of domestic Canadian politics, but it also involved a series of founding bargains that did not neatly fit into any nationally bounded history. Between the 1840s and the 1940s, over a half million Chinese emigrated to settlement nations in the Americas and Australasia.[6] Anti-Chinese laws and migrants' ability to evade and mitigate discriminatory legal systems connect Canada's history with those of other settler nations.[7] In the United States, Chinese-Anglo political factions also collaborated to control Chinese immigration interpreter posts.[8] Chinese slipped into Cuba, Panama, Peru, and Australia despite anti-Chinese immigration laws.[9] Chinese in Mexico dealt with anti-Chinese policies, including expulsion, but also made alliances with mainstream politicians. Chinese Mexicans also often slipped over the U.S. border, at times with the complicity of Mexican officials.[10] These patterns suggest the need to further explore the circulation of politics within the Pacific world. They also should prompt a rethinking of the place of the disenfranchised in political history. As the nations of the Americas and Australasia first globalized border controls, Chinese migrants developed an equally globalized but also intrinsically local political expertise. Political brokerage made the first global group of illegal immigrants possible.

NOTES

ABBREVIATIONS

| | |
|---|---|
| BCA | British Columbia Archives and Records Service |
| CCRC | Chinese Canadian Research Collection, University of British Columbia Archives |
| CCVOHP | Chinese Canadian Veterans Oral History Project, Chinese Cultural Centre of Greater Vancouver |
| Chung Collection | Wallace B. Chung and Madeline H. Chung Collection, University of British Columbia Library |
| DHGB | *Da Han Gong Bao* (*Chinese Times*) |
| Jianada Huaqiao Shi | References to this work are to Ma Sen's 1973 translation unless otherwise noted. |
| LAC | Library and Archives of Canada |
| Lew v. Lee | David Lew v. Wing Lee. Supreme Court of Canada Appeal, 1924. |
| MIRC | "Minutes of Inquiries Regarding Chinese Merchants Attempting to Enter Canada on the *Empress of China*," Chung Collection |
| RCCF | Royal Commission to Investigate Alleged Chinese Frauds and Opium Smuggling on the Pacific Coast Fonds |
| SRR | Survey of Race Relations Collection, Hoover Institution Archives, Stanford University |
| UBC | University of British Columbia Library Rare Books and Special Collections |
| VCA | Vancouver City Archives |
| Wong Papers | Foon Sien Wong Papers, UBC |

INTRODUCTION

1. Wolf, "Aspects of Group Relations in a Complex Society: Mexico," 1065–1078; Peck, *Reinventing Free Labor*; Breton, *Governance of Ethnic Communities*, 61–93; Zucchi, *Italians in Toronto*; Patrias, *Patriots and Proletarians*; Harney, "Commerce of Migration"; Harney, "The Padrone and the Immigrant"; Higham, "Introduction"; Greene, *American Immigrant Leaders*, 1–16.
2. Con et al., *From China to Canada*, 55.
3. Ibid., 42–147; Pfaelzer, *Driven Out*.
4. Following conventions in the field, the first date indicates the passage of the legislation and the last date is the conclusion of its active enactment. The Chinese head tax charged Chinese immigrant laborers an entry fee of $50, which by 1904 had risen to $500. The Chinese Immigration Act of 1923 barred the entry of all Chinese starting in July 1924, which accounts for the overlap in dates. Between 1924 and 1947 Erika Lee found that only 15 Chinese received exemptions from the 1923 law permitting them to enter Canada: the Canadian-born, diplomats, merchants, and students. Lee, "Enforcing the Borders," 78.
5. Con et al., *From China to Canada*, 42–147. *New York Times*, 27 Nov. 1885.
6. Holder, "The Chinaman in American Politics." *New York Times*, 9 Sept. 1900, 20 April 1902. Arthur Train, "Mock Hen and Mock Turtle," *Tutt and Mr Tutt*, 43-88. Macdonald and O'Keefe, *Canadian Holy War*, 77-90. McIllwain, *Organizing Crime in Chinatown*, 127–185.
7. The United States made Asian immigrants ineligible for naturalization, whereas in Canada judges used their discretion to keep Chinese immigrants' naturalization rates low. The following Western states and provinces denied persons of Chinese descent the right to vote for various periods of time even if they were native-born or naturalized citizens: British Columbia, Saskatchewan, California, Oregon, and Idaho. Chang, "Asian Americans and Politics," 16–18; Con et al., *From China to Canada*, 45–46, 145; Yee, "Chinese Business in Vancouver," 28; Ward, *White Canada Forever*, 41; Keyssar, *The Right to Vote*, 141; Chan, *Asian Americans*, 47; Wai-Man, *Portraits of a Challenge*, 152.
8. See McKeown, *Chinese Migrant Networks*; Ho-Jung, *Coolies and Cane*; Kwong, *Chinatown*; Yu, *To Save China*; Ling, *Chinese St. Louis*; Lai, *Becoming Chinese American*; and Ngai, "History as Law and Life."
9. This book makes extensive use of Chinese-language historical documents, sources that scholars throughout North America have underutilized. It builds on Madeline Hsu's *Dreaming of Gold, Dreaming of Home*; and Yong Chen's *Chinese San Francisco*. The two primary sets of Chinese sources are the sole surviving Chinese newspaper from British Columbia for the 1915–1945 period, *Da Han Gong Bao* (*Chinese Times*), and brokers' personal papers. A global Chinese emigrant fraternal association, the Chinese Freemasons (Chee Kung Tong, Zhigongtang), published *Da Han Gong Bao*. This group had no relation to the English Freemasons. In

reading *DHGB*, I kept in mind that all Chinese Canadian newspapers were party organs. However, the Freemasons' large membership and independence from China's main political parties also made the *DHGB* a paper for middle-of-the-road immigrants' opinion. At least half of Chinese Canadians were Freemason members (Con et al., *From China to Canada*, 111). The long period of time that the *Da Han Gong Bao* was published (1907–1992) suggests that its news appealed to many Chinese Canadians. Before late 1915, the paper was called *Da Han Ri Bao (Chinese Daily News)*. "Interview with Lum Hing, translator for the *Chinese Times*," 1924, box 24, file 24-6, SRR. In 1924, *Da Han Gong Bao* claimed a circulation of 4,000. Huang, "Gender, Race, and Power," 12–14. Two of British Columbia's other Chinese papers, *Xin Minguo Bao* and *Jianada Chenbao*, acted as organs of the right and left wings, respectively, of China's Nationalist Party, but only a few issues and news clippings have survived. Chinese newspapers from before 1914 seem to be lost. Lo and Lai, *Chinese Newspapers Published in North America*, 112–113.

10. On alternative public spheres, see Hansen, "Foreword," ix–xli.
11. Mar, "Beyond Being Others," 13–34; Ward, *White Canada Forever*; Anderson, *Vancouver's Chinatown*; Patricia E. Roy's trilogy, *A White Man's Province, The Oriental Question*, and *The Triumph of Citizenship*; Li, *Jianada Huaqiao Shi*; Con et al., *From China to Canada*; Chan, *Gold Mountain*; Helly, *Les Chinois à Montréal*; Yee, *Saltwater City*; Li, *Chinese in Canada*; Ng, *Chinese in Vancouver*; Huang and Wu, *Huaqiao, Huaren Shi*.
12. Robert Harney, *If One Were to Write a History: Selected Writings by Robert Harney*, ed. Pierre Anctil and Bruno Ramirez (Toronto: Multicultural History Society of Ontario, 1991); Peck, *Reinventing Free Labor*; Zucchi, *Italians in Toronto*; Patrias, *Patriots and Proletarians*; Bodnar, *The Transplanted*; Breton, *Governance of Ethnic Communities*; Greene, *American Immigrant Leaders*; John Higham, ed., *Ethnic Leadership in America* (Baltimore, Md.: Johns Hopkins University Press, 1978); Cohen, *Making a New Deal*; McKeown, *Chinese Migrant Networks*; Ho-Jung, *Coolies and Cane*; Kwong, *Chinatown, New York*; Yu, *To Save China*; Ling, *Chinese St. Louis*; Lai, *Becoming Chinese American*.
13. This book's conception of brokers and brokerage relations was inspired by histories of modern China because few historians of Canada and the United States have fully explored ethnic leadership as a mediating force. I take an anthropological approach, which examines brokers and brokerage as part of an evolving set of social structures. Given shifting historical contexts, brokers' changing and multiple roles cannot be reduced to a single form of dominance or a single theoretical approach. Therefore, I argue in favor of a more complex conception of race relations politics, which focuses on the ongoing construction of immigrants' relationships to both societies. This meeting of different worlds involved social structures that arose from interacting forces: the brokers themselves, ordinary Chinese, and their Canadian allies. I also explore how the brokers' representative power within race relations politics often

expressed controversial patterns of dominance rooted both in immigrant and in wider Canadian society. Conceptually, histories of what scholars term China's local elites provide the closest parallels to Chinese Canadian brokerage. The concept of elites in China's local societies covers a wide range of dominant mediating figures who aided ordinary people in their dealings with the state. On "nonofficial" local elites as a central mediating force in modern Chinese history, see Esherick and Rankin's introduction to *Chinese Local Elites*, 1–24; Macauley, *Social Power and Legal Culture*, 1–17; Goodman, *Native Place, City, and Nation*. See also Wolf's theoretical definition of political "cultural brokers" as seeking simultaneous leadership in separate minority and mainstream settings in "Aspects of Group Relations in a Complex Society: Mexico." Few Canadian studies have explored ethnic leadership's mediating power for nonvoting immigrants with a sophistication comparable to historical studies of China's local elites' relations with the state and the wider society. See Peck, *Reinventing Free Labor*; Breton, *Governance of Ethnic Communities*, 61–93; Zucchi, *Italians in Toronto*; Patrias, *Patriots and Proletarians*; Harney, "Commerce of Migration"; Harney, "The Padrone and the Immigrant"; Sangster, *Dreaming of What Might Be*. The U.S. history field's coverage of immigrant political brokerage shares the Canadian focus on the enfranchised. See Sterne, "Beyond the Boss."

14. *Eighth Census of Canada, 1941*, 3:128–129.
15. Barman, *West Beyond the West*, 429. Con et al., *From China to Canada*, 301. Anderson, *Vancouver's Chinatown*, 1–106.
16. Rumbaut, "Assimilation and Its Discontents."
17. See note 7. Also see Mar, "Beyond Being Others," 13–34.
18. This conception of Chinese as part of a shared Pacific world history of Canada and the United States complements more conventional accounts of the anti-Asian Exclusion Era that see Chinese as separate from the larger society because of mainstream discrimination and cultural differences. Takaki, *Strangers from a Different Shore*; Chan, *Gold Mountain*.
19. Ma argues that Yip's power came from the fraternal association that supported his control over Chinese in British Columbia, the Chinese Freemasons. Its leadership overlapped with Yip's political party, the Baohuanghui (Chinese Empire Reform Association). The Chinese Freemasons were involved in illegal immigration on both sides of the U.S.–Canada border. Ma, *Revolutionaries, Monarchists, and Chinatowns*, 76–77, 94, 122, 125, 135–136; Kim and Markov, "The Chinese Exclusion Laws."
20. *Washington Post*, 8 Jan. 1905.
21. Ma, *Revolutionaries, Monarchists, and Chinatowns*, 110–112, 118, 128–130; Li Li, "A History of the Overseas Chinese in China by David Li," translated by Ma Sen, box 25, file 54, CCRC; Tsai, *Hong Kong in Chinese History*, 222; Larson, "New Source Materials on Kang Youwei and the Baohuanghui," 171, 178, 190.
22. Worden, "A Chinese Reformer in Exile," 158–164.

23. MIRC, 2:716, 920–921, 929, 1294–1298, 3451 (1911); RCCF, RG 33-146, vol. 1; "Chinese Merchants Attempting to Enter Canada," LAC; Yee, "Chinese Business in Vancouver," 31–32, 40–44.
24. I take as a starting premise that ideas about "race" are what historians call social constructions: an expression of a society's social distribution of inequality in a particular place and time.
25. RCCF, 6:2940, 2944–2947, 2951, 2955–2957, 2964, 2974; 7:3089–3096; MIRC, 2:646–649, 676–677.
26. *Report of Mr. Justice Murphy*, 21–53; *Vancouver World*, 17–18 Jan. 1911; *Vancouver Daily Province*, 19 Dec. 1910; Morton, *In the Sea of Sterile Mountains*, 220.
27. MIRC, 2:644–646, 656–661, 911–912; 3:1294–1300, 1653 (1911).
28. *Vancouver Daily Province*, 24 Jan. 1911.
29. *Vancouver World*, 16 Jan. 1911; MIRC, 2:924–926; RCCF, 6–21.
30. Ward, *White Canada Forever*; Anderson, *Vancouver's Chinatown*; Roy, *A White Man's Province*; Roy, *The Oriental Question*; Roy, *The Triumph of Citizenship*; Li, *Jianada Huaqiao Shi*; Con et al., *From China to Canada*; Chan, *Gold Mountain*; Helly, *Les Chinois à Montréal*; Yee, *Saltwater City*; Li, *Chinese in Canada*; Ng, *Chinese in Vancouver*; Huang and Wu, *Huaqiao, Huaren Shi*.
31. Lee, "Orientalisms in the Americas," 235–256.
32. Con et. al, *From China to Canada*, 7; Chan, *Asian Americans*, 5–6.
33. Raushenbush, "The Great Wall of Chinatown," *Survey Graphic* 56.3 (1 May 1926): 154–158, 221
34. "Office File Questionnaires Chinese—Pacific Coast (U.S.) + Canada," Survey Interview Questionnaires (ca. Jan. and Feb. 1924), box 17, file 17-2, SRR; Winifred Raushenbush to Dr. Yick Pang Lew, 22 Feb. 1924, box 17, file 17-2, SRR; Chuichi Ohashi of Japanese Consulate, San Francisco, to Merle Davis, 6 Feb. 1924, box 14, file 14-11, SRR; Winifred Raushenbush, "Interview, Herbert Wang," 25 Mar. 1924, box 24, file 24-24, 6, SRR; *DHGB*, 14 Feb. 1924; Mears, "The Survey of Race Relations"; Merle Davis to Premier of British Columbia, Sir John Oliver, 3 Dec. 1923, box 13, file 13-1, SRR. On relations between the survey and the Chicago School of Sociology, see Yu, *Thinking Orientals*; and Okihiro, *Teaching Asian American History*, 39–40.
35. Park, "Human Migration and the Marginal Man"; Yu, *Thinking Orientals*, 96–102.
36. Canada: Ward, *White Canada Forever*; Roy, *A White Man's Province*; Anderson, *Vancouver's Chinatown*. In *Les Chinois à Montréal*, Helly explores the dual French-English contexts of relations in Montreal. United States: Lee, *At America's Gates*; Takaki, *Strangers from a Different Shore*.
37. To date, the majority of books from the China school about Chinese Canadians are historical overviews. These include Li, *Chinese in Canada*; Con et al., *From China to Canada*; Chan, *Gold Mountain*; Li, *Jianada Huaqiao Shi*; and Huang and Wu, *Huaqiao, Huaren Shi*. Historians of the China school have also focused on local Chinese communities, for example, Paul

Yee's popular pictorial history, *Saltwater City*, and Wing Chung Ng's *Chinese in Vancouver*, which explores the diverse history of Chinese Canadian identities. Ma's *Revolutionaries, Monarchists, and Chinatowns* stands out as an exception in the China school because of the breadth of its transnational perspective. Examples of works about the United States include Ma, *Revolutionaries, Monarchists, and Chinatowns*; Hsu, *Dreaming of Gold, Dreaming of Home*; Chen, *Chinese San Francisco*; and McKeown, *Chinese Migrant Networks*.

38. This study builds on Chinese American studies that have begun to explore Chinese-language sources, especially Hsu's *Dreaming of Gold, Dreaming of Home*; and Chen's *Chinese San Francisco*.
39. Kay J. Anderson, "Creating Outsiders, 1875–1903," in *The History of Immigration and Racism in Canada: Essential Readings*, ed. Barrington Walker (Toronto: Canadian Scholars Press, 2008), 90–104.
40. From a transpacific perspective, Chinese Canadian transnationalism appeared similar to Chinese Americans; see Hsu, *Dreaming of Gold, Dreaming of Home*, although Chinese Canadian transnationalism adds a U.S.–Canada dimension. For a working definition of transnational migrant, see Schiller, "Transmigrants and Nation-States." The concept of a transnational life builds upon work presented in Smith, *Mexican New York*, 1–17.
41. *Eighth Census of Canada, 1941*, 3:164, 534; 4:176–177, 293, 422–423; 7:1018–1033.
42. *DHGB*, 1915–1945.
43. Chan, "'Orientalism' and Image Making," 37–46.
44. Liang, *Xin Dalu Youji*, 233; RCCF, 1:6–7 (1910), RG 33-146, vols. 1–6, LAC; *Vancouver World*, 16–17 Jan. 1911; *Vancouver Daily Province*, 19 Dec. 1910; Wong, "The Chinese."
45. Con et al., *From China to Canada*, 6.
46. *Da Han Gong Bao* regularly reported on news from Chinese American communities.
47. "Visit, the Lam family" March 1924, box 24, file 24-20, SRR and "Visit Miss Hellaby, Anglican missionary," 1924, box 24, file 24-21, SRR. On the SRR as a Canadian source, see Mar, "From Diaspora to North American Civil Rights," 102–120. See also Yu, *Thinking Orientals*.
48. *DHGB*, 10 July 1943; Hansen, *Mingling of the Canadian and American Peoples*, 1:263.
49. MIRC, 2:716, 920–921, 924–926, 929, 1294–1298, 3451; "Chinese Merchants Attempting to Enter Canada," 1:6–21, 65–66, 120–121, 452–453, 459, 489, LAC; *Vancouver World*, 16 Jan. 1911; *Report of Mr. Justice Murphy*, 3–4, 13, 21–46.
50. RCCF, 6:2964, LAC; MIRC, 2:798–800; *Vancouver World*, 17 Jan. 1911.
51. Carty and Ward, "The Making of a Canadian Political Citizenship," 67; and Smith, "National Political Parties."

52. Backhouse, *Colour-Coded*, 3–17. See also Anderson, *Vancouver's Chinatown*, 8–33, on policies that expressed Anglo cultural hegemony over Chinese.
53. On China's legal history, see Macauley, *Social Power and Legal Culture*, 1–17, 100–145. On Chinese American legal activism, see McClain, *In Search of Equality*; Fritz, "A Nineteenth Century 'Habeas Corpus Mill,'" 55–80; Anderson, *Vancouver's Chinatown*, 136–137.
54. *David Lew v. Wing Lee (Rong Li)*, Supreme Court of Canada Appeal, 1924, RG 125, vol. 508, file 4956, LAC.
55. DHGB, 25 Sept. 1924.
56. Ashworth, *The Forces Which Shaped Them*, 75–82; Lai, "The Issue of Discrimination in Education"; Yee, *Saltwater City*, 52–53; Stanley, "White Supremacy, Chinese Schooling, and School Segregation"; Stanley, "Bringing Anti-Racism into Historical Explanation." Erez Manela describes the backdrop, a global trend of anti-colonial nationalism, in *The Wilsonian Moment*.
57. Chuichi Ohashi of Japanese Consulate, San Francisco, Letter to Merle Davis, SRR. Park stated this opinion in a Japanese-language newspaper. Many well-educated Chinese could read Japanese, and news traveled quickly across the West Coast's tightly networked Chinese communities.
58. DHGB, 14 Feb.1924; Raushenbush, British Columbia Major Documents, box 24, files 24-1 through 24-35. SRR.
59. Subsequent Chinese interviews in Seattle and San Francisco revealed parallel patterns of researcher management and selective information. Vancouver's Chinese newspapers circulated there. See C.H. Burnett, Seattle Chinese interviews major documents, box 27, folders 24-:18, 27, 33–34, 36–50. SRR; Raushenbush, "Their Place in the Sun"; Raushenbush, "The Great Wall of Chinatown," 154–158, 221; Gjerde, "New Growth on Old Vines." The impact of the Chicago School and the survey is especially marked in the fields of Asian Canadian and Asian American studies; see its most conceptually influential historical text, Takaki, *Strangers from a Different Shore*. In *Thinking Orientals*, Henry Yu documents that the Chicago School had a long-term impact on geography, sociology, social psychology, history, and Asian American studies, "where repudiation covers a long-standing appropriation," 186–197. Canadian historians explored the influence of the Chicago School on the development of immigration sociology starting at McGill University in the 1930s, but the survey's conceptual impact suggests an earlier West Coast starting point. See Shore, *Science of Social Redemption*; and Palantzas, "A Chicago Reprise in the Champagne Years of Canadian Sociology."
60. Roy, *The Oriental Question*, 67–77.
61. Canada's 1921 Census found that 42 percent of Chinese in British Columbia over age ten could only speak Chinese, with slower rates of linguistic assimilation across the board for Asian compared with European immigrants. *Sixth Census of Canada, 1921*, 2:546–547.

62. Anderson, *Vancouver's Chinatown*, 124–125; Liang, *Xin Dalu Youji*, 230–231; *DHGB*, 1915–1945 (news, advertisements, crime reports); Ito, *Issei*, 758; CCVOHP, Jane Ng and Amos Lee, interview with Bing Wong, 14 Aug. 1996; Lim, *West Coast Chinese Boy*, 6–8, 19, 37–41; Marquis, "Vancouver Vice," 246–254; Ray, *I Have Lived Here*, 292–312; Barman, *The West beyond the West*, 259; Wong, Nations at War Scrapbook; *DHGB*, 1920s–1940s; Marlatt and Itter, *Opening Doors*; Ann Lee, interview.
63. McInnes, *Oriental Occupation of British Columbia*, 37–38.
64. Yee, *Saltwater City*, 86–95; Huang with Jeffery, *Chinese Canadians*, 30–47, 70–79; CCVOHP, Roy Mah interview.
65. On the globalized anti-Chinese gatekeeping, see McKeown, *Melancholy Order*; and Lee, "Hemispheric Orientalism."
66. On the United States, see Lee, *At America's Gates*, 1–18.
67. Gabaccia, "Is Everywhere Nowhere?"; Hansen, *Mingling of the Canadian and American Peoples*, 263.
68. Gabaccia, "Is Everywhere Nowhere?"
69. See Anderson, *Vancouver's Chinatown*, 8–33.

## CHAPTER ONE

1. For a discussion of the U.S. system's difficulties in stopping Chinese illegal immigration, see Lee, *At America's Gates*, 189–220.
2. Adam McKeown, "Ritualization of Regulation," argues that the similar U.S. system was intended to systematically humiliate Chinese. See this chapter's conclusion for a discussion of the wider impact of the Chinese case.
3. On the U.S. sorting process, see Calavita, "Collisions at the Intersection of Gender, Race, and Class"; and McKeown, "Ritualization of Regulation," 377–403.
4. Lai, "A 'Prison' for Chinese Immigrants."
5. Ito, *Issei*, 617, writes of Japanese immigrants as "deaf and dumb" in an English-speaking country.
6. Gordon, "Patronage, Etiquette, and the Science of Connection," 1–4.
7. Hodgetts et al., *Biography of an Institution*, 9.
8. Order in Council 2050, 14 Oct. 1910, vol. 1001, RG 2, LAC, microfilm reel T-5013; Order in Council 794, 12 Apr. 1911, vols. 2–40, RG 2, LAC, microfilm reel T-5014.
9. The evidence of how Chinese Canadians traded for influence is presented throughout this chapter. Diane Newell found that British Columbia's wealthiest Chinese Canadian merchants (e.g., Chang Toy) often attempted to influence public policy through white intermediaries. Newell, "Beyond Chinatown."
10. RCCF, 7:3115 (1911).
11. Dawson, *Civil Service of Canada*, 1–92. As Alan Gordon argues, Canada's political historians have regarded patronage as central to the party system, though few have probed the complex give and take of patronage as a system of multiple,

mutual, but often asymmetric relations. See "Patronage, Etiquette, and the Science of Connection." J. E. Hodgetts et al. note that political parties did not keep written records of these local negotiations to prevent embarrassment at elections, so they have received much less study than the top-down dealings of high-level party leaders. See Hodgetts et al., *Biography of an Institution*, 9.
12. Dawson, *Civil Service of Canada*, 1–89; Whitaker, *The Government Party*, xx–xxii; Order in Council 2050, 14 Oct. 1910; Order in Council 794, 12 Apr. 1911.
13. Dawson, *Civil Service of Canada*, 1–89; Whitaker, *The Government Party*, xx–xxii; Hodgetts et al., *Biography of an Institution*, 9.
14. MIRC, 6:2969, 7:3089–3101 (1911); Agreement, David Lew with Arthur McEvoy, 2 Sept. 1908, BCA.
15. Morton, *In the Sea of Sterile Mountains*, 136.
16. MIRC, 6:2969 (1911).
17. This story comes from the 1901 habeas corpus case *In re Fong Yuk*. See Hunter and Lampman, *"In re Fong Yuk" British Columbia Law Reports* 8(1902):118–121; J. Lee, "Lee Mong Kow (1863–1924)." http://members.shaw.ca/leesassociationvictoria/mongkow.htm. Accessed 26 October 2006. The description of indentured Chinese prostitutes and servant girls as "female slavery" was generally acknowledged among Chinese Canadians in Victoria because so many were abused. Gordon (Won) Cumyow interview, in Marlatt and Itter, *Opening Doors*, 19.
18. Copy of Agreement, David Lew with Arthur McEvoy, 2 Sept. 1908.
19. MIRC, 7:3160–3161 (1911); *Report of Mr. Justice Murphy*; Morton, *In the Sea of Sterile Mountains*, 219–222.
20. Liang, *Xin Dalu Youji*, 233; Lee, "Enforcing the Borders," 54–86.
21. MIRC, 7:3166–3171 (1911).
22. *Vancouver World*, 7 Feb. 1911.
23. Ma, *Revolutionaries, Monarchists, and Chinatowns*, 49, 57–58, 62, 76, 79–80, 92, 128, 130, 133–136, 161; Li, *Jianada Huaqiao Shi*, 183–185; Larson, "Articulating China's First Mass Movement"; Larson, "New Source Materials on Kang Youwei and the Baohuanghui," 151–198.
24. This is evidenced by the decision to have a Royal Commission and by the lobbying efforts on both sides to manage the accusations and counter-accusations. *Report of Mr. Justice Murphy*, 5–21.
25. *Vancouver World*, 20 Jan. 1911.
26. Roy, *A White Man's Province*, 234–235; Morton, *In the Sea of Sterile Mountains*, 219–221.
27. Heroic stature: Lew met with Prime Minister Laurier in 1910 to discuss immigration matters. In the 1950s, Foon Sien Wong's pilgrimages to Ottawa to talk directly with immigration officials won extensive press coverage and attention because of their groundbreaking nature. MIRC, 2:823, 4:1754–1757 (1911); *Vancouver Daily Province*, 24 Jan. 1911, 9; Ng, *Chinese in Vancouver*, 75–76. On CERA, see Ma, *Revolutionaries, Monarchists, and Chinatowns*; on Yip and the

boycott, see Larson, "Articulating China's First Mass Movement." Compromised positions: *Da Han Gong Bao* and other Chinese-language newspapers often reported the compromised positions of interpreters who worked for the state. They apparently printed public criticisms of Yip's conduct. MIRC, 2:639 (1911). On idealism, see Larson, "Articulating China's First Mass Movement," which argues that CERA hoped to transform China's citizens into modern, active nation makers prepared for democracy.

28. Yip had been the acting interpreter since 1902 but was formally appointed in 1904. RG 2, ser. 1, vol. 2-27, LAC, microfilm reel T-5001; Order in Council 1688, "Appointment of Yip On, Chinese Interpreter, Vancouver," 19 Sept. 1904; RCCF, 1:452 (1911).
29. Larson, "Articulating China's First Mass Movement."
30. Ibid.; Wang, *In Search of Justice*, 134–159.
31. Wang, *In Search of Justice*, 138–139.
32. Ibid., 141–142.
33. Larson, "Articulating China's First Mass Movement," 20; Liang, "Ji Huagong Jinyue," 487.
34. *DHGB*, 16 June 1924.
35. *Washington Post*, 25 June 1905.
36. For discussions of the boycott's influence in China, see Wang, *In Search of Justice*; Wong, *China's Anti-American Boycott Movement*; and McKee, *Chinese Exclusion versus the Open Door Policy*.
37. Worden, "A Chinese Reformer in Exile," 158–164.
38. Ibid., 158–164; *Washington Post*, 26 June 1905; *New York Times*, 26 June 1905, 7; Lee, *At America's Gates*, 84–85.
39. RCCF, 1:78–79, 122 (1910); *Vancouver Daily Province*, 22 Dec. 1910.
40. The ruling federal party's local riding association usually voted on nominations for civil service positions, so the appointment of Chinese interpreters who eased illegal immigration at Canada's two chief Pacific entry points should not be seen as coincidental.
41. Yip was a central figure in CERA's Commercial Corporation, a party investment fund that sold shares to Chinese throughout China, the Americas, and Southeast Asia. Li, *Jianada Huaqiao Shi*, 184–185; Ma, *Revolutionaries, Monarchists, and Chinatowns*, 110.
42. Besides the 1905 U.S. boycott, Yip helped to lead a Chinese boycott of Japan between 1908 and 1910. Yip's connection to the Japanese boycott's organizer, the Canton Merchants Self-Government Society (SGA's Yueshang Zizhi Hui), strongly suggests a tie to the SGA's boycott of San Francisco in 1910. Boycotts of foreign goods were accompanied by exhortations for Chinese to buy Chinese products. Tsai, *Hong Kong in Chinese History*, 214–215, 220–221; *New York Times*, 12 May 1910; *Washington Post*, 4 Aug. 1910.
43. *Vancouver World*, 4 Jan. 1911.

44. Ma, *Revolutionaries, Monarchists, and Chinatowns*, 110–111, 116; Larson, "Articulating China's First Mass Movement," 14.
45. *Report of Mr. Justice Murphy*, 30–32.
46. Reports mention a single previous Chinese immigration interpreter at Vancouver, Charlie Yip Yen (also known as Yip Yuen, or Yip Ren). RCCF, 1:65 (1910).
47. Ma describes this faction as a dominant group of businessmen affiliated with the Chinese Freemasons, which allowed them to maintain control over Vancouver's and Victoria's Chinese populations during the late nineteenth and early twentieth centuries, until 1910–1911. Ma, *Revolutionaries, Monarchists, and Chinatowns*, 82, 94, 135–136.
48. Ibid., 84–153; Con et al., *From China to Canada*, 101–117.
49. *Vancouver World*, 17, 25 Jan. 1911.
50. Brown and Cook, *Canada, 1896–1921*, 179–185; Morton, *In the Sea of Sterile Mountains*, 221; Roy, *A White Man's Province*, 202–207, 234–236.
51. *Vancouver World*, 7, 9, 11, 13 Jan. 1911; *Vancouver Sun*, 25 Sept. 1924; *Vancouver Daily Province*, 25 Sept. 1924; *DHGB*, 25, 26, 27, 29, 30 Sept., 1 Oct. 1924; Macdonald and O'Keefe, *Canadian Holy War*, 78–81, 103. Lew's role as the official Chinese interpreter for the Royal Commission that explored Chinese losses in Vancouver's anti-Asian riot underlined that the young, unofficial Chinese lawyer was considered among the best legal interpreters of his generation. Department of Labour, *Report by W. L. Mackenzie King*, 3.
52. On litigation masters, see Macauley, *Social Power and Legal Culture*.
53. *Vancouver World*, 7, 9, 11, 13 Jan. 1911.
54. Lew's call built on the findings of a Royal Commission (1907–1908) that reported excessive patronage, graft, and incompetence in civil service dealings with immigrants. Dawson, *Civil Service of Canada*, 74–81.
55. MIRC, 2:643–646, 732, 745, 958; 6:2741–2746.
56. *Vancouver World*, 4, 5, 7, 9, 11, 13 Jan. 1911.
57. Yee, "Chinese Business in Vancouver," 40–41; Yee, *Saltwater City*, 33.
58. MIRC, 2:926 (1911); *Vancouver World*, 17, 25 Jan. 1911; *Vancouver Daily Province*, 16 Jan. 1911.
59. Lew had a formal association with Gordon Grant's law practice, which was run by T. R. E. McInnes's brother W. W. B. McInnes, a former Liberal commissioner of the Yukon, ex-Member of the Provincial Legislature and ex-MP, a respected political figure, and a leader of Vancouver's Asiatic Exclusion League. Grant was the former secretary of the Asiatic Exclusion League and a former member of Vancouver's Liberal Party executive. J. W. de B. Farris routinely handled Chinese labor contracts and related business, such as inquests, civil lawsuits, and immigration cases, and was known as a prominent young Liberal. Lew Fonds, Lew to Owyang King, 8 June 1909; Lew to J. W. de B. Farris, 2 Aug. 1909; *Vancouver World*, 25 Jan. 1911. T. R. E. McInnes was an attorney for *In re Chin Chee*, a 1905 habeas corpus case involving Chin Chee, a ten-year

resident of Vancouver, who was denied entry to Canada on the grounds that he had contracted trachoma during a visit to China. Victory in the case helped to establish stronger reentry rights for "home-coming" residents of Canada. See Lampman and Bass, *British Columbia Law Reports*, "In re Chin Chee." 9(1905):400–401; Bass, "*In re Lee Him*" 15(1911):163–165, 390; Roy, *A White Man's Province*, 201.

60. MIRC, 3:1316 (1911).
61. *Vancouver World*, 20 Jan. 1911; *Vancouver Daily Province*, 16 Jan. 1911.
62. MIRC, 2:656–657, 811–812 (1911); *In re Fong Yuk and the Chinese Immigration Act*, 118–121. On the United States, see McKeown, "Ritualization of Regulation," 390–391.
63. Bass, "In re Lee Him," 163–165, 390.
64. *Vancouver World*, 13, 17, 31 Jan., 2 Feb. 1911; Lew Fonds, Lew to Lee Kee [Lee Saifan], 27 June, 4 Aug. 1907; Yee, "Chinese Business in Vancouver," 40–41; RCCF, "Chinese Merchants Attempting to Enter Canada," 146 (1910).
65. Roy, *A White Man's Province*, 185–202.
66. *Vancouver World*, 11 Jan. 1911, 3; MIRC, 7:3467 (1911).
67. *Vancouver World*, 10, 23, 24 Jan. 1911; Ma, *Revolutionaries, Monarchists, and Chinatowns*, 49, 57–58, 62, 76, 79–80, 82, 92, 110–111, 116, 128, 130, 135–136, 161.
68. Josie Lee and Vivian Wong, interview. A search of the General Registers of Chinese Immigration could not confirm the exact year, possibly because he arrived under an alternate name. This account sets his arrival in the specific context of 1910, the year recalled by his family. Accounts of F. S. Wong's age conflict, but he was born probably between 1899 and 1902. Wong, "The Life and Times of Foon Sien."
69. MIRC, 2:643–818, 953–957.
70. Lee and Wong, interview.
71. *Vancouver World*, 13 Jan. 1911. At the time, Yip On and Bowell were colluding to extort money from arriving Chinese who sought head tax exemptions, such as merchants and their sons. Yip delayed them until they paid his price, and only after they had his "approval" did Bowell agree to process them. Dawson, a historian of Canada's civil service, noted that a Royal Commission in 1908 found that many civil servants considered petty graft or bribery to be a job perquisite. Dawson, *Civil Service of Canada*, 74–81.
72. The procedure comes from LAC, RG 76 (Immigration Branch), vol. 590, file 827835, microfilm reel C-10661, Department of Trade and Commerce regarding Chinese Immigration Act (and Transferring the Administration of the Act from the Trade and Commerce Department to Interior on 2 October 1911); Chinese Immigration Service, "Form for Chinese Parent's Examination," 1910–1911; Form C.I. 18, "Form for Chinese Claiming to Be Merchant Son's Examination," 1910–1911; *Vancouver World*, 13 Jan. 1911; Lee and Wong, interview.

73. *DHGB*, 25 Jan. 1923.
74. Department of Trade and Commerce regarding Chinese Immigration Act, 1885–1911. RG 76, vol. 590. LAC; Department of Trade and Commerce, *Chinese Immigration Act*, 6; Department of Trade and Commerce, Form C.I. 17, "Chinese Claiming Merchant Exemption Questionnaire."
75. Con et al., *From China to Canada*, 157; Low, *Memories of Cumberland Chinatown*, 91–92.
76. Con et al., *From China to Canada*, 157.
77. Department of Trade and Commerce, Chinese Immigration Act, 1885–1911, 12. Canada barred foreign contract workers with the Alien Labour Act of 1897, an act that Parliament revised and strengthened in 1905. Buchignani and Indra, "Vanishing Acts," 420–421; Peck, *Reinventing Free Labor*, 90.
78. Miki, *Redress*, 23.
79. *Vancouver World*, 1 Feb. 1911.
80. RCCF, 6:2741–2747 (1911).
81. Con et al., *From China to Canada*, 157.
82. Ibid.
83. Chan, *Gold Mountain*, 187.
84. Roy, *A White Man's Province*, 234.
85. The less stringent criteria for the reentry of Canadian residents were reinforced by the *In re Chin Chee* habeas corpus case of 1905. *British Columbia Law Reports* 11 (1905): 400–401.
86. RCCF, "Chinese Merchants Attempting to Enter Canada," 146 (1910); Liang, *Xin Dalu Youji*, 232.
87. Liang, *Xin Dalu Youji*, 233.
88. Roy, *A White Man's Province*, 61; *Report of Mr. Justice Murphy*, 29.
89. Yee, "Chinese Business in Vancouver," 32, 42, 65–72.
90. Williams, "Hong Kong and the Pearl River Delta *Qiaoxiang*"; Lee, *At America's Gates*, 176; Yee, "Chinese Business in Vancouver," 42; Waite, "Between Three Oceans," 334–335; Brown and Cook, *Canada, 1896–1921*, 200–201.
91. RCCF, 6:2726 (1911); *Report of Mr. Justice Murphy*, 51.
92. Department of Secretary of State, "In the County Court Judge's Criminal Court," RG 6E, vol. 574, file 246-2, LAC; "Before His Honour Judge Lampman, Victoria, British Columbia, Tuesday, January 30, 1917"; *Rex v. Ho Hee et al.*, "Testimony of Lee Mong Kow, taken at above trial" (hereafter "Testimony of Lee Mong Kow"), 1–30. Other steamship lines also used the Chinese agent system. Yee, "Chinese Business in Vancouver," 41; Stanley, "Defining the Chinese Other," 155–156. It is unclear whether Chinese paid higher ticket prices than did Anglo Canadians.
93. Kwong and Miščević, *Chinese America*, 82–85.
94. Ma, *Revolutionaries, Monarchists, and Chinatowns*, 76–77; *Ethnic Index* (Ottawa: LAC, 1986), 1:86–90, 104; Lee, "Enforcing the Borders."

95. Peck, *Reinventing Free Labor*, 94–96; Lee, "Enforcing the Borders," 54–86; Williams, "Hong Kong and the Pearl River Delta *Qiaoxiang*," 262–264; MIRC, 2:920 (1910).
96. RCCF, 1:17, 131–132, 152 (1910).
97. Roy, *A White Man's Province*, 235–236. Bennett McCardle dates the use of pictures on new Chinese immigration entry documents from 1912. McCardle, "The Records of Chinese Immigration at the National Archives of Canada."
98. RCCF, 1:6–7 (1910); *Vancouver World*, 16, 17 Jan. 1911; *Vancouver Daily Province*, 19 Dec. 1910.
99. RCCF, 1:7–8 (1910).
100. *Vancouver World*, 17 Jan. 1911; *Vancouver Daily Province*, 17, 31 Jan. 1911.
101. *Vancouver World*, 20 Dec. 1910, 4 Jan. 1911.
102. *Vancouver World*, 23 Dec. 1910; *Vancouver Daily Province*, 23, 24 Dec. 1910.
103. Williams, "Hong Kong and the Pearl River Delta *Qiaoxiang*," 261–263; *Report of the Royal Commission on Chinese and Japanese Immigration*, 9; Con et al., *From China to Canada*, 82–83.
104. Wong Que, file P-1402, and Yong Hor, file P-01413, Probate Files, 1893–1941, BCA, microfilm reel B-2546.
105. RCCF, "Chinese Merchants Attempting to Enter Canada," 114–142 (1910).
106. *Report of Mr. Justice Murphy*, 30–42.
107. Philip Kuhn describes the similar U.S. system of paper sons in *Chinese among Others*, 220–221.
108. For the procedures, see LAC, Department of Trade and Commerce, Chinese Immigration Act, 1885–1911.
109. MIRC, 2:777–779, 933 (1911).
110. Ibid., 786–787; Williams, "Hong Kong and the Pearl River Delta *Qiaoxiang*," 262–264.
111. RCCF, 1:31 (1910); "Chinese Merchants Attempting to Enter Canada," 153–154, 169–180, 142–143, 52–65, 20–21.
112. RCCF, 1:122 (1910).
113. Ibid., 78–79; *Vancouver Daily Province*, 22 Dec. 1910; Roy, *The Oriental Question*, 234.
114. "Form to Be Used when Examining a Person of Chinese Origin Who Claims Exemption as a Merchant," Department of Trade and Commerce, Chinese Immigration Act, Form C.I. 27, 1910–1911, LAC.
115. *Vancouver Daily Province*, 26 Jan. 1910.
116. RCCF, 1:24 (1910); "Form for Chinese Parent's Examination," Department of Trade and Commerce, Chinese Immigration Act, 1885–1911; "Form for Chinese Claiming to Be Merchant Son's Examination," 1910–1911.
117. Department of Trade and Commerce, Chinese Immigration Act, 1885–1911; Chinese Immigration Service, Form C.I. 9 (1910).
118. McKeown, "Ritualization of Regulation," 377–403.

119. Monthly Payrolls, 1910–1911, Department of Trade and Commerce, Chinese Immigration Act, 1885–1911; *Report of Mr. Justice Murphy*, 44.
120. RCCF, 1:71 (1910), 2:725 (1911); *Vancouver World*, 10 Jan. 1911; *Vancouver Daily Province*, 23 Dec. 1910; Mar, "Beyond Being Others," 20. From at least 1890 to 1914–1915, Canada's government processed arriving Chinese in an immigration building at the foot of Burrard Street, near Pier A and Pier B. This building was sometimes referred to as the "detention shed," a term used for earlier buildings that held Chinese arrivals in San Francisco (before Angel Island opened in 1910) and in Seattle. Later, entering Chinese were held at an immigration building on the waterfront at the foot of Thurlow Street that was built in 1914–1915. Canada's immigration department used this building until 1975. Megan Schlase, Archivist, City of Vancouver Archives, email to author, 15 January 2008.
121. The Chinese Empire Reform Association is the English name for a Chinese political party that called itself first Baohuanghui (Protect the Emperor Society), which existed from 1899 to 1906, and then the Constitutionalist Association (Diguo Xianzheng Dang), which existed after 1906.
122. Ma, *Revolutionaries, Monarchists, and Chinatowns*, 49, 57–58, 62, 76, 79–80, 82, 92, 128, 130, 135–136; Yee, *Saltwater City*, 46.
123. Larson, "Articulating China's First Mass Movement."
124. Yee, *Saltwater City*, 46; Worden, "A Chinese Reformer in Exile," 69; Ma, *Revolutionaries, Monarchists, and Chinatowns*, 110–111, 130; Li, *Jianada Huaqiao Shi*, 184–185.
125. Con et al., *From China to Canada*, 111.
126. Ma, *Revolutionaries, Monarchists, and Chinatowns*, 135–136, 169.
127. *Vancouver Daily Province*, 17 Jan. 1911; Ma, *Revolutionaries, Monarchists, and Chinatowns*, 125–130; Li, *Jianada Huaqiao Shi*, 183–185; Con et al., *From China to Canada*, 76.
128. Ma, *Revolutionaries, Monarchists, and Chinatowns*, 110, 116; U.S. Department of Commerce and Labor, Bureau of Manufactures, *Monthly Consular and Trade Reports* (Washington, D.C.: Government Printing Office, Oct. 1908), 337:50; Tsai, *Hong Kong in Chinese History*, 209.
129. Worden, "A Chinese Reformer in Exile," 217–225; Ma, *Revolutionaries, Monarchists, and Chinatowns*, 128–129.
130. Li, *Jianada Huaqiao Shi*, 184–185.
131. Ma, *Revolutionaries, Monarchists, and Chinatowns*, 111.
132. Ibid., 130–131, 135–136.
133. Ibid., 126–127; Tsai, *Hong Kong in Chinese History*, 216–220.
134. *New York Times*, 30, 31 May, 5 June 1910; *Washington Post*, 30 May, 4 Aug., 2 Oct. 1910.
135. Ma, *Revolutionaries, Monarchists, and Chinatowns*, 111, 135–136.
136. Ibid., 138–139; Tsai, *Hong Kong in Chinese History*, 220–223.
137. *Vancouver World*, 24 Jan. 1911.

138. *Vancouver World*, 13, 17, 31 Jan., 2 Feb. 1911; Lew Fonds, Lew to Lee Kee [Lee Saifan], 27 June, 4 Aug. 1907; Yee, "Chinese Business in Vancouver," 40–41; RCCF, "Chinese Merchants Attempting to Enter Canada," 146 (1910).
139. Roy, *A White Man's Province*, 188–189.
140. *Vancouver World*, 13, 31 Jan. 1911.
141. Roy, *A White Man's Province*, 190; Joan M. Jensen, *Passage from India: Asian Indian Immigrants in North America* (New Haven, Conn.: Yale University Press, 1988), 66; Lew Fonds, D. Lew to Lee Kee, 4 Aug. 1907.
142. Roy, *A White Man's Province*, 185–226; Jensen, *Passage from India*, 57–82
143. RCCF, "Chinese Merchants Attempting to Enter Canada," 146 (1910).
144. *Vancouver World*, 31 Jan. 1911.
145. *Vancouver World*, 2 Feb. 1911.
146. Ibid.
147. Ibid., 17 Jan. 1911.
148. Kornel Chang, "Enforcing Transnational White Solidarity: Asian Migration and the Formation of the U.S.–Canadian Boundary," *American Quarterly* 60.3 (2008): 671–696.
149. *Washington Post*, 19 Sept. 1909, and its reiteration, 4 Mar. 1910. The press coverage claimed a total closing of the border, but passage from Vancouver was still open to Chinese merchants with appropriate certificates.
150. *Washington Post*, 19 Sept. 1909, 4 Mar. 1910.
151. Bass, "In re Lee Him," 163–165, 390.
152. Following changing U.S. practice, immigration officials usually isolated Chinese detainees while questioning them. They also barred family members and third-party mediators from speaking with the detainees. MIRC, 2:656–657, 811–812 (1911); *In re Fong Yuk and the Chinese Immigration Act*, 118–121. On the United States, see McKeown, "Ritualization of Regulation," 390–391.
153. Lew probably served as the Chinese legal advisor for these cases, though the case reports only mention the white lawyers of record, who were Lew's friends Tom McInnes and J. W. de B. Farris. Bass, "In re Lee Him," 163–165, 390. For *In re Chin Chee*, see Bass, *British Columbia Law Reports*, 11(1905):400–401.
154. *Vancouver Daily Province*, 24 Jan. 1911.
155. Ng, *Chinese in Vancouver*, 75–77.
156. Roy, *A White Man's Province*, 199.
157. Worden, "A Chinese Reformer in Exile," 69.
158. *Vancouver Daily Province*, 24 Jan. 1911.
159. Ibid.; Worden, "A Chinese Reformer in Exile," 158. The argument about trade is inferred from the context of the 1910 Chinese boycott of San Francisco, along with CERA's frequent reference to this argument.
160. *Vancouver World*, 7 Jan. 1911.
161. The dominion Secret Service, also known as the dominion police, handled domestic spying and security matters. In 1920, it merged into the Royal Canadian Mounted Police. Mount, *Canada's Enemies*, 12.

162. MIRC, 2:644–647, 742 (1911).
163. Ibid., 824.
164. Ibid., 818.
165. Ibid., 647, 818.
166. Ibid., 647; Lew Fonds, Lew to P. L. Prentis, 26 May 1909.
167. Li, *Jianada Huaqiao Shi*, 181; Ma, *Revolutionaries, Monarchists, and Chinatowns*, 91.
168. MIRC, 2:676–677 (1911).
169. Ibid., 649–651, 847.
170. RCCF, 15:45 (1910).
171. *Report of Mr. Justice Murphy*, 11–12.
172. Ibid., 34–39.
173. Ibid.; RCCF, 1:117 (1910); *Vancouver Daily Province*, 21 Dec. 1910.
174. *Report of Mr. Justice Murphy*, 31, 40–41, 117.
175. MIRC, 2:716 (1911); *Vancouver World*, 10 Jan. 1911; *Vancouver Daily Province*, 10 Jan. 1911.
176. *Vancouver World*, 4 Jan. 1911; *Vancouver Daily Province*, 4 Feb. 1911.
177. MIRC, 2:750 (1911).
178. *Vancouver Daily Province*, 31 Dec. 1910.
179. RCCF, 6:2940–2947, 2964 (1911).
180. The demand is inferred from the contexts of the CERA/SGA-influenced U.S. 1905 boycott and the related boycott of 1910.
181. The U.S. interest can be inferred from the coverage in the *New York Times* and *Washington Post*, which would have reached Canada as part of syndicated U.S. news that English Canadian papers regularly reprinted. An online search of the *Toronto Star* of 1905 for "China" and "boycott" resulted in sixty-four hits, http://www.pagesofthepast.ca/Default.asp (accessed 23 Aug. 2008).
182. Tsai, *Hong Kong in Chinese History*, 220; *New York Times*, 12 May 1910.
183. *Washington Post*, 2 Oct. 1910.
184. The records of Lew's investigation do not say whether it was the British consuls in Hong Kong and Guangzhou who handled Canada's foreign policy who chose to interfere.
185. LAC, Department of Trade and Commerce regarding Chinese Immigration Act (1910–1911), had very brief policy guidelines so local officials and party leaders would have been expected to improvise the rest.
186. *Vancouver World*, 29 Dec. 1910.
187. Con et al., *From China to Canada*, 299.
188. Chen, *Being Chinese, Becoming Chinese American*, 27–30; Ma, *Revolutionaries, Monarchists, and Chinatowns*, 30–31, 49.
189. Chinese Canadian Historical Society, *Historic Study of the Society Buildings in Chinatown* (Vancouver, B.C.: Chinese Canadian Historical Society, 2005), 55.
190. *Vancouver Daily Province*, 26 Jan. 1911.
191. Ma, *Revolutionaries, Monarchists, and Chinatowns*, 26, 91–92.

192. MIRC, 2:648 (1911): 648.
193. Ibid., 684–685.
194. Ibid., 858.
195. RCCF, "Chinese Merchants Attempting to Enter Canada," 1:1–180 (1910).
196. Ibid., 136–143.
197. Ibid., 1–180.
198. Ibid., 452.
199. MIRC, 2:872 (1911); *Vancouver World*, 28, 29 Dec. 1910; *Vancouver Daily Province*, 29 Dec. 1910.
200. *Report of Mr. Justice Murphy*, 42–46; MIRC, 2:928, 7:3111–3114, 3145, 3435 (1911); *Vancouver World*, 10–14 Jan. 1911.
201. *Report of Mr. Justice Murphy*, 5–6.
202. *Vancouver World*, 23, 24 Jan. 1911; MIRC, 2:648–649 (1911); *Vancouver World*, 7 Jan. 1911.
203. MIRC, 2:920–923, 927–929, 7:3089–3101, 3443 (1911); *Vancouver World*, 11 Jan., 2 Feb. 1911.
204. MIRC, 2:920–921 (1911).
205. Ibid.
206. Ibid.
207. Ibid., 739, 1016–1017; *Vancouver World*, 14 Jan. 1911.
208. MIRC, 2:648–649, 844, 902 (1911). The response to Lew can be inferred from the response to Tom Chue Thom's letter of support for Lew, 7:3089–3101 (1911); *Vancouver World*, 26 Jan. 1911; *Vancouver Daily Province*, 26 Jan. 1911.
209. MIRC, 3:1016–1017, 2.648–649, 844, 902 (1911).
210. MIRC, 2:648–649 (1911); *Vancouver World*, 7, 12 Jan. 1911.
211. MIRC, 2:924 (1911); *Vancouver Daily Province*, 12 Jan. 1911. Spelling and grammar from Thom's original letter.
212. MIRC, 2:925–926 (1911); *Vancouver Daily Province*, 12 Jan. 1911.
213. MIRC, 7:3089–3101 (1911).
214. Ibid., 3094.
215. *Report of Mr. Justice Murphy*, 19, shows conflict among the Liberal Party factions regarding the appointment of lawyers to assist Lew's initial investigation; logically, parallel conflict would have occurred over the staffing of the Royal Commission.
216. On Murphy and McCrossan as Liberals, see Parker, *Who's Who and Why*, 945, and Castell, *Canadian Annual Review of Public Affairs*, 579.
217. RCCF, 1:386 (1910).
218. *Report of Mr. Justice Murphy*, 5, 48–53.
219. *Vancouver Daily Province*, 16 Dec. 1910.
220. *Vancouver World*, 4–7 Jan. 1911.
221. *Vancouver Daily Province*, 22, 29 Dec. 1910; *Report of Mr. Justice Murphy*, 3–4, 12, 32–34.

222. *Vancouver World*, 4–6 Jan. 1911.
223. Ibid., 4–7 Jan. 1911.
224. Ibid., 7 Jan. 1911.
225. Ibid., 9 Jan. 1911. McCrossan is inferred to be the questioner from the context. Ibid., 7 Jan. 1911.
226. Ibid., 12 Jan. 1911.
227. Ibid.
228. Ibid., 9 Jan. 1911.
229. MIRC, 2:796–800 (1911).
230. *Vancouver World*, 12 Jan. 1911.
231. Ibid., 26 Jan. 1911.
232. MIRC, 7:3166–3174 (1911).
233. *Ethnic Index*, 1:86–90, 104; Lee, "Enforcing the Borders."
234. MIRC, 2:839, 7:3467 (1911); *Vancouver Daily Province*, 11 Jan. 1911.
235. MIRC, 2:839, 7:3467 (1911); *Vancouver Daily Province*, 11 Jan. 1911.
236. *Vancouver World*, 17 Jan. 1911; *Vancouver Daily Province*, 19 Dec. 1910; *Report of Mr. Justice Murphy*, 25–28.
237. *Report of Mr. Justice Murphy*, 42.
238. *Vancouver World*, 18 Jan. 1911; Morton, *In the Sea of Sterile Mountains*, 220; *Report of Mr. Justice Murphy*, 23.
239. *Vancouver World*, 17 Jan. 1911.
240. Dawson, *Civil Service of Canada*, 1–89; Hodgetts et al., *Biography of an Institution*, 9; Whitaker, *The Government Party*, xx–xxii.
241. *Vancouver World*, 17, 20 Jan. 1911.
242. Ibid., 1 Feb. 1911; *Vancouver Daily Province*, 2 Feb. 1911.
243. *Vancouver World*, 1 Feb. 1911.
244. Davies, *From Sourdough to Superstore*, 20–21.
245. *Vancouver World*, 14, 25 Jan. 1911; Lew Fonds, Lew to Owyang King, 8 June 1909.
246. *Vancouver World*, 17 Jan. 1911.
247. *Vancouver World*, 1 Feb. 1911.
248. *Report of Mr. Justice Murphy*, 42–46.
249. Ibid., 5–21.
250. Ibid., 51–52.
251. *Vancouver World*, 7 Jan. 1911.
252. Department of Trade and Commerce regarding Chinese Immigration Act (and Transferring the Administration of the Act from the Trade and Commerce Department to Interior on 2 October 1911), RG 76, vol. 590, file 827835, LAC, microfilm reel C-10661.
253. Jack Wai Yen Lee, "Lee Mong Kow (1863–1924)" http://members.shaw.ca/leesassociationvictoria/mongkow.htm. Accessed 26 October 2006.; "Invoices of Yip Kew Him, Canadian Pacific and Department of Immigration Interpreter, 1916–1941," Chung Collection.

254. Department of Trade and Commerce regarding Chinese Immigration Act, LAC.
255. Roy, *A White Man's Province*, 235–236; McCardle, "The Records of Chinese Immigration at the National Archives of Canada," 163–171; *Da Han Ri Bao*, 26 Aug. 1914.
256. Cameron, "Canada's Struggle with Illegal Entry."
257. Barman, *The West beyond the West*, 268; Cameron, "Canada's Struggle with Illegal Entry," 51–60.
258. *DHGB*, 12 Apr. 1919.
259. Percy Reid, Chief Controller of Chinese Immigration, Vancouver, to Deputy Minister, Dept. of Immigration and Colonization, Ottawa, Ont., 17 June 1924, Department of Immigration and Colonization-Registration under Sec. 18 Chinese Imm. Act of Chinese Born in Canada, RG 13-A-2, vol. 1958, files 1924–1204, LAC.
260. *DHGB*, 25 Sept. 1924; *Vancouver Daily Province*, 25 Sept. 1924.
261. *Vancouver Daily Province*, 25 Sept. 1924.
262. Foster, "Romance of the Lost."
263. Vancouver Board of Trade, Media Release, 3 Mar. 2004, http://www.boardoftrade.com/vbot_page.asp?pageid=1196 (accessed 25 Aug. 2008).
264. Morton, *In the Sea of Sterile Mountains*, 221.
265. Davies, *From Sourdough to Superstore*, 72.
266. Trade reciprocity with the United States was the election's deciding issue. Morton, *In the Sea of Sterile Mountains*, 221–222; Roy, *A White Man's Province*, 234–235.
267. Chung Collection, box 15, folder 7, "Documents and Ephemera Related to Community and Social Activities of Yip Sang and His Family," UBC.
268. Vancouver Board of Trade, Media Release, 3 Mar. 2004, http://www.boardoftrade.com/vbot_page.asp?pageid=1196 (accessed 25 Aug. 2008).
269. Delgado, "At Exclusion's Southern Gate," 183–208.
270. On patronage generally, see Gordon, "Patronage, Etiquette, and the Science of Connection."
271. Lee, *At America's Gates*, 177–178.
272. Hamilton, *Sobering Dilemma*; Morton, *At Odds*.
273. Yee, "Chinese Business in Vancouver," 92–114.
274. *New York Times*, 17 Aug. 1904, 18 June 1913.
275. Holder, "The Chinaman in American Politics."
276. Mary Roberts Coolidge, *Chinese Immigration* (New York: Holt, 1909), 315–320, 331, 413, 417–419. The party system of government politicized many levels of civil service during the nineteenth and early twentieth centuries, so Chinese behaved like other aspirants to official favor and sought political sponsors to compete for influence in the immigration service. Wong, *Sweet Cakes, Long Journey*, 190–198.
277. Lee, *At America's Gates*, 68–69, 199–200.

278. Senate Commission on Industrial Relations, *Final Report and Testimony*, 6001–6344.
279. Lee, *At America's Gates*, 58–63; Senate Commission on Industrial Relations, *Final Report and Testimony*, 6001–6344.

## CHAPTER TWO

1. *DHGB*, 26 Sept. 1924; Macdonald and O'Keefe, *Canadian Holy War*, 78–82, 89–90, 95, 102–104, 214.
2. Lew is the subject of two publications: a brief encyclopedia entry and a sensationalized popular account of a tong war based on English-language sources: Timothy J. Stanley, "Lew, David Hung Chang," in *Dictionary of Canadian Biography Online*, vol. 15, ed. Ramsay Cook and Réal Bélanger (Toronto and Laval, Canada: University of Toronto Press and University of Laval, 2005), http://tinyurl.com/yftzqa4 (accessed 5 Feb. 2009); Macdonald and O'Keefe, *Canadian Holy War*, 78–82, 89–90, 95, 102–104, 214. This discussion of legal interpreters counters Canadian views of the Exclusion Era, which have conceived of the law as a repressive force, but it also expands upon a wider Canadian and U.S. literature that sees Chinese as legal agents. Li, *Chinese in Canada*, 31–43; Backhouse, *Colour-Coded*, 132–172; Walker, *Race, Rights and the Law*, 51–121; Mosher, *Discrimination and Denial*; Marquis, "Vancouver Vice"; McLaren, "Race and the Criminal Justice System." Other literature focuses on successful court challenges to anti-Chinese laws in the United States: Salyer, *Laws Harsh as Tigers*; McClain, *In Search of Equality*; Lee, *At America's Gates*; Pfaelzer, *Driven Out*, 291–334; Ngai, "History as Law and Life"; Todd M. Stevens, "Brokers between Worlds: Chinese Merchants and Legal Culture in the Pacific Northwest, 1852–1925" (Ph.D. diss., Princeton University, 2003). Comparable court challenges in Canada often failed. See Backhouse, *Colour-Coded*, 132–172; Donald W. Fetherston, "Contradictions of Immigration Law-Making: Chinese Immigration to Canada and the Early Supreme Court of British Columbia" (Ph.D. diss., University of Hawaii, 1996), 68–141. Chinese Canadian court challenges have been less studied, but it appears that the principle of equal protection under the law was interpreted with more judicial restraint. A smaller part of this literature has traced ethnic "firsts," such as the first Chinese in Canada to become lawyers in the 1940s and 1950s. See Backhouse, "Gretta Wong Grant."
3. Brockman, "Exclusionary Tactics."
4. Canada's provincial law societies excluded Chinese from the legal profession on racial grounds, while most U.S. states barred all foreigners from practicing law. Since Chinese in the United States were by law prohibited from naturalizing, only U.S.-born Chinese American citizens could practice law, and very few did. A. M. Hendrickson, *Rules for Admission to the Bar in the Several States and Territories of the United States in Force January 1, 1922*, 11th

ed. (St. Paul, Minn.: West, 1922), 3–221; Wong, *Sweet Cakes, Long Journey*, 192; Joseph Gaston, *Portland, Oregon: Its History and Builders* (Chicago: Clarke, 1911), 3:347.

5. *Vancouver Sun*, 24 Oct. 1924. The paper referred to Lew as "the young Chinese lawyer."

6. Police Court Notebook, box 2, 1906–1925, UBC; "Foon Sien Wong's Appointment as Provincial Court Interpreter," news clipping in Nations at War Scrapbook, box 1 (ca. 1920s), Wong Papers.

7. Gruen, *Roman Politics and the Criminal Courts*, 1.

8. Chinese Canadians' use of legal brokers was similar to the system of informal legal brokerage in China. See Macauley, *Social Power and Legal Culture*, 1–17, 100–194.

9. Ibid., 1–17.

10. McLaren, "Race and the Criminal Justice System"; Marquis, "Vancouver Vice," 246–252; Mosher, *Discrimination and Denial*, 63–81, 138–174; Carstairs, *Jailed for Possession*, 16–34.

11. *DHGB*, 30 Sept. 1924, 3.

12. Won Alexander Cumyow Fonds, box 2, Police Court Notebook, 1906–1925, folder 1-7, UBC; Cumyow Fonds, box 1, journal transcription of English material in letterbook, folder 1-4, UBC; Chung Collection, folders 35, 15, 17, 18, UBC; 1907 Chinese and English Letterbook of David Lew, record no. E/D/L58, BCA; Gordon Won Cumyow interview, in Marlatt and Itter, *Opening Doors*, 15–20; Wo Sang in Acct. with David C. Lew Re: *Rex v. Yet Sun and Chin Gim*, 12 June (ca. 1907–1909), Lew Fonds, BCA; David Lew to J. A. Russell, Esq., 12 June (undated, 1907 by sequence), BCA, Lew Fonds: David Lew to Wong Lung, 18 June (1907 by sequence); David Lew to Yah Tin Luck, 12 June 1909; David Lew to J. W. de B. Farris, 2 Aug. 1909; David Lew to L. B. Campbell, Chief of Provincial Police, 2 Aug. 1909; Yip Quene, "Jang Jack and G. Yom's Car Case to Mr. A. Henderson," folder 0035-02, 1, 1933, Chung Collection; Peddlers Association and Legal Cases, box FOLDR-0023, folders 0023-8 and 9, Chung Collection; *DHGB*, 26, 29 Sept. 1924, 15 Apr. 1925.

13. David Lew to Li Jia (ca. 1906–1909), Lew Fonds, BCA, translated by Begin Zen.

14. *DHGB*, 7 Nov. 1923; A. L. Joliffe to Percy Reid, 12 Dec. 1923, RG 76, vol. 590, file 827835, microfilm reel C-10661, LAC.

15. A. L. Joliffe to Percy Reid, 12 Dec. 1923, LAC.

16. *DHGB*, 11 Apr. 1930.

17. Raushenbush, "Interview with J. A. Russel [*sic*], Barrister, Criminal Lawyer for Chinese," 2, draft version, SRR.

18. Ibid.; David Lew to J. A. Russell, Esq., 12 June (ca. 1907), Lew Fonds.

19. *Vancouver Sun*, 17 Aug. 1971. See also New York attorney Arthur Cheney Train's satire of Chinese legal interpreting, "Mock Hen and Mock Turtle," in his *Tutt and Mr. Tutt*, 43–88.

20. Wong, *Sweet Cakes, Long Journey*, 190–198.
21. "In the County Court Judge's Criminal Court, before His Honour Judge Lampman, Victoria, British Columbia, Tuesday, January 30, 1917," RG 6, vol. 574, file 246-2, part 2, LAC; *Rex v. Ho Hee et al.*, "Testimony of Lee Mong Kow," 1–30.
22. Hunter and Lampman, "*In re Fong Yuk.*" *British Columbia Law Reports*, 8(1902):118–121; *Vancouver Sun*, 14, 15 Apr. 1925. In the 1925 case *Rex v. Chong Sing*, the Chinese Freemasons hired extra Chinese legal interpreters, who probably helped Anglo defense attorney Frank Higgins catch court interpreter Foon Sien Wong's denial that an association of Chinese from Panyu existed.
23. Farkas, *Bury My Bones in America*, 79.
24. See Lew's complaint that the usual policy was not followed for one case. Lew to CERA President, and Lew Kwong, Secretary, and Special Committee, 27 June (ca. 1906–1909), Lew Fonds, BCA.
25. David Lew to J. A. Russell, Esq., 12 June (ca. 1907); David Lew to Wong Lung, 18 June (ca. 1907), Lew Fonds, BCA.
26. *DHGB*, 29 Sept., 1 Oct. 1924.
27. See Starkins on Foon Sien Wong's ties in *Who Killed Janet Smith?* 56, 255. C. H. Burnett's interviews with Seattle Chinese in 1924 also linked Chinese association graft to better U.S. legal treatment of their members. Major Documents 27-27, 27-42, 27-43, 27-44, 27-48, 27-49, SRR. Mary Coolidge found anti-Chinese laws in San Francisco to be pretexts for official extortion between 1892 and 1906 (*Chinese Immigration*, 417–422). Ma found that the Chinese Freemasons' national "Translators' Lodge" in 1903 came close to monopolizing U.S. legal interpreting in San Francisco (*Revolutionaries, Monarchists, and Chinatowns*, 91–92). For information on Chicago, see McKeown, *Chinese Migrant Networks*, 210, 211, 217; for New York, McIllwain, *Organizing Crime in Chinatown*, 71–79, 100–103, 106–126.
28. Stevens, "Brokers between Worlds," 16–58; McFie, *Vancouver Island and British Columbia*, 382–383.
29. Janet Mary Nicol, "Canadian First: The Life of Won Alexander Cumyow 1861 to 1955," http://www.cchsbc.ca (accessed 13 June 2006).
30. Watts, *History of the Legal Profession in British Columbia*, 53–58.
31. A good number of Chinese Canadian legal interpreters had legal training as clerks in law offices and/or university education: Foon Sien Wong (UBC, La Salle University Law School of Chicago), J. P. Sam (University of Toronto, Trinity College), Inglis Hosang (UBC, University of California Law School, Inns of Court in London, the Sorbonne; he also had been a barrister in London and Hong Kong), Won Alexander Cumyow (clerking), Gordon Won Cumyow (unspecified legal training, probably law school and clerking). Jing Feng Huang, "Dao Huang Wenfu Zong Zhang Qiangu'," box 26, file 13, CCRC; *Vancouver Sun*, 14 Apr. 1925; "Death Claims Chinese Lawyer," *Graduate Chronicle* (1945): 14, UBC; Nicol, "Canadian First," 1; Brockman, "Exclusionary Tactics," 519–522.

32. Macauley, *Social Power and Legal Culture*, 1–17.
33. Won Alexander Cumyow Fonds, Police Court Notebook, 1906–1925, UBC. Ordinary Chinese workers' earnings of about $30 per month have been extrapolated from wages reported by Liang Qichao, a visiting Chinese official from Guangdong, in his memoir *Xin Dalu Youji* in *Jindai Zhongguo Shiliao Congkan*, vols. 96–97, 228–229; *Report of the Royal Commission on Chinese and Japanese Immigration*, 55, 135; Yee, "Chinese Business in Vancouver," 105–106.
34. Gordon Won Cumyow interview, in Marlatt and Itter, *Opening Doors*, 15–20.
35. McLaren, "Race and the Criminal Justice System"; Mosher, *Discrimination and Denial*, 63–81, 138–174; Carstairs, *Jailed for Possession*, 16–34; Cole and Chin, "Emerging from the Margins of Historical Consciousness," 327.
36. Coolidge, "Chinese Immigration," 417-421. Holder, "The Chinaman in American Politics," 226–237; Marquis, "Vancouver Vice."
37. Marquis, "Vancouver Vice."
38. Quene Yip, "Jang Jack and G. Yom's Car Case to Mr. A. Henderson," 1933, Chung Collection; Peddlers Association and Legal Cases, Chung Collection; Lew to Mah Sam Yuen, Yah Tin Luck Chinese Theatre, 12 June 1909, Lew Fonds; McLaren, "Race and the Criminal Justice System," 404; Raushenbush, "Interview with J. A. Russel[l]," 30 Apr. 1924, Box 24, File 24-27, SRR.
39. Gompers and Morrison, *Some Reasons for Chinese Exclusion*, 6.
40. The legislation passed in 1903 and was enacted in 1904. *Revised Statutes of Canada*, 1741.
41. Ngai, "History as Law and Life"; Stevens, "Brokers between Worlds."
42. Yee, "Chinese Business in Vancouver," 92–114.
43. Cumyow Fonds, journal transcription of English material in letterbook, box 1, folder 1-4.
44. Lew Fonds, BCA: David Lew to Yah Tin Luck, 12 June 1909; Lew to J. W. de B. Farris, 2 Aug. 1909; Lew to L. B. Campbell, Chief of Provincial Police, 2 Aug. 1909; Lew to Charles B. Jones and G. T. Rant, 18 Aug. [1909].
45. *Report of the Royal Commission on Chinese and Japanese Immigration*, 135, 188–189. Lew Fonds: David Lew to Yah Tin Luck, 12 June 1909; Lew to J. W. de B. Farris, 2 Aug. 1909; Lew to L. B. Campbell, 2 Aug. 1909.
46. Lew Fonds: Lew to Yah Tin Luck, 12 June 1909; Lew to J. W. de B. Farris, 2 Aug. 1909; Lew to L. B. Campbell, 2 Aug. 1909; *Daily Province*, 2 Aug. 1909. Lew's letters refer to an accident at a brick factory that killed two Chinese workers. The letters show that he helped to lobby for an official inquest into the accident. He arranged for a white lawyer to represent the Chinese contractor. Lew himself represented the dead Chinese workers' families at the inquest and in probate. He also helped both families to file civil lawsuits of $1,500 against the brick company. Report of the Coroner's Inquisition, B.C. Attorney General, Inquisitions, GR 1327, reel B2384, file 133-1909, BCA; *Daily Province*, 4 Aug. 1909; British Columbia Supreme Court (Vancouver), Probate Files, 1893–1941, GR 1415, reel B2546, file P01413 "Yong Hor" and file P1402 "Wong Kue" (1909).

47. On the United States, see Stevens, "Brokers between Worlds," iii, 92–153.
48. Leier, *Red Flags and Red Tape*, 128–129.
49. Lew Fonds: Lew to J. W. de B. Farris, 2 Aug. 1909; Lew to L. B. Campbell, 2 Aug. 1909; *Daily Province*, 2 Aug. 1909.
50. Report of the Coroner's Inquisition, BCA, 1–16; *Daily Province*, 4 Aug. 1909.
51. Lew Fonds: Lew to Macdonald, Killam, and Parris, Barristers, 30 Aug. 1909; British Columbia Supreme Court (Vancouver), file P01413 and file P1402. The results of the civil lawsuits are unknown.
52. M. M. Fernie and District Historical Society, "The Strikebreakers on Vancouver Island: Chinese Strikebreakers," *King Coal: B. C.'s Coal Heritage*, http://collections.ic.gc.ca/kingcoal (accessed 16 Dec. 2005); Roy, *The Oriental Question*, 254–255.
53. *DHGB*, 12 Apr. 1919.
54. Ibid., 1, 9 Apr., 14 June 1919; Creese, "Exclusion or Solidarity?" 320–321.
55. Ward, *White Canada Forever*, 41.
56. *Report of the Royal Commission on Chinese and Japanese Immigration*, 160–161, 235; Raushenbush, "Interview with J. A. Russel[l]," SRR; Liang, *Xin Dalu Youji*, 233.
57. Yee, "Chinese Business in Vancouver," 105.
58. Lew Fonds: Lew to Vancouver General Hospital Chairmen and Directors, 6 Oct., 12 Nov. 1908.
59. Quene Yip, "Jang Jack and G. Yom's Car Case to Mr. A. Henderson," 1933, Chung Collection; Peddlers Association and Legal Cases, Chung Collection, UBC; Lew Fonds: Lew to Mah Sam Yuen, Yah Tin Luck Chinese Theatre, 12 June 1909. John McLaren suggests that Chinese could expect fair treatment in civil cases. McLaren, "Race and the Criminal Justice System," 404.
60. Stevens as well as McClain and McClain note that scholars have regarded the Chinese population in the United States as aloof from the popular legal culture, with the exception of court challenges to racial discrimination and Chinese businesses' reliance on civil law. Stevens, "Brokers between Worlds," iii–iv; McClain and McClain, "The Chinese Contribution to the Development of American Law," 3-24; Con et al., *From China to Canada*, 31–32, 39.
61. Con et al., *From China to Canada*, 39.
62. Li, *Jianada Huaqiao Shi*, 123–128; Con et al., *From China to Canada*, 32, 39, 108–109, 165; Oropeza, "La Discriminación en México," 47–56. As products of transnational conflict, strife between the Chinese Nationalist Party and the Chinese Freemasons also likely occurred elsewhere in the Americas, Australasia, and England, where Chinese immigrants had established branches of both organizations. *DHGB*, 20 Mar. 1924.
63. *DHGB*, 30 Sept. 1924.
64. Ibid.
65. Winifred Raushenbush, "Interview with Dr. Y. P. Lew," 4 Feb. 1924, SRR.

66. *DHGB*, 17, 22 Apr. 1925; Con et al., *From China to Canada*, 108–109; Raushenbush, "Interview with Dr. Y. P. Lew," 4 Feb. 1924, Box 24, File 24-5, SRR.
67. Quene Yip, "Jang Jack and G. Yom's Car Case to Mr. A. Henderson," 1933, Chung Collection; Peddlers Association and Legal Cases, Chung Collection.
68. Yip, "Jang Jack and G. Yom's Car Case." The name of the legal assistant is listed phonetically as "Fushien" with a notation that it is not spelled correctly; given the small number of legal assistants, this was probably Foon Sien Wong.
69. Con et al., *From China to Canada*, 136; Peddlers Association and Legal Cases, 1933–1937, Chung Collection; Police Court Notebook, 1906–1925, Box/File 1-7, Cumyow Papers; Lew Fonds, David Lew to J. C. McRae, Police Chief of Winnipeg, 8 Feb. 1909; Starkins, *Who Killed Janet Smith?* 58–59, 159, 254–255.
70. Lew Fonds, David Lew to J. C. McRae, 8 Feb. 1909.
71. Starkins, *Who Killed Janet Smith?* 1–2; Davies, *From Sourdough to Superstore*, 72; S. Moreley Wickett, "City Government in Canada," *University of Toronto Studies in History and Economics* 2 (1907): 10–11.
72. For a more detailed account of Foon Sing Wong's experience, see Starkins, *Who Killed Janet Smith?*
73. Ibid.
74. Chung Collection, box 35, file 1, "Yungaohua Zhonghua Huiguan Wei Yingjiu Huang Huan Sheng An Jin Zhi Zheng Xin Lu," 16 May 1925, 1–23.
75. *Vancouver Sun*, 9 Sept. 1924.
76. The Nations at War Scrapbook, Wong Papers, Box 1., includes Chinese news clippings of poetry and matchmaking advertisements and English poems printed on cards with the University of British Columbia's logo and Wong's address. Some of the Chinese poems and advertisements are under Wong's pen name of "Wen Hu," an allusion to his English poetic moniker, "Tiger."
77. McKeown, *Chinese Migrant Networks*, 178–223; McIllwain, *Organizing Crime in Chinatown*, 183–187.
78. *DHGB*, 25, 27 Oct. 1924. Timothy J. Stanley, "Lew, David Hung Chang."; Macdonald and O'Keefe, *Canadian Holy War*, 78–82, 89–90, 95, 102–104, 214.
79. Li, *Jianada Huaqiao Shi*, 180.
80. *DHGB*, 30 Sept. 1924, 3.
81. Ibid., 7 Oct. 1924, 3; Li, *Jianada Huaqiao Shi*, 180, 91–93; Ito, *Issei*, 758, 843; *Vancouver Sun*, 3 May 1924, 10; Marquis, "Vancouver Vice," 251.
82. *Vancouver Sun*, 13, 15, 16, 20, 26, 28 Jan., 2 May 1924.
83. Kevin B. Walmsley, "State Formation and Institutionalized Racism: Gambling Laws in Nineteenth and Early Twentieth Century Canada," *Sport History Review* 29 (1998): 77–85.
84. Ibid.

85. *DHGB*, 30 Sept. 1924. On Freemason-Nationalist rivalries, see Con et al., *From China to Canada*, 165; Kim and Markov, "The Chinese Exclusion Laws"; McIllwain, *Organizing Crime in Chinatown*, 75–76, 32, 33, 102, 136–137, 140–146, 172; Oropeza, "La Discriminación en México"; *DHGB*, 30 Sept., 1 Oct. 1924.
86. Morton, *In the Sea of Sterile Mountains*, 231.
87. *DHGB*, 29 Sept. 1924.
88. Walmsley, "State Formation," 81–84; McLaren, "Race and the Criminal Justice System," 405–418.
89. Li, *Jianada Huaqiao Shi*, 180, 91–92.
90. *Vancouver Sun*, 3 May 1924, 10, noted that arrested Chinese paid court fines of $20–$30, plus the cost of an interpreter.
91. Yee, "Chinese Business in Vancouver," 76–79; VCA, Add. MSS 1108, Yip Family and Yip Sang Ltd. Fonds, box 612-F-7, files 4, 5, "[Account book of] Yuan Li gambling house—parts 1 and 2," 1924; box 612-G-1, files 2, 3, "[Account book of] An Li gambling house—parts 1 and 2," 1925; box 612-G-1, file 4, "[Account book of] Kwong Loy gambling den," 1925.
92. Marquis, "Vancouver Vice," 246–261.
93. *DHGB*, 29 Sept. 1924, 3.
94. "Liao Hongxiang Yu Hai Wu Zhi," *DHGB*, 28 Nov. 1923; Li, *Jianada Huaqiao Shi*, 180, 91–92.
95. *DHGB*, 14 Oct. 1924, 3.
96. Ibid., 25 Sept. 1924.
97. Ibid., 29 Sept. 1924.
98. Ibid., 26, 29 Sept. 1924.
99. Ibid.
100. *Lew v. Lee*, Case on Appeal [factum], 1924, "Proceedings at Trial," 7.
101. Yip Family and Yip Sang Ltd. Fonds., Add. MSS 1108, Business and Financial Records, box 612-D-3, files 4, 5; box D-4, files 1, 5; box D-6, files 2, 4, VCA.
102. Nanaimo Community Archives, Malaspina-University College, and Nanaimo Community Heritage Commission. "Nanaimo Chinatowns [*sic*] Project: Introduction." http://chinatown.mala.bc.ca/introduction.asp (accessed 30 March 2010). *Lew v. Lee*, Case on Appeal [factum], 1924, "Proceedings at Trial," 7.
103. *Lew v. Lee*, Case on Appeal [factum], 1924, "Proceedings at Trial," 2–3.
104. *DHGB*, 26 Sept., 17 Oct. 1924; *David Lew v. Wing Lee*, Supreme Court of Canada Appeal, 1924, RG 125, vol. 508, file 4956, LAC; Case on Appeal [factum], F. S. Cunliffe (Thompson, Cote, Burgess and Thompson, Ottawa Agents) and Arthur Leighton (Nellis, Thompson and Ellis, Ottawa Agents) in the Supreme Court of Canada on Appeal from the Court of Appeal for British Columbia, David Lew (Plaintiff/Appellant) and Wing Lee (Defendant/Respondent), 27 May 1924 (Vancouver: Murray and Chapman, 1924), 1–126.

105. *Vancouver Daily Province*, 26 Sept. 1924. *DHGB*, 20, 26, 27 Sept. 1924. British Columbia's liquor regulations at this time subjected alcohol to government taxes but did not prohibit it. Starkins, *Who Killed Janet Smith?* 139–140.
106. *DHGB*, 20, 27, 29 Sept. 1924; *Vancouver Daily Province*, 26 Sept. 1924.
107. *Vancouver Sun*, 19, 20 Sept. 1924.
108. *DHGB*, 20, 26 Sept. 1924. *Vancouver Daily Province*, 26 Sept. 1924.
109. *DHGB*, 26 Sept., 2 Oct. 1924.
110. C. H. Burnett, "Interview with Mr. Fred H. Lysons, Attorney," 29 July, 5, 22 Aug. 1924, Box 27, File 27-192. SRR. The CPR's records were not consulted because at the time of this book's research they were not deposited in an archive.
111. *Vancouver Sun*, 29 May 1924, 1.
112. *DHGB*, 29 Sept., 1 Oct. 1924; *Vancouver Daily Province*, 27 Sept. 1924.
113. *DHGB*, 29 Sept. 1924; Macdonald and O'Keefe, *Canadian Holy War*, 78–82; Ann Lee, interview; journal transcription of Chinese material in letterbook, folder 1-5, Cumyow Papers.
114. Most Chinese "slave girls" as they were called, were indentured immigrants, bound to serve their employer for a period of years until their contracts expired. A good number but not all of these women became involved in prostitution or suffered abuse. See Lucie Cheng Hirata, "Free, Indentured, Enslaved: Chinese Prostitutes in Nineteenth-Century America," and Karen Van Dieren, "The Response of the WMS." Gordon Cumyow interview, in Marlatt and Itter, *Opening Doors*, 15–20. In 1924, the British Columbia legislature passed a law barring Chinese from employing white and First Nations females. The political context of the Janet Smith Bill is discussed in Scott Kerwin, "The Janet Smith Bill of 1924 and the Language of Race and Nation in British Columbia," *BC Studies* 121 (1999): 83–114.
115. *DHGB*, 29 Sept. 1924.
116. Gordon Cumyow interview, in Marlatt and Itter, *Opening Doors*, 15–20.
117. *DHGB*, 26 Sept., 2 Oct. 1924.
118. Ibid., 30 Sept., 2, 6 Oct. 1924; Roy, *The Oriental Question*, 48.
119. *Lew v. Lee*, Lord Buckmaster, Privy Council Appeal no. 20 of 1925: *Wing Lee Appellant v. David Lew*, since deceased now represented by Yick Pang Lew, the Administrator of his Estate: From the Supreme Court of Canada: Judgment of the Lords of the Judicial Committee of the Privy Council, 11 May 1925 (London: Harrison and Sons, 1925).
120. Nanaimo Community Archives et al, "Nanaimo Chinatowns [*sic*] Project: Introduction."; *Lew v. Lee*, Cunliffe and Leighton, Case on Appeal; "Plan—Surveying Property Adjacent to Intersection of Pine and Hecate Streets, Nanaimo," 1924. LAC.
121. *DHGB*, 3 Sept., 4 Nov. 1924.
122. *Vancouver Sun*, 25 Apr. 1925.
123. *DHGB*, 30 Sept. 1924.

124. Ibid., 13, 14 Apr. 1925. Chong's lawyers were Frank Higgins and A. M. Harper. The eminent J. P. Sam was from Toronto, a graduate of Trinity College, University of Toronto.
125. *Vancouver Sun*, 23 Apr. 1925.
126. Ibid., 15, 24 Apr. 1925; *Vancouver Daily Province*, 24 Apr. 1925; *DHGB*, 13–18, 20–24 Apr. 1925; Macdonald and O'Keefe, *Canadian Holy War*, 89–90, 102–104. It is possible that Lew's death had nothing to do with politics, because he was also having a very public affair with a married Chinese Canadian woman, Nellie Ho (Lan Jiao Jie). *DHGB*, 26, 27, 29 Sept. 1924; *Vancouver Sun*, 22 Apr. 1925; *Vancouver Daily Province*, 26 Sept. 1924.
127. *Vancouver Star*, 25 Feb. 1925, Box 2, File 2-1, "Correspondence Portfolio#2", Whaun Papers. The strategy to legalize Chinese gambling followed the "Deady" cases in the United States; see Ralph James Mooney, "Matthew Deady and Federal Judicial Response to Racism in the Early West," in Charles McClain, Ed. *Chinese Immigrants and American Law* (Garland Publishing: New York & London, 1994). 1: 241–317.
128. Nine out of ten Chinese in Vancouver were male according to Canada's Census of in 1921. Con et al., *From China to Canada*, 306.
129. Van Dieren, "The Response of the WMS."

## CHAPTER THREE

1. *DHGB*, 18 Oct., 6, 11, 21 Nov. 1922; 25 Jan. 1923.
2. Ibid., 6 Nov. 1922.
3. Ibid., 11 Oct. 1922.
4. These revolutions included anti-imperialist nationalism in China, Hong Kong, and India, as well as the rise of organized labor. *DHGB*, 19, 27 Sept., 6, 2 Nov. 1922.
5. Ibid., 18 Oct., 22 Nov. 1922.
6. Ashworth, *The Forces Which Shaped Them*, 75–82; Lai, "The Issue of Discrimination in Education"; Yee, *Saltwater City*, 52–53; Stanley, "White Supremacy, Chinese Schooling, and School Segregation"; Stanley, "Bringing Anti-Racism into Historical Explanation."
7. *DHGB*, 18 Oct. 1922.
8. This conception expands on David Strand's analysis of urban Chinese society in the 1920s and Erez Manela's discussion of the global movement for anti-colonial nationalism after the First World War. Strand, "Mediation, Representation, and Repression: Local Elites in 1920s Beijing," in Esherick and Rankin, *Chinese Local Elites*, 216–238; Manela, *The Wilsonian Moment*, 3–17.
9. *DHGB*, 20 Oct. 1922.
10. Ibid., 12 Oct. 1922.
11. Ibid., 25 Oct. 1922.
12. Yee, *Saltwater City*, 52–53.

13. *DHGB*, 11 Oct. 1922.
14. Stanley, "White Supremacy, Chinese Schooling, and School Segregation," 292–241; Stanley, "Bringing Anti-Racism into Historical Explanation," 159–161; Low, *The Unimpressible Race*, 113–123; Lai, "The Issue of Discrimination in Education."
15. There is controversy over the May Fourth movement's parameters. Its main events took place between 1917 and 1921, but preludes began as early as 1915 with reaction to Japan's Twenty-One Demands, and its postlude is sometimes dated to 1925's May Thirtieth movement. Chow, *The May Fourth Movement*, 5–6.
16. Manela, *The Wilsonian Moment*, 3–17.
17. Ashworth, *The Forces Which Shaped Them*, 75–82; Lai, "The Issue of Discrimination in Education"; Stanley, "White Supremacy, Chinese Schooling, and School Segregation"; Stanley, "Bringing Anti-Racism into Historical Explanation"; Low, *The Unimpressible Race*, 112–123.
18. These revolutions included, starting in 1916, a more inclusive and assertive labor movement, which was to some degree inspired by global socialist movements and events such as the Winnipeg general strike. Actions in Vancouver in sympathy with the strike generated great excitement among Chinese. *DHGB*, 16–21 June 1919. *Da Han Gong Bao* covered the strikes in Vancouver and Winnipeg in great detail from June through July 1919, capturing the revolutionary mood, even if it is unclear how many Chinese participated. Chinese shingle mill workers had already unionized and held strikes to defend their interests. Yee, *Saltwater City*, 68; Yee, *Chinatown*, 44; Creese, "Exclusion or Solidarity?" 320–321. Another social movement was the global rise of anti-imperialist nationalism in Asia at the end of the First World War, what Erez Manela calls the "Wilsonian moment," which strongly influenced the politics of China's Nationalist revolution in Canada; see also Con et al., *From China to Canada*, 158–161.
19. The most detailed scholarship on the school strike views the strike's politics in the more conservative terms of Chinese merchant activism and the rise of a second generation of locally born Chinese, echoing Chinese American historians' belief that West Coast Chinese conservatism and merchant class domination precluded populist activism. See Stanley, "White Supremacy, Chinese Schooling, and School Segregation"; Stanley, "Bringing Anti-Racism into Historical Explanation." Chen, *Being Chinese, Becoming Chinese American*, 119–127, 133–145, sees the defense of Confucianism and of class hierarchies, along with anti-leftist sentiments, as being keystones of Chinese American identity. However, her reading takes the claims of newspapers expressing these sentiments as the dominant position, when it is also possible to interpret their aggressive defense of traditional merchant-brokers' elite authority as part of a dialogue. On the egalitarian moment and its "failures," see Seager and Roth, "British Columbia and the Mining West"; David Jay Bercuson, *Confrontation*

*at Winnipeg: Labour, Industrial Relations, and the General Strike* (Montreal: McGill-Queen's University Press, 1974), 187–195; Bryan Palmer, *Working Class Experience: Rethinking the History of Canadian Labour, 1800–1991* (Toronto: McClelland and Stewart, 1992), 196–213.

20. Zhonghua Huiguan, which is the equivalent of the Chinese American Six Companies in San Francisco.
21. Li, *Jianada Huaqiao Shi*, 214; Liu, "Yubu Huaqiao Sanshi Nian Fendou Shi Ji," 6.
22. Lai, "The Issue of Discrimination in Education." Low, *The Unimpressible Race*, 113–123. Laura McKeen, Executive Secretary, San Francisco International Institute of the YMCA Service Bureau for Foreign-Speaking People, Letter to Eliot G. Mears, 29 May, 1927. Box 6, File 6-4, SRR.
23. Low, *The Unimpressible Race*, 113–123; Letter to Professor C. E. Rugh from William Greenwell, principal, Lincoln School, Oakland," 13 Nov. 1924, SRR.
24. Lai, "The Issue of Discrimination in Education."
25. Ann Lee, interview; "Statement by J. M. Campbell, Principal of one of the schools in the city of Victoria, British Columbia, made in a letter to Professor T. H. Boggs," 28 May 1925, SRR.
26. *Victoria Daily Times*, 6 Sept. 1922.
27. Chow, *The May Fourth Movement*, 263. Lai, "The Issue of Discrimination, 57.
28. *Victoria Daily Times*, 9 Oct. 1922.
29. *Daily Colonist*, 8 Oct. 1922.
30. Lai, "The Issue of Discrimination in Education."
31. *Daily Colonist*, 12 Oct. 1922.
32. Charles Hirschman, "The Impact of Immigration: Looking Backwards to the Future," *Border Battles: The U.S. Immigration Debates, Social Science Research Council*, 28 July 2006, http://borderbattles.ssrc.org/Hirschman/index2.html (accessed 6 Feb. 2009). The fields of social science were also connected across the U.S.–Canada border. In 1921, two of the founding thinkers of immigration studies, University of Chicago sociologists Robert Park and Ernest Burgess, established the parameters of the second-generation problem as part of their field-defining discussion of the problem of assimilation in their groundbreaking *Introduction to the Science of Sociology*. See Rumbaut, "Assimilation and Its Discontents," 185–186, 193. On impact of U.S. culture in British Columbia, see Barman, *The West beyond the West*, 259.
33. Nasaw, *Schooled to Order*, 87–89.
34. *DHGB*, 3 June 1923.
35. The exact connection between the Canadian and U.S. Tongyuanhui cannot be determined from the Canadian evidence. However, the Chinese Canadian Club was formed during a period of CACA expansion across the United States, and observers referred to both the San Francisco and Victoria Tongyuanhui as "native sons parlors." Chung, "The Chinese American Citizens' Alliance," 35.

36. The CCC had lodges in Vancouver and Victoria since 1914. (Receipt for membership for the Chinese Canadian Club, Chung Collection; *DHGB*, 3 June 1923.) The CSA's presence in Vancouver and Victoria dates to at least 1916. (Guy Funn Chan to Thomas Moore Whaun, 5, 14 Oct. 1916, Whaun Papers.) It is unclear whether these two groups had any connection to an earlier Chinese Canadian group in British Columbia, the "Citizens Association," which represented naturalized and Canadian-born Chinese. The "Citizens Association" appeared influential in 1910, when prominent merchant Shen Man served as its president. RCCF, 30 Sept. 1910, RG 33-146, vol. 2, box 2, LAC.
37. Raushenbush, "Interview with Harry Hastings regarding the school strike and other matters," 26, 30 May 1924, box 24, file 24-32, SRR.; Raushenbush, "Interview with Joe Hope, president of the Chinese Canadian Club," 26 May 1924, box 24, file 24-33; and Raushenbush, Interview with Cecil Lee, a native son who is married to a Hakkla," 26 May–1 June 1924, box 24, file 24-34. SRR.
38. *DHGB*, 18 Oct. 1922.
39. Ibid., 27 Sept. 1922; Liu Guangzu, "Yubu Huaqiao Sanshi Nian Fendou Shi Ji," 6; Lai, "The Issue of Discrimination in Education."
40. *DHGB*, 19 Sept. 1922.
41. Ibid., 22 Feb. 1923.
42. Ibid., 11 Nov. 1922.
43. Interview with Harry Hastings, SRR.
44. *DHGB*, 22 Nov. 1922.
45. "Political India a Huge Problem," *Victoria Daily Times*, 28 Sept. 1922.
46. *Victoria Daily Times*, 6 Oct. 1922; *DHGB*, 19 Sept. 1922.
47. Jonathan D. Spence, *The Search for Modern China* (New York: Norton, 1990), 332–333; Carroll, *Concise History of Hong Kong*, 97; Tsang and Yui-Sang, *Modern History of Hong Kong*, 88.
48. Bumstead, "1919," 3, 27–44; Kealey, "1919."
49. *DHGB*, June–July 1919.
50. The involvement of nonwhite workers in the various strikes of 1919 has been mentioned only briefly by historians: Creese, "Exclusion or Solidarity?" 320–321; Seager and Roth, "British Columbia and the Mining West," 252.
51. *DHGB*, 14 June 1919.
52. In China, the influence of Communist Party and Nationalist Party activism on both class and anti-imperialist nationalist lines encouraged workers to use their labor as a tool to strike against their worker-master relations to British society in both Canada and China.
53. *DHGB*, 1, 9 Apr. 1919.
54. The description of Exclusion Era Chinese having a worker-master relation to mainstream Canada comes from labor organizer Roy Mah (Ma Guo Guan). Roy Mah, interview with Chris Lee and Douglas Quan, 1 Aug. 1996, CCVOHP.
55. *DHGB*, 20 Oct. 1922.

56. Ibid., 6, 20 Oct. 1922.
57. *Victoria Daily Times*, 9, 13, 23 Oct. 1922; *DHGB*, 21 Oct. 1922.
58. Liu, "Yubu Huaqiao Sanshi Nian Fendou Shi Ji," 6.
59. Li, *Jianada Huaqiao Shi*, 214.
60. *DHGB*, 18 Oct., 2 Nov. 1922.
61. Ibid., 2 Nov. 1922.
62. Ibid.
63. Ibid., 18 Oct. 1922.
64. Ibid., 2 Nov. 1922.
65. Ibid., 18 Oct. 1922.
66. Ibid.
67. Raushenbush, "Interview with Harry Hastings."
68. *DHGB*, 18 Oct. 1922.
69. Ibid.
70. Ibid., 2 Nov. 1922.
71. *DHGB*, 2 Nov. 1922.
72. Dikotter, "Racial Discourse in China," 12–33.
73. *DHGB*, 2 Nov. 1922.
74. Ibid., 21 Nov. 1922.
75. Ibid; 22 Nov. 1922.
76. Ibid.
77. Chow, *The May Fourth Movement*, 84–170, 260–261.
78. Raushenbush, "Interview with Gershon Lew, the Hottest Bolshevik in Vancouver," May 1924, box 24, file 24-29, SRR; *Chinese Times (Da Han Gong Bao)* Chronological Research Index, files 4-1 to 5-2, CCRC, boxes 4–5.
79. *DHGB*, 22 Feb. 1923.
80. Ibid., 31 Mar. 1923.
81. Ibid., 23 Nov. 1922.
82. Ibid., Jan. 1923.
83. Ibid., 23 Nov. 1922.
84. Ibid.
85. Ibid., 3 Nov. 1922.
86. Ibid., 6 Nov. 1922.
87. Ibid. The author simply listed as "Song" was probably Lambert Sung because his activities later in 1924 suggest that he was a leader of stature so established that he needed no introduction. Ibid., 14 Feb. 1924.
88. Ibid., 3 Nov. 1922.
89. Ibid., 6 Nov. 1922.
90. Ibid., 8 Nov. 1922.
91. Ibid., 8 Jan. 1923.
92. Guy Funn Chan to Thomas Moore Whaun, 5, 14 Oct. 1916, Whaun Papers. By 1924, the offshoot's members were integrated back into the larger CSA. Chinese Students Alliance Dinner Program, 24 Nov. 1924, Vivian Wong Papers.

93. *DHGB*, 11 Nov. 1922.
94. Ibid., 25 Jan. 1923.
95. Josie Lee and Vivian Wong, interview; Chinese Students Alliance Dinner Program, 24 Nov. 1924; *DHGB*, 25 Jan. 1923.
96. *DHGB*, January 25, 1923, 2-3.
97. *DHGB*, 30 Jan. 1923.
98. Ibid., 30 Jan., 17 Feb. 1923.
99. Chinese Immigration, vol. 590, microfilm reel C-10661, file 827821, RG 76, LAC.
100. Lee Bick interview, in Huang with Jeffery, *Chinese Canadians*, 24; An Autobiographical Sketch Delivered by Tom Moore Whaun on Channel 10, 17 Nov. 1972, Whaun Papers, folder 2-2; *New York Times*, 22 Aug 1925; Con et al., *From China to Canada*, 158–161.
101. *DHGB*, 27 Apr. 1923.
102. Sarah Carter, *Aboriginal People and Colonizers of Western Canada to 1900* (Toronto: University of Toronto Press, 1999), 163–164.
103. *DHGB*, 27 Apr. 1923.
104. Roy, *The Oriental Question*, 55–76.
105. Ibid., 75.
106. Stanley, "Bringing Anti-Racism into Historical Explanation," 163–164; Chinese Immigration, microfilm reel C-10661, LAC.
107. *DHGB*, 4 Sept. 1923.
108. Ashworth, *The Forces Which Shaped Them*, 81–82; Lai, "The Issue of Discrimination in Education," 63; "Chinatown Is Shrinking," *Vancouver Sun*, 15 Jan. 1959, Wong Papers, box 4, Brown Scrapbook, news clipping.
109. Seager and Roth, "British Columbia and the Mining West," 231–267; Bercuson, *Confrontation at Winnipeg*, 187–195; Palmer, *Working Class Experience*, 196–213; Andrew Parnaby, *Citizen Docker: Making a New Deal on the Vancouver Waterfront, 1919–1939* (Toronto: University of Toronto Press, 2008).
110. Roy, *The Oriental Question*, 55–89; *DHGB*, 23 Oct. 1924.
111. *Daily Colonist*, 14 Oct. 1922. The paper also printed numerous letters from Chinese and English readers about the boycott between September 1922 and April 1923.
112. Ibid., 6 Apr. 1923.
113. *DHGB*, 18 Oct. 1922; Li, *Jianada Huaqiao Shi*, 214.
114. *DHGB*, 27 Apr. 1923.
115. Ibid., 2 Nov. 1922.
116. Low, *The Unimpressible Race*, 115–123.
117. Chen, *Being Chinese, Becoming Chinese American*, 119–127, 134–145.
118. Creese, "Working Class Politics, Racism, and Sexism," 90.
119. Con et al., *From China to Canada*, 160.
120. *DHGB*, 16 June 1924.
121. Chow, *The May Fourth Movement*, 171–196, 269–337.

CHAPTER FOUR

1. Winifred Raushenbush to Dr. Yick Pang Lew, 22 Feb. 1924; Chuichi Ohashi to Merle Davis, 6 Feb. 1924, SRR; "Office File Questionnaires Chinese—Pacific Coast (U.S.) + Canada" (ca. Jan. and Feb. 1924), SRR; Raushenbush, "Interview with Herbert Wang," 25 Mar. 1924, SRR; *DHGB*, 14 Feb. 1924.
2. Mears, "The Survey of Race Relations"; Merle Davis to Sir John Oliver, 3 Dec. 1923, box 13, "Correspondence British Columbia (Canada) file 13-1, SRR.
3. *DHGB*, 14 Feb. 1924.
4. On relations between the survey and the Chicago School of Sociology, see Yu, *Thinking Orientals*; and Okihiro, *Teaching Asian American History*, 39–40.
5. Robert Park's *The Immigrant Press and Its Control* depended on ethnic leaders for information, a practice that continued in the Pacific Coast Survey of Race Relations. Park, *The Immigrant Press and Its Control*, xxxiv, 150–166.
6. Based on Raushenbush's position that "the sociologist is a scientist" who collects life histories, which are "simply [an opportunity] for someone to write or tell the story of their life," she appears not to have realized the possibility that her subjects would not be naïve. Her earlier work with Park on *The Immigrant Press and Its Control* depended on ethnic leaders for information about the non-English press, allowing her Japanese informant Shiko Kusama of the Japanese Association of California to steer the discussion of Japanese Americans away from the transnational outlooks which historian Eiichiro Azuma found were prevalent in Japanese American communities. Park, *The Immigrant Press and Its Control*, xxxiv, 150–166; Azuma, *Between Two Empires*.
7. Yu, *Thinking Orientals*, 93–185.
8. Mar, "From Diaspora to North American Civil Rights," 114–115; Raushenbush, "Dinner Mr. Louie Houie, President of the Merchants Association," 2 Apr. 1924, box 24, file 24-26, SRR; Raushenbush, "Mr. Thomas Moore Whaun Audience," 7 May 1924, box 24, file 24-28, SRR; Raushenbush, "Interview with Harry Hastings."
9. See Ronald Takaki's acclaimed *Strangers from a Different Shore*, which quoted survey interviews extensively as the authentic voices of early Asian Americans; See also Stanley, "By the Side of Other Canadians."
10. Mar, "From Diaspora to North American Civil Rights," 97–102; Yu, *Thinking Orientals*, 93–148. Yu argues that the Chicago sociologists also enlisted Asian American students as their in-house native informants and cultural brokers starting in the 1930s, but his account is more concerned with individual Asian Americans' performance of roles according to white researchers' expectations, which gained them entry into academic careers, than with possible collective Asian American community agendas.
11. This figure was compiled from major documents and a list of the lost minor documents relating to the survey's research in British Columbia. The Survey did not always identify these subjects as "brokers." Documented evidence of an

interviewee's leadership in Anglo-Chinese brokerage relations served as this book's criteria for "broker" status. Raushenbush, British Columbia Major Documents, 30 Jan.–4 June 1924, box 24, files 24-1 through 24-35, SRR; The list of Chinese Canadian interviewees in the British Columbia minor documents, which appear lost, comes from Aparna Mukherjee, "A Register of the Survey of Race Relations Records," Hoover Institution Archives, Stanford University, http://content.cdlib.org/view?docId=tf2q2n98s9&doc.view=entire_text&brand=oac (accessed 18 Nov. 2008).

12. *DHGB*, 14 Feb. 1924.
13. Mar, "Beyond Being Others," 17.
14. Quoted in Stanley, "Bringing Anti-Racism into Historical Explanation"; Stanley, "White Supremacy, Chinese Schooling, and School Segregation."
15. Yu, *Thinking Orientals*, 19–46; Raushenbush, Letter to Dr. Yick Pang Lew, 22 Feb. 1924.
16. *DHGB*, 14 Feb. 1924; Raushenbush, "Interview with Dr. Y. P. Lew," 4 Feb. 1924, SRR; Con et al., *From China to Canada*, 165.
17. *Sixth Census of Canada, 1921*, 4:511; LAC, "Census Undercount," Memorandum to W. J. Egan, file 23635, RG 76, microfiche C-4785; Snyder, "Neighborhood Gatekeepers." The Census estimated that 42.04 percent of the 21,144 Chinese that it counted in British Columbia could not speak English. However, the immigration department discovered 31,116 Chinese in British Columbia in 1924, so the Census almost certainly undercounted non-English-speakers and illegal immigrants. The most conservative estimate would presume that all undercounted Chinese did not speak English. That would raise the non-English-speaking percentage to 61.87 percent, indicating that over one-third of the Chinese population could speak and understand English.
18. *DHGB*, 14 Feb. 1924.
19. Only one Chinese interview subject approached her independently. Raushenbush, interview with Cecil Lee, 26 May–1 June 1924, SRR.
20. *DHGB*, 14 Feb. 1924.
21. Shore, *Science of Social Redemption*, 24–37.
22. Mar, "From Diaspora to North American Civil Rights," 112; Yu, *Thinking Orientals*, vi–90. Yu discusses the survey in relation to ideas about the "Oriental problem" and Orientalism in U.S. society.
23. *DHGB*, 14 Feb., 4 Mar. 1924.
24. The North American approach to immigration studies can be read as part of the broader trend toward continental studies of Canada within interwar era scholarship described by Berger, *The Writing of Canadian History*, 137–159; Das, *Hindustani Workers on the Pacific Coast*; Yamato Ichihashi, *Japanese in the United States* (Stanford, Calif.: Stanford University Press, 1932).
25. Mears, "The Survey of Race Relations."
26. "A Brief History of the University of British Columbia," University of British Columbia Archives, http://www.library.ubc.ca/archives/hist_ubc.html (accessed 18 Nov. 2008).

27. *DHGB*, 4 Mar. 1924, 3.
28. Ibid.; "Office File Correspondence British Columbia (Canada)," 1924, Box 13, File 13-2, SRR; John Nelson to Merle Davis, 1 Oct. 1924, box 11, File 11-5; "Report of Donations," Apr.–Nov. 1924, box 13, file 13-2, SRR; "Office File Minutes of Meetings British Columbia (Canada)," box 16, file 16-3, SRR; "Minutes of the B.C. Council re Oriental Survey, held at the Board of Trade Council Chamber this evening at 8 o'clock," 14 Sept. 1923, box 16, file 16-3, SRR.
29. Woods, "John Nelson," 1–14.
30. Ibid., 4–5; *DHGB*, Oct. 1924.
31. Roy, *The Oriental Question*, 44–53.
32. Woods, "John Nelson," 3–8.
33. Toy, "Whose Frontier?" pars. 14–26; *DHGB*, 4 Mar. 1924; Gross, *Richard Rorty*, 67–71.
34. Gross, *Richard Rorty*, 67–72; Thomas et al., *Polish Peasant in Europe and America*; Park, *The Immigrant Press and Its Control*, xxxiv. Raushenbush's training at Chicago consisted of apprenticeship rather than classes because women generally could not pursue academic careers. She also had staffed the Chicago Commission on Race Relations, which in 1922 published the book *The Negro in Chicago*. In 1923, she started work with Park on organizing the Survey of Race Relations.
35. *DHGB*, 4 Mar. 1924.
36. Kivisto, "What Is the Canonical Theory of Assimilation?"; Persons, *Ethnic Studies at Chicago*, 60–75; Toy, "Whose Frontier?" par. 44.
37. Roberts, "Shovelling Out the 'Mutinous.'"
38. See chapter 3 about the CCC and CSA.
39. Ye, *Seeking Modernity*. The Vancouver readership of the journal *Chinese Students' Monthly* reflects the linkage between Vancouver's Chinese student group and the American CSA. A memento in the Vivian Wong Papers, a Chinese Students Alliance Dinner Program, 24 Nov. 1924, lists Vancouver's Chinese Students Alliance as part of the Chinese Students Alliance of Canada.
40. The two groups had the same Chinese name, Tongyuanhui, and they formed around the same time, but their relationship is unclear.
41. Thomas Moore Whaun to Mrs. James Rorty (Winifred Raushenbush), 25 Mar. 1968, box 1, Whaun Papers, UBC. His response to this assumption is inferred by Raushenbush's discussion of the sociologist's scientific objectivity in Raushenbush to Yick Pang Lew, 22 Feb. 1924.
42. Burnett, Seattle Chinese major documents.; "Interview with Esther Wong, native-born Chinese, San Francisco, California," 1 July 1924, box 28, file 28-239, SRR; Raushenbush, "Great Wall of Chinatown," 154–158, 221.
43. *DHGB*, 14 Feb. 1924.
44. The survey's "General Principles and Definitions" aimed to "help 'Discover America' for Americans."

45. "Chinese Questionnaire—Canada"; "Description of the Survey's Advantages for Chinese," both in "Office File Questionnaires Chinese – Pacific Coast (U.S.) + Canada," box 17, file 17-2, SRR; Raushenbush to Yick Pang Lew, 22 Feb. 1924.
46. "Visit Miss Hellaby, Anglican missionary," interview by Raushenbush, 10 Mar. 1924; "Dinner Mr. Louie Houie," 1; Con et al., *From China to Canada*, 305.
47. Raushenbush gave Cecil Lee great credence because she believed that he had approached her independently, but Lee was a CCC leader, and his testimony appeared to be part of the community plan. Cecil Lee and Joe Hope, interviews by Raushenbush, 26 May 1924, SRR.
48. Raushenbush: "Conversation with waiter," 9 Feb. 1924, box 24, file 24-2, SRR; "Visit, the old men's home," 1 Apr. 1924, box 24, file 24-25, SRR.
49. Raushenbush, "Conversation with waiter."; Lo and Lai, *Chinese Newspapers Published in North America*, x.
50. Raushenbush, "Interview with Joe Hope," 3.
51. The notion of elites engaging in discursive performances of their status in order to influence others to action comes from Woods, "Rethinking Elites."
52. See, for example, Ward, *The Writing on the Wall*; and the Canadian film *Secrets of Chinatown*, directed by Fred Newmeyer (Victoria, B.C.: Northern Production, 1935).
53. Roy, *A White Man's Province*, 64–81; Roy, *The Oriental Question*, 90–130.
54. DHGB, 14 Feb. 1924.
55. Ibid.
56. Ibid. Raushenbush, "Interview with Cecil Lee." Ko, "Interview with Chris Lee and Douglas Quan."
57. DHGB, 14 Feb. 1924.
58. Ibid.
59. Ibid.
60. Yee, "Chinese Business in Vancouver," 50.
61. *Vancouver World*, 11 Feb. 1911; *Nanaimo Free Press*, 4 Dec. 1922.
62. Roy, *The Oriental Question*, 60–61, 110–129.
63. Raushenbush, "Dinner Mr. Louie Houie."
64. Dikotter, *Discourse of Race*.
65. Raushenbush, "Interview with Mr. [Tom] Moore Whaun Advertising Manager of the Canada Morning News," 13 Feb. 1924, box 24, file 24-7.
66. "An Autobiographical Sketch Delivered by Tom Moore Whaun on Channel 10, Nov. 17, 1972," box 1, Whaun Papers; "Jiaxiang Tang Huan Yan Huang Song Mao Xueshi," unidentified Chinese news clipping (ca. 1921), box 2, Whaun Papers, UBC.
67. Whaun was elected vice president of the British Columbia Chinese Students Alliance in 1916. This was an organization for Chinese Canadian high school and university students in Vancouver, which that year extended to Victoria.

Guy Funn Chan to Thomas Moore Whaun, 5, 14 Oct. 1916, box 1, Whaun Papers.
68. Whaun, "An Autobiographical Sketch," 1.
69. Raushenbush, "Visit: Home of Mr. [Ko] Wing Kan," 20 Feb. 1924, box 24, file 24-13, SRR.
70. Raushenbush, "Interview, Herbert Wang."
71. Raushenbush, "Interview with Mr. [Tom] Moore Whaun."
72. Huang, "Gender, Race, and Power," 48–56.
73. Raushenbush, BC Major Documents. *DHGB*, 19, 27 Sept.; 2,3,4,6,11,21,22,23 November 1922; 3,8 25 Jan.; 22 Feb 1923; 14 Feb. 1924. "Jiangxia Tang Huan Yan Huang Song Mao Xue Shi," ca. 1921. Box 1, Whaun Papers.
74. Raushenbush, "Interview with Mr. Moore Whaun."
75. Ibid.
76. Raushenbush, "Call, T. M. Whaun," 5 Mar. 1924, box 24, file 24-17, SRR.
77. Raushenbush, "Interview Gershon Lew, the Hottest Bolshevik in Vancouver," May 1924; "Mr. Thomas Moore Whaun Audience," 3.
78. Raushenbush, "Interview with Harry Hastings," draft version, 5–6.
79. He was probably referring to Marcus Aurelius, not Antonius. The former was a Stoic philosopher-emperor famous for his *Meditations*. The latter is better known as Mark Antony, Caesar's friend and a member of the second triumvirate, who was no philosopher and left no writings.
80. Raushenbush, "Call T. M. Whaun," 5.
81. Raushenbush, "Mr. Thomas Moore Whaun Audience," 3.
82. Raushenbush, "Call T. M. Whaun," 1.
83. Raushenbush, "Visit Home of Mr. Ko Wing Kan," 1.
84. Raushenbush, interview with Cecil Lee, 4.
85. Raushenbush, "Visit the Lam family."
86. Raushenbush, "Interview with Cecil Lee," 4–5.
87. Raushenbush, "Luncheon, Miss Hosang."
88. Raushenbush, "Interview: Herbert Wang," 1–4.
89. Ibid.
90. Raushenbush, "Visit, the old men's home," 1–6.
91. Raushenbush, "Interview with Lew Shong Kow, ex-president of the Chinese Empire Reform Association," 30 Jan. 1924, 4. box 24, file 24-1, SRR.
92. Raushenbush, "Interview, Herbert Wang," 22 Feb. 1924, 5.
93. Raushenbush, "Interview with Cecil Lee," 3.
94. C. H. Burnett, box 27, folders 18, 27, 33–34, 36–50, SRR; "Interview with Esther Wong," 1 July 1924, SRR; Raushenbush, "Great Wall of Chinatown," 154–158, 221.
95. C. H. Burnett, "Interview of Pany Lowe," 5 July 1924, 4, box 28, file 28-242, SRR.
96. Hansen, *Mingling of the Canadian and American Peoples*, 263. Park and his associates concluded that Asians' experience on the Pacific Coast could be described

as a variation of a generalized race relations cycle which presumed permanent settlement to be normative. Persons, *Ethnic Studies at Chicago*, 60–76.

97. *DHGB*, 14 Feb. 1924.
98. At the time, naturalization as a British subject was a privilege, not a right, and judges in British Columbia often considered Chinese undesirable for citizenship. Macdonald and O'Keefe, *Canadian Holy War*, 90.
99. Con et al., *From China to Canada*, 119.
100. Government of Canada, "An Act Respecting Chinese Immigration," (Ottawa: Acland, 1925), Immigration Branch, LAC, microfilm, C-10661, 305.
101. Spence, *The Search for Modern China*, 334–342.
102. See Rowe, "'The Mysterious Oriental Mind.'"
103. Whaun, "An Autobiographical Sketch," 1.
104. *Daily Province*, "*Totem* 1927 with clippings," n.d. (ca. 23 June 1923); *Vancouver Sun*, 23 June 1923, file 827821, LAC.
105. Wong Tung Mow (Thomas Moore Whaun) to Lord Byng, Governor General of Canada, 23–29 June 1923, file 827821, LAC.
106. Raushenbush, "Interview with Mr. Moore Whaun," 2.
107. Whaun, "An Autobiographical Sketch," 1.
108. Raushenbush, "Interview with Mr. Moore Whaun," 2.
109. Raushenbush, "Interview with Lew Shong Kow," 4.
110. Raushenbush, "Call T. M. Whaun," 1.
111. Raushenbush, "Mr. Thomas Moore Whaun Audience," draft, 4.
112. Francis, *National Dreams*, 45.
113. *Jianada Chen Bao*, 5 Nov. 1927.
114. Raushenbush, "Interview with Mr. Moore Whaun," 2.
115. China's Communist Party had an alliance with the Nationalists and had considerable influence over the Nationalist Party's left wing.
116. *Da Han Gong Bao* had regular crime reports and occasional pictorial content at least since 1915, the earliest date of the issues that have been preserved. *Jianada Chenbao*'s sole surviving issue left in Canada (5 Nov. 1927) did not have more pictorial content or crime reports than other Chinese newspapers.
117. Raushenbush, "Visit Miss Hellaby," 2.
118. Raushenbush, "Visit the Lam family," 3. Mary Lam said that membership in the students club was open to any graduate of a school beyond the primary grades.
119. Ibid, 3.
120. Raushenbush, "Thomas Moore Whaun Audience," 2.
121. Ibid., 3. United Church of Canada. Woman's Missionary Society. *They Came Through: Stories of Chinese Canadians*. (Toronto: Literature Dept. and Committee on Missionary Education, United Church of Canada) circa 1940s.
122. Raushenbush, "Tea with Harry Hastings, the half-breed Chinese intellectual of Victoria," 26, 30 May 1924, box 24, file 24-31, SRR.
123. Raushenbush, interview with Joe Hope, 1.

124. *DHGB*, 3 June 1923.
125. Raushenbush, interview with Harry Hastings, 1.
126. Lai, "The Issue of Discrimination in Education."
127. *DHGB*, 19 Sept., 2 Nov. 1922. See Chow, *May Fourth Movement*, on on anti-colonial nationalist protests in China.
128. Raushenbush, interview with Harry Hastings, 1–4.
129. *DHGB*, 18 Oct. 1922.
130. Raushenbush, interview with Cecil Lee, 3.
131. Raushenbush, interview with Harry Hastings, draft, 5–6.
132. *Da Han Gong Bao* ran a daily section called "News from Other Chinatowns" that covered U.S. Chinese news; this was a common practice among Chinese immigrant newspapers in Canada and the United States.
133. Chen, *Chinese San Francisco*, 208–214.
134. C. H. Burnett, box 27, folders 18, 27, 33–34, 36–50, SRR.
135. On Japanese American transnationalism, see Azuma, *Between Two Empires*; and on the survey's view of Japanese Americans, see Raushenbush, "Their Place in the Sun," 141–145, 203.
136. Raushenbush, "Dinner Mr. Louie Houie," 6.
137. Ohashi to Davis, 6 Feb. 1924.; *DHGB*, 14 Feb. 1924.
138. Ohashi to Davis, 6 Feb. 1924.
139. Ibid.
140. Raushenbush, "Their Place in the Sun," 141–145, 203.
141. Ibid.
142. Toy, "Whose Frontier?" pars. 34–50.
143. Boggs, "Oriental Penetration into B.C."
144. Informal Reception Given by the Chinese Students Alliance of Canada, 24 Nov. 1924, Vivian Wong Papers.
145. Woods, "John Nelson," 5–14.
146. Ibid., 12.
147. Ibid., 8–14.
148. *Totem*, 38.
149. Whaun Papers, box 1: Laura E. Jamieson to Whaun, 9 Mar. 1929. Whaun Papers, box 2: "International Club Gives Reception for Noted Speaker [Bertrand Russell]," news clipping, 19 Oct. 1929; "Huang Song Mao Xueshi Xuanchuan Zhi Rexin," news clipping. Vivian Wong Papers: Chinese Students Alliance Dinner Program, 24 Nov. 1924.
150. Whaun to Esther Raushenbush, 7 Feb. 1968; Winifred Rorty (née Raushenbush) to Whaun, 21, 25 Mar., 30 May, 16 Oct. 1968. Whaun Papers.
151. "Notes from an Address by Miss Raushenbush," Conference File: Findings Conference, 21–26 Mar. 1925, 13, SRR.
152. The survey concluded that native-born youth, i.e., second-generation Asian immigrants, became completely Americanized in their consciousness, though discrimination and lack of opportunity could encourage the retention of

otherwise fading Asian cultural ties. They found the brokers to be most fascinating because of the stories of consciousness that they articulated. Mears, *Tentative Findings of the Survey of Race Relations*, 21-26 March, 1925, box 4, file 4-7, SRR; Park, "Human Migration and the Marginal Man."

153. Minutes of the Closed Convention of the Survey of Race Relations, 23 Mar. 1925, box 4, file 4-10, SRR; Robert Park, "Address on Methods of Research" (findings presented at Little Theatre, Stanford University, 25 Mar. 1925), 7, box 4, file 4-11, SRR. Raushenbush triaged the data into major and minor documents. The major documents were copied and preserved, and many of the minor documents were eventually lost.

154. Toy, "Whose Frontier?" par. 7.

155. The major documents had notations that they were to be copied to multiple survey team members, including Park, Emory Bogardus, Roderick McKenzie, and others, depending on the content. For example, see Raushenbush, "Interview with Mrs. Yip Quong," 26, Feb. 1924, 1, box 24, file 24-11.

156. "'East by West': Our Windows on the Pacific," *Survey Graphic* 56.3 (1 May 1926).

157. Yu, *Thinking Orientals*, 5–12, 186–204.

158. Raushenbush, "Great Wall of Chinatown," 154–158, 221.

159. Ibid., 221.

160. Park, "Address on Methods of Research," 1–12; "Minutes of the Closed Convention of the Survey of Race Relations," 45–62; Persons, *Ethnic Studies at Chicago*, 45–97.

161. Ronald Takaki's *Strangers from a Different Shore* is the most influential synthesis of this Asian American history perspective; it quotes the Survey of Race Relations extensively. On the influence of the Chicago School's view of Asians, see Yu, *Thinking Orientals*, 186–200.

162. The Survey of Race Relations became a founding event in North American immigration studies. The Chicago School also shaped Canada's first domestic sociological studies of immigrants in the 1930s and 1940s. See Yu, *Thinking Orientals*, 186; Shore, *Science of Social Redemption*. The Chicago School's concepts also strongly influenced the first book-length sociological study of Japanese and Chinese Canadians to be published by a Canadian academic press: Charles H. Young et al., *The Japanese Canadians* (Toronto: University of Toronto Press for Canadian National Committee for Mental Hygiene, Canadian Institute of International Affairs, 1938). Starting in the 1950s, Canadian and U.S. immigration historians who desired to write history "from the bottom up" turned to the Chicago School for guidance. Consequently, Chicago themes of assimilating ethnic identities, race relations, and local social ecologies came to define much of the domestic agenda of immigration studies within the new social history of Canada and the United States. By the 1960s and 1970s, immigration historian Jon Gjerde wrote in a 1999 literature review, one could speak of the Chicago School as the most influential founding school of U.S. immigration history.

Canadian and American historical scholarship interacted constantly, so the Chicago School concepts shaped the founding paradigms of Canadian immigration history as well. In 2006, an electronic search of books scanned by the Google Corporation turned up forty-two books in American history that cited the Survey of Race Relations; http://books.google.com (accessed 4 Dec. 2006).

163. For discussions of scientific racism, see popular Social Darwinist Lothrop Stoddard's *The Rising Tide of Color*; and on eugenics in Canada, see McLaren, *Our Own Master Race*. Within Vancouver's Chinese-language press, constant exhortations to "save China" and save the "Han race" reflected that a great many Chinese immigrants shared Social Darwinist beliefs, though they did not mention this to survey researchers. On Social Darwinism in China, see Dikotter, *Discourse of Race*.

164. Raushenbush, "Great Wall of Chinatown," 155.

165. Yu, *Thinking Orientals*, 111–123; Persons, *Ethnic Studies at Chicago*, 98–110.

166. Yu, *Thinking Orientals*, 188–189; William Petersen, "Success Story, Japanese American Style," *New York Times Magazine* (9 Jan. 1966): 20–21, 33, 36, 38, 40–41, 43.

167. Persons, *Ethnic Studies at Chicago*, 28–110, notes that Chicago sociologists believed that the process of assimilation was "inevitable," but they remained politically "complacent" about when it would eventually overcome racial or cultural barriers.

168. Park, "Human Migration and the Marginal Man."

169. Higham, "Introduction," 1; Breton, *Governance of Ethnic Communities*, 61–93.

170. Rumbaut, "Assimilation and Its Discontents."

171. Peck, *Reinventing Free Labor*; Harney, "The Padrone and the Immigrant"; Cohen, *Making a New Deal*; Sterne, "Beyond the Boss."

172. Farquar and Hevia, "Culture and Postwar American Historiography of China."

173. Okihiro, "Is Yellow Black or White?"

174. A WorldCat database search of books about the model minority concept found 1,041 entries; http://tinyurl.com/yfj5fqa (accessed 2 Feb. 2009). A search of articles in the EbscoHost databases in relevant fields of the social sciences and humanities found 763 articles about the model minority concept;http://tinyurl.com/yf75oof (accessed 2 Feb. 2009).

CHAPTER FIVE

1. Roy, *The Triumph of Citizenship*, 148–185; Chan, *Gold Mountain*, 145–147; Li, *Chinese in Canada*, 90–91; Yee, *Saltwater City*, 105; Keshen, *Saints, Sinners, and Soldiers*, 3–4; Con et al., *From China to Canada*, 198–201; Wong, *Americans First*; Mar, "From Diaspora to North American Civil Rights"; Maxwell, "A Cause Worth Fighting For"; Lee, "The Road to Enfranchisement"; Mar, "Beyond Being Others," 15, 24–34. For a dissenting view, see Patrias, "Race, Employment Discrimination, and State Complicity."

2. On the postwar Canadian, global, and local human rights movements, see Lambertson, *Repression and Resistance*, 3–6; Ignatieff, *The Rights Revolution*, 1–6; Bangarth, "'We Are Not Asking You to Open Wide the Gates for Chinese Immigration.'"

3. *DHGB*, 15 Aug. 1944; Con et al., *From China to Canada*, 301; *Eighth Census of Canada, 1941*, 4:534, 524, 164, 130; Lee Bick (Li Biru) interview, in Huang with Jeffery, *Chinese Canadians*, 25.

4. Report of the Chinese Canadian Historical Society, Contractor to City of Vancouver, *Historic Study of the Society Buildings in Chinatown* (July 2005): A70; Barman, *The West beyond the West*, 268; *DHGB*, 11 Dec. 1930; CCRC, box 6, Chinese Times—Subject Index, file 6-19, "Notes and Survey Prepared from CT by Researcher Tim Brook" (n.d.).

5. Yee and Newell note that Chinese merchants depended on Chinese workers as clients for much of their business. Yee, "Chinese Business in Vancouver"; Newell, "Beyond Chinatown"; Josephine Lee and Vivian Wong, interview.

6. Report of the Chinese Canadian Historical Society, Contractor to City of Vancouver, A70; Barman, *The West beyond the West*, 265–275; *DHGB*, 11 Dec. 1930; CCRC, box 6, Chinese Times—Subject Index, file 6-19, "Notes and Survey Prepared from CT by Researcher Tim Brook" (n.d.).

7. Con et al., *From China to Canada*, 181–183.

8. Gordon Won Cumyow interview, in Marlatt and Itter, *Opening Doors*, 15–20; Con et al., *From China to Canada*, 165; *DHGB*, 25 July 1930.

9. Szonyi, "Mothers, Sons, and Lovers," 50.

10. For the Japanese invasion of China, including Guangdong, and Chinese Canadian news reports and responses, see Quan Liu, *Guangdong Huaqiao Huaren Shi* (Guangzhou: Guangdong Remin Chubanshe, 2002), 246–250; Chen et al., *Taishan Xianzhi*, 12–13; *DHGB*, 19 Oct. 1937, 29 Aug., 8–10 Dec. 1942, 30 Jan. 1943, 22 May 1944.

11. *DHGB*, 10, 12, 13 July 1943, 24 Aug. 1944.

12. Other racial minority protests: Jagpal, *Becoming Canadians*, 126–127; Dhami, *Maluka*, 329–333; Michael D. Stevenson, *Canada's Greatest Wartime Muddle* (Montreal: McGill-Queen's University Press, 2001), 37–50.

13. *DHGB*, 6, 15 July, 2, 5 Aug. 1943.

14. Ibid., 15 July, 5 Aug. 1943. Chinese coal miners at Union Bay went on strike until the federal government, which controlled wages, agreed to pay them the same wages as white workers received. "Coal Miners (Chinese)—Union Bay, British Columbia," RG 27, vol. 421, file 279, LAC.

15. *DHGB*, 15 Aug., 2 Sept. 1944; *Xin Minguo Bao*, 26 Aug. 1944. *Da Han Gong Bao* counted 3,500 to 4,000 Chinese of military age in British Columbia. Marjorie Wong's *The Dragon and the Maple Leaf* found that, in September 1944, Canada called up 1,061 Chinese Canadians in British Columbia, of whom 273 reported, about half of whom were fit to serve. Wong found that the total for British Columbia Chinese enlistments, voluntary and conscripted combined,

was only about 400, 9. Roy, *The Triumph of Citizenship*, 154, lists the number of active protesters against Chinese Canadian conscription in Vancouver as 400. Further, few Chinese immigrants volunteered.

16. *Vancouver Daily Province*, 30 Jan. 1945, VCA, news clipping file; "Young Chinese Anxious to Fight—and Vote," unidentified newspaper, 22 Aug. 1944; *Vancouver Daily Province*, 22 Aug. 1944, 21 Dec. 1945; VCA, news clipping file, "Units Served Far Apart, Came Home on the Same Train," unidentified newspaper, 21 Dec. 1945.
17. *DHGB*, 10, 12, 13 July 1943.
18. Ibid., 19 Oct. 1937, 29 Aug., 8–10 Dec. 1942, 30 Jan., 2, 29 June 1943.
19. Ibid., 10 July 1943.
20. Roy, *The Triumph of Citizenship*, 148–185; Chan, *Gold Mountain*, 145–147; Li, *Chinese in Canada*, 90–91; Yee, *Saltwater City*, 105; Anderson, *Vancouver's Chinatown*, 170–173. On the popular image of the Second World War as Canada's "good war," see Keshen, *Saints, Sinners, and Soldiers*, 3–4.
21. Roy, *The Triumph of Citizenship*, 150–151, 156–158.
22. Keshen, *Saints, Sinners, and Soldiers*, 14–18; Roy, *The Triumph of Citizenship*; news clipping, Foon Sien Wong, "Why 'East Meets West,'" *Vancouver Sun*, 19 Oct. 1940, box 4, Foon Sien Wong Papers.
23. On anti-Communism and the wartime management of immigrants, see "Overseas Chinese—Activities, Organizations," 1943–1948, RG 25, ser. G-2, vol. 3314, folder 9820-40, LAC; Kordan, "Ethnicity, the State, and War," 1–12, 138–186. On the presumption of "foreignness": Patrias, "Race, Employment Discrimination, and State Complicity," 9–42.
24. Chinese papers in Vancouver, San Francisco, and New York frequently reprinted each others' articles, including articles by Chinese Canadians. Nations at War Scrapbook; news clippings, Foon Sien Wong, "Jinji jue jiao wu yi xuan zhan" (three-part article), *Xin Minguo Zhou Bao* (New York), n.d. (ca. late 1930s); Wong, "Xin Shidai" (four-part column), reprinted in an unidentified newspaper (probably *Xin Minguo Bao* of Victoria, Canada) from the U.S. publication *Meiguo Yazhou Zazhi*; news clipping, Wong, "Xitele kuang yan xia zhi shijie mian mian guan" (ca. Sept. 1939–May 1940), unidentified newspaper (probably *Xin Minguo Bao*); news clipping, Wong, "Jingji jue jiao wu yi xuan zhan" (three-part article), *Xin Minguo Zhou Bao* (New York) (ca. late 1930s). Examples of *Da Han Gong Bao* reprinting content from Chinese newspapers in San Francisco and New York: 29 June, 23 Mar. 1943, box 1, Wong Papers.
25. *DHGB*, 13 July 1943.
26. Wong, *Americans First*, 121–122, 173–175.
27. Nations at War Scrapbook; news clipping of Wong's column in *Xin Minguo Bao*, "Riqian Zhan Shi Guan Zhi" (ca. 1942), box 1, Wong Papers. On the wartime censorship policy: Keshen, *Saints, Sinners, and Soldiers*, 14–18; Foon Sien Wong, "The Chinese Canadians," (unpublished manuscript, n.d., ca. 1960s), part "Way of Life," 2, Wong Papers, box 4; Western Board of Directors

of the Canadian Council of Christians and Jews, Minutes of Meeting, 21 Feb. 1960, box 4, Wong Papers. Foon Sien Wong's "Goal for 1959," an unidentified news clipping, shows that Canada censored Chinese Canadian media and communications through established Chinese community leaders like Wong, who censored for the national War Services Department between 1939 and 1945.

28. Osborne, *Unwanted Soldiers*; Chan, *Gold Mountain*, 144, 146; Con et al., *From China to Canada*, 200. Yee and Roy briefly note the conflict over military service. Chan also notes that 8,000 men were of eligible age, but only about 500 served (144). Some works, such as *Unwanted Soldiers*, have focused most on the Chinese who chose to serve with no guarantees of equal rights. Yee, Roy, Maxwell, and Mar note the conflict, but a more complete story of Chinese Canadians' resistance to military service remains to be written. Roy, *The Triumph of Citizenship*, 154–155; Mar, "From Diaspora to North American Civil Rights," 218–224; Maxwell, "A Cause Worth Fighting For," 38–39; Veterans Affairs Canada, "Heroes Remember: Chinese-Canadian Veterans," http://www.vac-acc.gc.ca/remembers/sub.cfm?source=collections/hr_cdnchinese (accessed 16 Feb. 2009); Osborne, *Unwanted Soldiers*.

29. This is the main argument in K. Scott Wong's *Americans First*.

30. Anderson, *Vancouver's Chinatown*, 172; Roy, *The Triumph of Citizenship*, 151–152; Yung, *Unbound Feet*, 260–270; Wong, *Americans First*, 46–54.

31. *DHGB*, 15 July 1943.

32. Ibid., 10, 12, 13 July 1943.

33. Keshen, *Saints, Sinners, and Soldiers*, 3–11.

34. I have located only two monograph-length studies of China-Canada relations: Ren, "Canadian Trade Commissioners in Shanghai"; Song and Dong, *Zhongguo yu Jianada: Zhong Jia Guanxi de Lishi Huigu*.

35. These figures are derived from the following: a definition of a "Canadian" as either a resident or a British subject born in Canada; 9 percent of Canadian residents were born outside of the British Empire; and 9 percent of the global Canadian-born population lived in the United States. *Eighth Census of Canada, 1941*, 3:258; Vedder and Gallaway, "Settlement Patterns of Canadian Immigrants," 77.

36. *DHGB*, 24, 30 Nov. 1939.

37. Avison, *American Dollars Are Hard to Get*, 1–16; Powell, "A History of the Canadian Dollar," 53–55.

38. Hansen, *Mingling of the Canadian and American Peoples*, 1:263.

39. Whynot, "Old Stamping Grounds," 4, 34; Azzi, *Walter Gordon*, 20; *DHGB*, 24, 30 Nov. 1939, 13 July 1943. Many Chinese immigrants had been sending remittances through Chinese remittance shops, which were part of the commerce of transnational migration. See Hsu, *Dreaming of Gold, Dreaming of Home*, 34–40. This pattern had analogues in other immigrant groups, such as the Italians. See Harney, "Commerce of Migration" and "The Padrone and the Immigrant."

40. Avison, *American Dollars Are Hard to Get*, 1; Powell, "A History of the Canadian Dollar," 53.
41. Gibbons, "Foreign Exchange Control in Canada."
42. Gibbons writes that the FECB's remittance policy authorized immigrants only to send "moderate amounts" to dependents and relatives outside Canada: "When larger amounts were applied for, evidence of need was required and, in the early days, of past remittancees. While payments of this type were never entirely stopped the policy was more restrictive in some periods than in others" ("Foreign Exchange Control in Canada," 42). Asian, Eastern European, Southern European, and British immigrants often remitted money to families abroad. They used Canadian banks for domestic purposes, but Asians, Southern Europeans, and Eastern Europeans often preferred to remit funds through ethnic firms, which offered services in their own languages and which could deliver money to their relatives more effectively than Canadian banks could.
43. Newell, "Beyond Chinatown," 258.
44. The Vancouver City Archives holds remittance business records for the period between 1923 and 1933 related to the Yip Family; http://tinyurl.com/ylpwptm (accessed 14 Feb. 2009).
45. *DHGB*, 12 Feb. 1940.
46. Ibid., 19 Oct. 1937, 23 July, 29 Aug. 1942.
47. China, Consulate, Canada, "Correspondence: Foreign Exchange Board," MG 10, ser. C2, vol. 4, file 22, LAC.
48. Li, *Jianada Huaqiao Shi*, 257.
49. *DHGB*, 20 Jan., 12 Feb. 1940.
50. Gibbons, "Foreign Exchange Control in Canada," 42.
51. *DHGB*, 13 July 1943.
52. Ibid., 27 Mar. 1940.
53. .The 30,000 figure comes from a Consulate estimate reported in DHGB, 15 Aug., 1944, which would have been based on the Consulate's 1940 registration and subsequent processing of FECB requests. Con et al., *From China to Canada*, 302.
54. *DHGB*, 20 Jan. 1940.
55. Con et al., *From China to Canada*, 191.
56. *DHGB*, 20 Jan. 1940.
57. Western Board of Directors of the Canadian Council of Christians and Jews, Minutes of Meeting, 21 Feb. 1960, box 4, Wong Papers; news clipping, Foon Sien Wong's "Goal for 1959," unidentified newspaper, box 4, Wong Papers; F. S. Wong, CBA Fundraising Appeal Letter, 30 Aug. 1938, Vivian Wong Papers; *DHGB*, 12 Feb. 1940.
58. *DHGB*, 29 June 1943.
59. Ibid., 23 July, 8, 9 Dec. 1942.
60. Ibid., 8 Jan. 1944.
61. Kwong, *Chinatown, New York*, 133–134.

62. *DHGB*, 22 Feb. 1943.
63. Ibid., 12 Feb. 1940, 22 Feb. 1943.
64. Kealey, "The Canadian State's Attempts," 433–436.
65. Roy and Anderson briefly mention the threat of a Chinese strike on 7 July 1943 with regard to Vancouver's war industries. They believe that this threat was immediately successful, with the result that no strike or protest movement occurred. They seem to misidentify pensions as one cause of this potential strike. According to *DHGB*, the strike did happen, and because the Chinese did not win, a longer-term protest movement developed. The errors came from the faulty translation within one of Roy's and Anderson's sources, a partial English index of *DHGB*, created in the 1970s to research *From China to Canada*. Further, different sources had different viewpoints. The *DHGB* reported that, in Vancouver's English-language press, the Chinese consul denied that any illegal "proposed strike" had happened, though in the Chinese-language press, the consul and the Chinese community recognized that the strike had indeed happened. See Roy, *The Triumph of Citizenship*, 152; Anderson, *Vancouver's Chinatown*, 172; *DHGB*, 6–8, 10, 12, 13, 15, 19 July, 2, 5 Aug. 1943; Chinese Times—Index (1936–1958), CCRC, box 5, folders 5–8, 13–14; Roy, *The Triumph of Citizenship*, 154–155; Mar, "From Diaspora to North American Civil Rights," 218–224; Maxwell, "A Cause Worth Fighting For."
66. *DHGB*, 8 July, 30 Aug., 2 Sept. 1943.
67. Kealey and Cruikshank, "Strikes in Canada."
68. *DHGB*, 6 July 1943.
69. Ibid.
70. *Vancouver News Herald*, 20 July 1943; news clipping, "Plan Parley on Tax Claims," 21 July 1943, VCA.
71. Granted, remittances had great difficulty reaching occupied China, but *Da Han Gong Bao*'s daily advertisements for this service between 1943 and 1944 indicates a continuing demand. To Chinese Canadians, even the slightest hope that they could save their loved ones made their attempts to send as much money as possible an urgent concern.
72. *DHGB*, 13 July 1943.
73. Application of Income Tax Act to Persons of Chinese Race Resident in Canada, 1941–1942, MG 10-C2, LAC; Bing-Shuey Lee to Hong Lee, 29 July 1942, and Li Chao to Gene Mah, 20 July 1942, MG 10-C2, vol. 3, file 11, LAC; news clipping, "Grant Exemptions: Chinese Will Benefit under New Income Tax Regulations," *Vancouver Daily Province*, 19 Mar. 1942, box 1, Wong Papers.
74. Application of Income Tax Act to Persons of Chinese Race Resident in Canada, 1941–1942, LAC.
75. "Grant Exemptions: Chinese Will Benefit under New Income Tax Regulations"; *Vancouver Daily Province*, 19 Mar. 1942.
76. *DHGB*, 10, 12, 13 July 1943; *Vancouver News Herald*, 20 July 1943.
77. *DHGB*, 13 July 1943.

78. Ibid.
79. Ibid., 15 July 1943; Anniversaries 2007, "Remembering Roy Mah," 14 July 2007, reprinted from the *Allied Worker* (the IWA newsletter), Aug. 2003, http://anniversaries07.ca/news/2007_07_01_archive.html (accessed 15 Feb. 2008).
80. *DHGB*, 10 July 1943.
81. Application of Income Tax Act to Persons of Chinese Race Resident in Canada, 1941–1942; *DHGB*, 10, 19 July 1943; *Vancouver News Herald*, 20 July 1943.
82. Yee, *Saltwater City*, 99.
83. *Vancouver News Herald*, 6 Aug. 1942; Wong, "Wu Zhi Bu De Ganxiang," *Xin Minguo Bao*, 14 Aug. 1942.
84. Wong, "Wu Zhi Bu De Ganxiang," *Xin Minguo Bao*, 14 Aug. 1942. The Chinese version omitted Wong's most pointed criticisms of class exploitation within the Chinese Canadian population. Con et al., *From China to Canada*, 199.
85. Josephine Lee and Vivian Wong, interview.
86. Jenny Lee, "Chinatown's Quiet Revolutionary," *Vancouver Sun*, 12 May 2007, reposted on *GungHaggisFatChoy*, http://gunghaggisfatchoy.com/blog/archives (accessed 4 July 2007).
87. *DHGB*, 8 July 1943.
88. Norbert McDonald, *Distant Neighbors: A Comparative History of Seattle and Vancouver* (Lincoln: University of Nebraska Press, 1987), 141–143; Morley, *Vancouver*, 190–192.
89. Roy, "The Soldiers Canada Didn't Want."
90. CCVOHP, Herbert Lim interview.
91. CCVOHP, Bing Wong interview.
92. Mar, "The Mar-Sue Family's Quest," 106.
93. Keshen, *Saints, Sinners, and Soldiers*, 41–120.
94. Ibid., 54.
95. Ibid., 55.
96. *Vancouver News Herald*, 20 July 1943.
97. *DHGB*, 10, 12, 13 July, 1943.
98. Patrias, "Race, Employment Discrimination, and State Complicity," 11, 20–21, 41. CCVOHP, Herbert Lim interview.
99. *DHGB*, 13 July 1943.
100. Anderson, *Vancouver's Chinatown*, 172.
101. Gray, "Woodworkers and Legitimacy," 122. Gray cited *National War Labor Board Proceedings* 11 (10–11 June 1943): 1012, 1007–1010; *DHGB*, 6 July 1943.
102. Keshen, *Saints, Sinners, and Soldiers*, 61.
103. *DHGB*, 6, 8 July 1943.
104. Ibid., 7, 8 July 1943.
105. Ibid.

106. Ibid., 8 July 1943.
107. Ibid., 13 July 1943.
108. Ibid.
109. Ibid.
110. *Vancouver News Herald*, 20 July 1943.
111. *DHGB*, 19 July 1943.
112. Ibid.
113. Chung Collection, pamphlet regarding Chinese fundraising in 1925 for the defense of Foon Sing Wong, box FOLDR-0035, file 1.
114. *Vancouver News Herald*, 20 July 1943.
115. Ibid.
116. News clipping file, "Plan Parley on Chinese Tax Claims," 21 July 1943, VCA.
117. Chinese Patriotic Leagues and Associations War Relief Files, Correspondence by City (ca. 1939–early 1940s), MG 10, vol. 4, ser. C2, files 9–18, LAC.
118. CCVOHP, Mah interview; "Roy Mah," in Huang and Jeffery, *Chinese Canadians*, 72–76.
119. CCVOHP, Bevan Jangze interview.
120. News clipping files, Ted Ward, "Special Wage Rate Cards Printed by Union Here for Chinese Members Who Help Build BC Ships," 25 Feb. 1943, VCA.
121. Ibid.
122. *DHGB*, 8 July 1943.
123. Ibid., 2 Aug. 1943. The intermediaries included "Huang Song," a possible reference to Whaun's Chinese name, Huang Song Mao. News clippings, "Chinese Workers Open Drive for Membership," Vancouver Daily *Province*, 16 Feb. 1948; "Chinese Labor Group in Drive to Join TLC," *Vancouver News Herald*, 16 Feb. 1948; "Chinese Here Start Union Movement," *Vancouver Sun*, 16 Feb. 1948; and "CCL Opposes New Chinese Labor Union," *Vancouver Sun*, 18 Feb. 1948, VCA. Con et al., *From China to Canada*, 199, dates a Chinese Trade Workers' Union to the Second World War, though their account shows a 1942 founding date, so it is possible that the group had some form of earlier organization that predated its 1943 protest. Li, *Jianada Huaqiao Shi*, 152, dates the founding of the Chinese workers group (Zhonghua Zhigong Lianhehui) led by Foon Sien Wong and Ma Shanyun to 1937 or 1938.
124. *DHGB*, 2 Aug. 1943.
125. Ibid.
126. Ibid., 1 Mar. 1944.
127. Ibid. The paper listed Huang Song as one of the participants, perhaps a reference to T. M.
128. Ibid.
129. Keshen, *Saints, Sinners, and Soldiers*, 61.
130. Kealey, "Strikes in Canada," 376–378.
131. *DHGB*, 15 July, 5 Aug. 1943. The *DHGB* did not report the outcome of the equal pay demand, so it probably did not succeed.

132. Ibid., 26 Oct. 1943.
133. *Vancouver News Herald*, 20 July 1943; news clipping, "Plan Parley on Tax Claims," 21 July 1943, VCA.
134. *DHGB*, 7, 8, 13, 15, 19, 20 July, 2 Aug., 30 Sept., 23, 26 Oct., 17 Dec. 1943, 28 Feb., 1 Mar. 1944.
135. Ibid., 13 July 1943.
136. Ibid., 12 Apr., 1, 2 May 1944; news clipping, "Chinese Named Union Organizer," 14 Apr. 1944, VCA.
137. Barman, *The West beyond the West*, 322–323; McInnis, *Harnessing Labor Confrontation*, 1–17.
138. McInnis, *Harnessing Labor Confrontation*, 41–42; *DHGB*, 1 Mar. 1944.
139. *DHGB*, 13 Mar. 1944.
140. News clipping, "Chinese Named Union Organizer," 14 Apr. 1944, VCA.
141. *DHGB*, 12 Apr. 1944.
142. Ibid., 10 July 1943. The *Eighth Census of Canada, 1941*, 3:164, counted East Indians under the rubric of "Asians other than Chinese and Japanese," a group that contained only 1,757 persons in 1941.
143. *DHGB*, 12 Apr., 1–2 May 1944.
144. Nations at War Scrapbook; news clipping, "Shengfu tongguo yaoan: Zhun yuan zheng huabing you xuanquan," *Xin Minguo Bao*, 2 Apr. 1945, box 1, Wong Papers.
145. "Shengfu tongguo yaoan: Zhun yuan zheng huabing you xuanquan," Wong Papers.
146. Lambertson, *Repression and Resistance*.
147. Kealey, "The Canadian State's Attempts," 434.
148. For a general argument about the rights revolution as a global and Canadian event, see Ignatieff, *The Rights Revolution*.
149. For a conventional account of the conscription crisis as a French-English issue, see Granatstein and Hitsman, *Broken Promises*.
150. Jagpal, *Becoming Canadians*, 126–127; Dhami, *Maluka*, 329–333; Stevenson, *Canada's Greatest Wartime Muddle*, 37–50; Stevenson, "Mobilisation of Native Canadians"; Wong, *The Dragon and the Maple Leaf*, 9, 218, 232–246; *DHGB*, 15 Aug. 1944.
151. Barman, *The West beyond the West*, 429; *DHGB*, 15 Aug. 1944. Canada's Census of 1941 found that one in twelve British Columbia residents was either Asian or First Nations, though by 1944 the number of Chinese counted by China's consulate in British Columbia, 30,000, was far greater than the Census count. Because the consulate vetted remittance requests, its figure was probably more accurate.
152. Mar, "From Diaspora to North American Civil Rights," 218–224; Maxwell, "A Cause Worth Fighting For," 24–41.
153. *DHGB*, 24 Sept. 1940; Mar, "From Diaspora to North American Civil Rights," 213–214; Memorandum, "Orientals—National War Services," RG 27, vol.

1489, file 2-184, LAC; Secret no. 1, Dept. of National War Services, 20 Nov. 1941, RG 27, file 2-184, vol. 1489, LAC; National Selective Service—Aliens—Chinese, RG 27, files 2-114-115, vol. 998, LAC; Maj. Gen. H. J. Riley to A. MacNamara (ca. 1943); E. G. Bjarnason to Wright, 12 July 1944; Charles Henry to Arthur MacNamara, Deputy Minister of Labour, 29 July 1943, all in LAC; CCVOHP, Daniel Lee interview; Roy, "The Soldiers Canada Didn't Want"; Wong, *The Dragon and the Maple Leaf*, 78–81. A small number of Chinese Canadians did enlist before the ban was lifted. Some were volunteers. Others were conscripted outside British Columbia in provinces where the ban on Chinese enlistment was not always consistently enforced. Roy, *The Triumph of Citizenship*, 152–155.

154. *DHGB*, 24 Aug. 1944.
155. Roy, "The Soldiers Canada Didn't Want."
156. Estimates of the Chinese Canadian military-age population varied considerably, but *Da Han Gong Bao* is probably a reliable source. *DHGB*, 15 Aug. 1944; Wong, *The Dragon and the Maple Leaf*, 8–9.
157. Ann Lee interview; *DHGB*, 24 Aug. 1944.
158. News clippings on conscription issue, income tax, and Chinese Canadian war effort, Summer 1944, box 1, Wong Papers; Mamie Moloney, "In One Ear," *Vancouver Sun*, 15 Aug. 1944; Roy Mah, "Chinese in Canada," Letter to Editor, *Vancouver Sun*, 15 Aug. 1944; Letter to Editor in response to "Soldiers' Mother," unidentified English newspaper, 22 July 1944; Charles Evans, "Chinese in City," Letter to Editor, *Vancouver Sun*, 4 Aug. 1944; Two Loggers, "Chinese in Canada," Letter to Editor, *Vancouver Sun*, n.d. (July or Aug. 1944); Mrs. H. Joe, "Racial Prejudice," *Vancouver Sun*, 3 Aug. 1944; Richard H. Chow, "Chinese-Canadians," *Vancouver Sun*, 4 Aug. 1944; Editorial, "Take It Easy," *Vancouver Sun*, 8 Aug. 1944; Fred Chun, "Chinese in Canada," *Vancouver Sun*, 4 Aug. 1944; "Human Being" and "Chinese Canadians," *Vancouver Sun*, n.d. (July or Aug 1944); Foon Sien Wong, "Chinese Cooperation," Letter to Editor, *Vancouver Sun*, 29 July 1944; Jimmy Yuen, "Chinese in Canada," *Vancouver Sun* (ca. July–Aug. 1944); Harry H. Leong, "Race Discrimination," *Vancouver Sun* (ca. July–Aug. 1944); Patrias, "Race, Employment Discrimination, and State Complicity," 11, 20–21, 41.
159. Foon Sien Wong, "Chinese Cooperation," Letter to Editor, *Vancouver Sun*, 29 July 1944.
160. Mamie Moloney, "In One Ear," *Vancouver Sun*, 15 Aug. 1944, 6.
161. Wong, *The Dragon and the Maple Leaf*, 78–79, 112–121.
162. CCVOHP, Roy Mah interview, Bevan Jangze interview.
163. CCVOHP, Roy Mah interview; Ann Lee interview; *DHGB*, 15 Aug., 2 Sept. 1944.
164. Ann Lee interview; Nations at War Scrapbook; news clipping, editorial on conscription, *Xin Minguo Bao* (ca. Aug. 1944), box 1, Wong Papers.
165. CCVOHP, Roy Mah interview, Bevan Jangze interview; *DHGB*, 24 Aug. 1944.

166. CCVOHP, Bevan Jangze interview.
167. *DHGB*, 24 Aug. 1944.
168. CCVOHP, Ann Lee interview.
169. *DHGB*, 15 Aug. 1944.
170. Granatstein and Hitsman, *Broken Promises*, 1, 164–172; Stevenson, "Mobilisation of Native Canadians"; Jagpal, *Becoming Canadians*, 126–127.
171. H. Keenleyside, for the USEA to Maj. Gen. L.R. LaFleche, Deputy Minister of National War Services, 9 Oct. 1941, "Orientals—National War Services," RG 27, vol. 1489, file 2-184, LAC; Justice Gillanders, Chairman of the Board (Draft/Mobilization), Toronto, to Maj. Gen. L. R. LaFleche, Assoc. Deputy Minister, Dept. of National War Services, 2 Oct. 1941, "Orientals—National War Services," RG 27, vol. 1489, file 2-184, LAC; "Conscription of Hong Wing Shu and Other Chinese Canadian citizens – Particular case," 4 Aug. 1942 to 23 Feb. 1948. RG 25, series G-2, vol 3037, file 4164-40, LAC; "Charlie" Woo Fay to Mobilization Board of Kingston, 13 Jan. 1945 and 4 Feb. 1945, "National Selective Service. Aliens – Chinese," RG 25, ser. G-2, vol. 3037, File 2-114-5, LAC.
172. H. Keenleyside, for the USEA to Maj. Gen. L.R. LaFleche, Deputy Minister of National War Services, 9 Oct. 1941; Justice Gillanders, Chairman of the Board (Draft/Mobilization), Toronto, to Maj. Gen. L. R. LaFleche, Assoc. Deputy Minister, Dept. of National War Services, 2 Oct. 1941.
173. M. Wong, *The Dragon and the Maple Leaf*, 9.
174. Nations at War Scrapbook box 1, Wong Papers; News clippings collection, box 1, Wong Papers.
175. News clipping, Fred Chun, "Chinese in Canada," *Vancouver Sun*, 4 Aug. 1944, box 1, Wong Papers.
176. Ann Lee interview.
177. CCVOHP, Bing Wong interview.
178. Wang, "*His Dominion and the Yellow Peril*," 77–82.
179. News clipping, "'No Vote, No Fight': City Chinese Oppose Call Up," unidentified newspaper, 23 Aug. 1944, box 1, Wong Papers; Roy, *The Triumph of Citizenship*, 154; Mike Howell, "Double Duty," *Vancouver Courier*, www.vancouvercourier.com/issues03/112o3/news/112103nn1.html (accessed 4 July 2007).
180. *DHGB*, 24 Aug. 1944.
181. "Reaching Out to First Nations Veterans," *Salute!* (Ottawa: Veterans Affairs Canada), Fall 2002, http://www.vac-acc.gc.ca/clients/sub.cfm?source=salute/fall2002/firstnation (accessed 16 Mar. 2009).
182. *DHGB*, 24 Aug. 1944.
183. CCVOHP, Roy Mah interview.
184. Foon Sien Wong, "The Chinese Canadians," unpublished manuscript, part 11, 10. ca. 1960s-1971, Josephine Lee Papers.
185. *DHGB*, 29 Aug. 1944.

186. Stevenson, *Canada's Greatest Wartime Muddle*, 43. Apparently, no legal action was taken against Chinese Canadians who did not comply with conscription until the case of Jimmy Che in 1945. *DHGB*, 9 Apr. 1945, Chinese Times—Index, box 5, folder 10, CCRC.
187. Wong, *The Dragon and the Maple Leaf*, 218.
188. *Xin Minguo Bao*, 3 Sept. 1948.
189. Keshen explains war policy in *Saints, Sinners, and Soldiers*, 14–18. On specific portrayals of Chinese Canadians, see note 16.
190. CCVOHP, Frank Wong interview.

CONCLUSION

1. Roy, *A White Man's Province*; Roy, *The Oriental Question*; Roy, *The Triumph of Citizenship*; Backhouse, *Colour-Coded*; Stanley, "Bringing Anti-Racism into Historical Explanation"; Stanley, "White Supremacy, Chinese Schooling, and School Segregation."
2. The literature's focus on majority policies toward Asian minorities and the latter's reaction arose only partly from the linguistic challenges of dealing with Asian-language evidence. Language barriers alone cannot explain why Chinese Canadians were not conceptually integrated into Canadian history. In 1982, Con et al.'s *From China to Canada* was the first national history of Chinese Canadians that used extensive research into Chinese-language sources. From a research standpoint, it is arguably one of the finest, most groundbreaking research projects on the topic. Almost thirty years later, few scholars have built on its insights.
3. Gabaccia, "Is Everywhere Nowhere?"; Gutiérrez and Hondagneu-Sotelo, "Introduction: Nation and Migration"; Hsu, "Transnationalism and Asian American Studies"; McKeown, *Melancholy Order*; Kuhn, *Chinese among Others*, 197–238.
4. See Patrias, *Patriots and Proletarians*; Avery, *Dangerous Foreigners*; Peck, *Reinventing Free Labour*; Harney, "The Commerce of Migration."
5. Hansen, *Mingling of the Canadian and American Peoples*, 263.
6. At least 120,000 emigrated to Canada, calculated as follows: 98,361 Chinese registered as entrants (1885–1949) in addition to 17,000 railway and gold rush era migrants plus several thousand illegal immigrants. The latter two groups are conservative estimates because no official count is available. The numbers in the other countries are as follows: United States, 150,000–200,000 (Census, 1870–1930); Australia, 100,000; New Zealand, 5,000; Cuba, 200,000; Mexico, 37,000; and Peru, 60,000 (Census, 1876–1940). "Introduction," from Immigrants from China, 23 June 2008, LAC, http://www.collectionscanada.gc.ca/databases/chinese-immigrants/index-e.html (accessed 2 July 2008); Con et al., *From China to Canada*, 296; Daniels, *Coming to America*, 240; Jupp, *The Australian People*, 197; Ng, "Chinese in New Zealand"; Ding, *Ancestors in the Americas*; McKeown, *Chinese Migrant Networks*, 48.

7. Erika Lee, "The 'Yellow Peril' and Asian Exclusion in the Americas," *Pacific Historical Review* 76.4 (2007): 537–562; Kuhn, *Chinese among Others*, 197–238; Lee, "Orientalisms in the Americas," 235–256.
8. Wong, *Sweet Cakes, Long Journey*, 180–197; Ma, *Revolutionaries, Monarchists, and Chinatowns*, 91.
9. Yun, *The Coolie Speaks*, 216–217; Siu, *Memories of a Future Home*, 39–40; McKeown, *Chinese Migrant Networks*, 25; Fitzgerald, *Big White Lie*.
10. Lee, "Enforcing the Borders"; Delgado, "At Exclusion's Southern Gate"; Morales, "Differencias Politicas."

BIBLIOGRAPHY

UNPUBLISHED PRIMARY SOURCES

*British Columbia Archives and Records Service (BCA)*

David C. Lew Fonds. 1907–1910.
Probate files. 1893–1941. Microfilm reel B-2546.

*Chinese Canadian Research Collection, University of British Columbia (CCRC)*

*Memorial Volume of Wong Foon Sien* (Vancouver, 1970), box 26, file 13.
David C. Lew Letterbook, 1907–1909.
Li Donghai. *Jianada Huaqiao Shi*. Box 25, file 54. Translated by Ma Sen, 1973 ["A History of the Overseas Chinese in Canada by David Li"].

*Chinese Cultural Centre Museum and Archives, Vancouver, British Columbia*

Chinese Canadian Veterans Oral History Project (CCVOHP)
Jangze, Bevan. "Interview with Chris Lee and Douglas Quan." Vancouver. 2 Aug. 1996.
Ko, John. "Interview with Chris Lee and Douglas Quan." Vancouver. 12 Aug. 1996.
Lee, Daniel. "Interview with Douglas Quan and Jane Ng." Vancouver. 12 Aug. 1996.
Lim, Herbert. "Interview with Theresa Ho and Jennifer Jang." Vancouver. 3 Aug. 1996.

Mah, Roy. "Interview with Chris Lee and Douglas Quan." Vancouver. 1 Aug. 1996.
Wong, Bing. "Interview with Jane Ng and Amos Lee." Vancouver. 14 Aug. 1996.
Wong, Frank, "Interview with Jane Ng and Amos Lee." Vancouver. 7 Aug. 1996.

*Hoover Institution Archives, Stanford University, Stanford, California*

Survey of Race Relations Collection (SRR). 1924. 38 boxes.
Burnett, C.H., "Interview of Pany Lowe, Social Document." 5 July 1924, box 28, file 28-242.
———. "Interview with Mr. Fred H. Lysons, Attorney." 29 July, 5, 22 Aug. 1924, Box 27, File 27-192
———. Seattle Chinese major documents, summer, 1924. box 27, folders 24-:18, 27, 33–34, 36–50.
Davis, Merle, Letter to Premier of British Columbia, Sir John Oliver. 3 Dec. 1923, box 13, file 13-1.
"Interview with Esther Wong, native-born Chinese, San Francisco, California." 1 July 1924, box 28, file 28-239
McKeen, Laura, Executive Secretary, San Francisco International Institute of the YMCA Service Bureau for Foreign-Speaking People, Letter to Eliot G. Mears, 29 May, 1927. Box 6, File 6-4.
"Minutes of the B.C. Council re Oriental Survey, held at the Board of Trade Council Chamber this evening at 8 o'clock." 14 Sept. 1923, box 16, file 16-3
"Office File Correspondence British Columbia (Canada)." 1924, Box 13, File 13-2,
"Office File Minutes of Meetings British Columbia (Canada)." box 16, file 16-3
"Office File Questionnaires Chinese—Pacific Coast (U.S.) + Canada, Survey Interview Questionnaires (ca. Jan. and Feb. 1924)." box 17, file 17-2.
"Office File Correspondence British Columbia (Canada)," 1924, Box 13, File 13-2
Nelson, John, Letter to Merle Davis, 1 Oct. 1924, box 11, File 11-5; "Report Donations," Apr.–Nov. 1924, box 13, file 13-2.
Ohashi, Chuichi of Japanese Consulate, San Francisco, Letter to Merle Davis, 6 Feb. 1924, box 14, file 14-11.
Raushenbush, Winifred. British Columbia Major Documents, box 24, files 24-1 through 24-35.
———. "Call, T. M. Whaun." 5 Mar. 1924, box 24, file 24-17

———. "Conversation with waiter, International Chop Suey." 9 Feb. 1924, box 24, file 24-2

———. "Dinner Mr. Louie Houie, President of the Merchants Association." 2 Apr. 1924, box 24, file 24-26

———. "Interview, Herbert Wang." 25 Mar. 1924, box 24, file 24-24.

———. "Interview with Cecil Lee, a native son who is married to a Hakkla. [Hakka]" 26 May–1 June 1924, box 24, file 24-34.

———. "Interview with Dr. Y. P. [Yick Pang] Lew, Dentist and President of the Chinese Benevolent Association; interpreter Seto More [Seto Ying Shek], agent of the Canadian Pacific Bureau, Ocean Travel." 4 Feb. 1924, Box 24, File 24-5.

———. "Interview with Gershon Lew, the Hottest Bolshevik in Vancouver." May 1924, box 24, file 24-29.

———. "Interview with Harry Hastings regarding the school strike and other matters." 26, 30 May 1924, box 24, file 24-32.

———. "Interview with J. A. Russel[l], barrister, criminal lawyer for the Chinese." 30 Apr. 1924, Box 24, File 24-27.

———. "Interview with Joe Hope, president of the Chinese Canadian Club." 26 May 1924, box 24, file 24-33.

———. "Interview with Lew Shong Kow, ex-president of the Chinese Empire Reform Association," 30 Jan. 1924. box 24, file 24-1,

———. "Interview with Mr. [Tom] Moore Whaun Advertising Manager of the *Canada Morning News* [*Jianada Chen Bao*]," 13 Feb. 1924, box 24, file 24-7.

———. "Interview with Mrs. Yip Quong," 26, Feb. 1924, 1, box 24, file 24-11.

———. Letter to Dr. Yick Pang Lew, 22 Feb. 1924, box 17, file 17-2.

———. "Luncheon, Miss Hosang." 19 Mar. 1924, draft version, 7, box 24, file 24-23.

———. "Mr. Thomas Moore Whaun Audience." 7 May 1924, box 24, file 24-28.

———. "Tea with Harry Hastings, the half-breed Chinese intellectual of Victoria," 26, 30 May 1924, box 24, file 24-31.

———. "Visit, the Lam family." March 1924, box 24, file 24-20.

———. "Visit Miss Hellaby, Anglican missionary." 1924, box 24, file 24-21.

———. "Visit: Home of Mr. Ko Wing Kan," 20 Feb. 1924, box 24, file 24-13,

———. "Visit, the old men's home," 1 Apr. 1924, box 24, file 24-25.

*Library and Archives of Canada, Ottawa, Ontario (LAC)*

China. Consulate. Canada. Chinese Patriotic Leagues and Associations War Relief files. MG 10.

———. Correspondence by City, circa 1939 to early 1940s. MG 10, ser. C2, vol. 4, files 9–18.
———. Correspondence: Foreign Exchange Board. MG 10, ser. C2, vol. 4, file 22.
"Chinese Merchants Attempting to Enter Canada," RCCF, RG 33-146.
Department of External Affairs. "Conscription of Hong Wing Shu and other Chinese Canadian citizens - Particular case." 4 Aug. 1942 to 23 Feb. 1948. RG 25, series G-2, vol. 3037, file 4164-40.
Department of External Affairs. Application of Income Tax Act to Persons of Chinese Race Resident in Canada. 1941–1942. RG 25-6-2, vol. 2883.
Department of Immigration and Colonization. Registration under Sec. 18 Chinese Imm. Act of Chinese Born in Canada. RG 13-A-2, vol. 1958.
Department of Labour. Coal Miners (Chinese)—Union Bay, British Columbia. RG 27, vol. 421, file 279.
———. Department of National War Services. 1941. RG 27, vol. 1489.
———. "Selective Service—Aliens—Chinese." RG 27, vol. 998.
Department of Secretary of State. Chief Press Censor. 1915–1920. RG 6, vol. 574.
Department of Trade and Commerce regarding Chinese Immigration Act. 1885–1911. RG 76, vol. 590, Files 827821 to 827835.
Immigration Branch. General Registers of Chinese Immigration. 1894. RG 76, ser. D2a, vol. 697. Microfilm reel C-9511.
"Introduction." From Immigrants from China, LAC, 23 June 2008. http://www.collectionscanada.gc.ca/databases/chinese-immigrants/index-e.html. Accessed 2 July 2008.
Orders-in-Council. 1910–1911. RG 2. Microfilm.
Royal Commission to Investigate Alleged Chinese Frauds and Opium Smuggling on the Pacific Coast (RCCF). RG 33-146, vols. 1–6.
Supreme Court of Canada Fonds. David Lew v. Wing Lee. Supreme Court of Canada Appeal, 1924. RG 125, vol. 508, file 4956.

*Private Collections*

Josephine Lee Papers. 1945–1971.
———. Foon Sien Wong, "The Chinese Canadians," unpublished manuscript, ca. 1960s–1971.
Vivian Wong Papers. 1922–1971.
———. Chinese Students Alliance Dinner Program, 24 Nov. 1924

*University of British Columbia (UBC), Vancouver*

Chung Collection.

———. "Documents and Ephemera Related to Community and Social Activities of Yip Sang and His Family." Box 15.
———. "Invoices of Yip Kew Him, Canadian Pacific and Department of Immigration Interpreter, 1916–1941." http://digitalcollections.library.ubc.ca/u?/coll0803-7,11715 & http://digitalcollections.library.ubc.ca/u?/coll0803-7,11976. Accessed March 20, 2010.
———. "Minutes of Inquiries Regarding Chinese Merchants Attempting to Enter Canada on the *Empress of China*" (MIRC). Box 33.
———. "Peddlers Association and Legal Cases, 1933–1937." Box 23.
———. "Receipt for membership for the Chinese Canadian Club." http://digitalcollections.library.ubc.ca/u?/coll0803-7,2719. Accessed 20 Mar. 2010.
———. Yip Quene. "Jang Jack and G. Yom's Car Case to Mr. A. Henderson." Box 35_02, File 1.
———. "Yungaohua Zhonghua Huiguan Wei Yingjiu Huang Huan Sheng An Jin Zhi Zheng Xin Lu," 16 May 1925. Box 35.
Thomas Moore Whaun Papers. 1916–1985.
Foon Sien Wong (Huang Wenfu) Papers. 1922–1971.
Won Alexander Cumyow Fonds, 1878–1992

*Vancouver City Archives (VCA)*

Newspaper clippings. 1937–1949.
Yip Family and Yip Sang Ltd. Fonds. 1895–1989.

INTERVIEWS

Joe, Andrew. Interview by author. Vancouver. 12 Aug. 2003.
Lee, Ann (pseudonym). Interview by author. Toronto. 6 Mar. 1999.
Lee, Josephine, and Vivian Wong. Interview by author. Vancouver. 29 June 1999.

PERIODICALS

*Da Han Gong Bao (Chinese Times)*, 1915–1950
*Da Han Ri Bao (Chinese Daily News)*, 1914–1915
*Daily Colonist*, 1922–1923
*Jianada Chen Bao (Canada Morning Post)*, 1927
*Nanaimo Free Press*, 1920–1924
*New York Times*, 1885–1911
*Toronto Star*, 1922
*Vancouver News Herald*, 1930s–1940s
*Vancouver Daily Province*, 1906–1945
*Vancouver Sun*, 1918–1945

*Vancouver World*, 1910–1911
*Victoria Daily Times*, 1922–1923
*Washington Post*, 1905–1911
*Xin Minguo Bao (New Republic)*, 1937–1945


GOVERNMENT DOCUMENTS

*Canada*

*Census of Canada, Sixth, 1921*, vol. 2: *Population*. Ottawa: Acland, 1925.
*Census of Canada, Eighth, 1941*. Ottawa: Cloutier, 1941.
Department of Labour. *Report by W. L. Mackenzie King, Commissioner, Appointed to Investigate into the Losses Sustained by the Chinese Population of Vancouver, B.C. on the Occasion of the Riots in That City in September 1907*. Ottawa: Dawson, 1908.
Department of Trade and Commerce, Canada. *Chinese Immigration Act As Amended to Date with Regulations Authorized by Orders in Council Based Thereon*. Ottawa: Government Printing Bureau, 1910.
*Report of Mr. Justice Murphy, Royal Commissioner Appointed to Investigate Alleged Chinese Frauds and Opium Smuggling on the Pacific Coast, 1910–1911*. Ottawa: Government Printing Bureau, 1911.
*Report of the Royal Commission on Chinese and Japanese Immigration*. Ottawa: Dawson, 1902.
*Revised Statutes of Canada, 1906*. Ottawa: Dawson, 1907.

*United States*

Gompers, Samuel, and Frank Morrison. *Some Reasons for Chinese Exclusion: Meat vs. Rice. American Manhood against Asiatic Coolieism. Which Shall Survive?* United States Senate, 57th Cong., 1st sess., Document no. 137. Washington, D.C.: Government Printing Office, 1902.
Senate Commission on Industrial Relations. *Final Report and Testimony*. Washington, D.C.: Government Printing Office, 1916.


OTHER PUBLISHED PRIMARY SOURCES

Ah-Ying [Qian Xingdun], Editor. *Fan Mei Hua Gong Jin Yue Wenxue Ji*. Beijing: Zhonghua Shu Ju, 1962.
Avison, T. L. *American Dollars Are Hard to Get: The Story of Foreign Exchange Control in Canada*. Toronto: Canadian Association for Adult Education and the Canadian Institute for International Affairs, 1941.
Bass, Oscar Chapman. "In re Lee Him." *British Columbia Law Reports* 15 (1911): 163–165.

Boggs, Theodore. "Oriental Penetration into B.C." *International Forum Review* 1.3 (July 1926): 11–19.
Coolidge, Mary Roberts. *Chinese Immigration*. New York: Henry Holt, 1909.
Hopkins, J. Castell, *The Canadian Annual Review of Public Affairs*, vol. 9, 1909, Toronto: Annual Review Publishing, 1910.
Das, Rajani Kanta. *Hindustani Workers on the Pacific Coast*. Berlin: De Gruyter, 1923.
Dawson, Robert MacGregor. *The Civil Service of Canada*. Oxford: Oxford University Press, 1929.
"'East by West': Our Windows on the Pacific." *Survey Graphic* 56.3 (1 May 1926).
Grant, Madison. *The Rising Tide of Color against White World Supremacy*. New York: Scribner's, 1920.
Holder, Charles Frederick. "The Chinaman in American Politics." *North American Review* 166 (Feb. 1898): 226–240.
Hunter, Gordon, and Oscar Chapman Bass. "*In re Fong Yuk* and the Chinese Immigration Act." *British Columbia Law Reports* 8(1902): 118–121.
Lampman, Peter Second and Oscar Chapman Bass, *British Columbia Law Reports*, "*In re Chin Chee*." 9(1905):400–401.
Liang, Qichao. "Ji Huagong Jinyue." 1905. Reprint in *Fan Mei Hua Gong Jin Yue Wenxue Ji*, edited by A. Ying. Beijing: Zhonghua Shu Ju, 1962.
———. *Xin Dalu Youji*. 1904. Reprint, Taipei, Taiwan: Wenhai Chubanshe, 1967.
Liu, Guangzu. "Yubu Huaqiao Sanshi Nian Fendou Shiji." In *Jianada Yuduoli Zhonghua Huiguan Huaqiao Xuexiao Chengli Liushi Zhounian Jinian Tekan*, 6. Victoria, B.C.: Special Publication, 1960.
McFie, Matthew. *Vancouver Island and British Columbia: Their History, Resources, and Prospects*. London: Longman, Green, and Roberts, 1865.
McInnes, Tom. *Oriental Occupation of British Columbia*. Vancouver: Sun, 1927.
Mears, Eliot Grinell. "The Survey of Race Relations." *Stanford Illustrated Review* (Apr. 1925): 380–381.
Newmeyer, Fred, dir. *Secrets of Chinatown*. Victoria, B.C.: Northern Production, 1935.
Park, Robert. "Human Migration and the Marginal Man." *American Journal of Sociology* 33.6 (1928): 881–893.
———. *The Immigrant Press and Its Control*. 1922. Reprint, Montclair, N.J.: Patterson Smith, 1971.
——— and Ernest W. Burgess. *Introduction to the Science of Sociology*. Chicago: University of Chicago Press, 1921.

Parker, C.W., *Who's Who and Why: A Biographical Dictionary of Men and Women of Canada and Newfoundland*. vols. 6 and 7, 1915–1916. Toronto: International Press, 1914.

Raushenbush, Winifred. "The Great Wall of Chinatown," *Survey Graphic* 56.3 (1 May 1926): 154–158, 221.

Raushenbush, Winifred. "Their Place in the Sun: Japanese Farmers Nine Years after the Land Laws." *Survey Graphic* 56 (1 May 1926): 141–145.

Senkler, E. C. *British Columbia Law Reports*, vol. 25. Victoria, B.C.: Colonist Printing and Publishing for the Law Society of British Columbia, 1919.

Stephen, Alexander Maitland. *War in China . . . What It Means to Canada*. Vancouver: China Aid Council and National Salvation League, 1937.

Stoddard, Lothrop. *The Rising Tide of Color against White World Supremacy*. New York: Scribner's, 1920.

Survey of Race Relations [Eliot G. Mears] *Tentative Findings of the Survey of Race Relations: A Canadian-American Study of the Oriental on the Pacific Coast*. Stanford, Calif.: Survey of Race Relations, Stanford University, 1925.

*Totem*. Vancouver: University of British Columbia, 1927.

Train, Arthur. *Tutt and Mr. Tutt*. New York: Scribner's, 1921.

United Church of Canada. Woman's Missionary Society. *They Came Through: Stories of Chinese Canadians*. Toronto: Literature Dept. and Committee on Missionary Education, United Church of Canada, circa 1940s.

Ward, Hilda Glynn. *The Writing on the Wall*. Vancouver: Sun, 1921.

Wong, Foon Sien. "Riqian zhan shi zhi guan zhi." *Xin Minguo Bao*, ca. 1941–1942.


SECONDARY SOURCES

Adachi, Ken. *The Enemy That Never Was; A History of Japanese Canadians*. Toronto: McClelland and Stewart, 1976.

Anderson, Kay. *Vancouver's Chinatown: Racial Discourse in Canada, 1875–1980*. Montreal: McGill-Queen's University Press, 1991.

Ashworth, Mary. *The Forces Which Shaped Them: A History of Education of Minority Group Children in British Columbia*. Vancouver: New Star, 1979.

Avery, Donald. *Dangerous Foreigners: European Immigrant Workers and Labour Radicalism in Canada, 1896–1932*. Toronto: University of Toronto Press, 1979.

Azuma, Eiichiro. *Between Two Empires: Race, History, and Transnationalism in Japanese America*. New York: Oxford University Press, 2005.

Azzi, Stephen. *Walter Gordon and the Rise of Canadian Nationalism*. Montreal: McGill-Queen's University Press, 1999.

Backhouse, Constance. *Colour-Coded: A Legal History of Racism in Canada, 1900–1950*. Toronto: University of Toronto Press for Osgoode Society for Canadian Legal History, 1999.

———. "Gretta Wong Grant: Canada's First Chinese-Canadian Female Lawyer." *Windsor Yearbook of Access to Justice* 15 (1996): 3–46.

Balla, Steven J., and John R. Wright, "Interest Groups, Advisory Committees, and Congressional Control of the Bureaucracy." *American Journal of Political Science* 45.4 (2001): 799–812.

Bangarth, Stephanie. "'We Are Not Asking You to Open Wide the Gates for Chinese Immigration': The Committee for the Repeal of the Chinese Immigration Act and Early Human Rights Activism in Canada." *Canadian Historical Review* 84.3 (2003): 395–422.

Barman, Jean. *The West beyond the West: A History of British Columbia*. Third Ed. Toronto: University of Toronto Press, 2007.

Bendix, Reinhard. *Max Weber: An Intellectual Portrait, with a New Introduction by Guenther Roth*. Berkeley: University of California Press, 1977.

Berger, Carl. *Sense of Power: Studies in the Ideas of Canadian Imperialism, 1867–1914*. Toronto: University of Toronto Press, 1970.

———. *The Writing of Canadian History: Aspects of English Canadian Historical Writing since 1900*, 2nd ed. Toronto: University of Toronto Press, 1986.

Bodnar, John. *The Transplanted: A History of Immigrants in Urban America*. Bloomington: Indiana University Press, 1987.

Bradwin, Edmund W. *The Bunkhouse Man*. Toronto: University of Toronto, 1972.

Breton, Raymond. *The Governance of Ethnic Communities: Political Structures And Processes in Canada*. New York: Greenwood, 1991.

"A Brief History of the University of British Columbia." University of British Columbia Archives. http://www.library.ubc.ca/archives/hist_ubc.html. Accessed 18 Nov. 2008.

Brockman, Joan. "Exclusionary Tactics: The History of Women and Visible Minorities in the Legal Profession in British Columbia." In *Essays in the History of Canadian Law*, vol. 6, *British Columbia and the Yukon*, edited by Hamar Foster and John McLaren, 508–561. Toronto: University of Toronto Press for the Osgoode Society, 1995.

Brook, Timothy. *Collaboration: Japanese Agents and Local Elites in Wartime China*. Cambridge, Mass.: Harvard University Press, 2005.

Brown, R. Craig, and Ramsay Cook. *Canada, 1896–1921: A Nation Transformed*. Reprint, Toronto: McClelland and Stewart, 1991.

Buchignani, Norman, and Doreen Indra. "*Vanishing Acts: Illegal Immigration in Canada as a Sometime Social Issue.*" In *Illegal Immigration in America*, edited by David W. Haines and Karen E. Rosenblum, 415–450. Santa Barbara, Calif.: Greenwood, 1999.

Buckner, Phillip. *Canada and the British Empire*. New York: Oxford University Press, 2008.

Bumstead, J. M. "1919: The Winnipeg General Strike Reconsidered." *Beaver* 74 (June–July 1994): 3–44.

Calavita, Kitty. "Collisions at the Intersection of Gender, Race, and Class: Enforcing the Chinese Exclusion Laws." *Law and Society Review* 40.2 (2006): 249–281.

Cameron, James D. "Canada's Struggle with Illegal Entry on Its West Coast: The Case of Fred Yoshy and Japanese Migrants Before the Second World War." *BC Studies* 147 (Summer 2005): 37–62.

*Canadian Encyclopedia*. Toronto: Historical Foundation of Canada, 2008. http://www.thecanadianencyclopedia.com/PrinterFriendly.cfm?Params=A1ARTA0001588. Accessed 6 July 2008.

Carroll, John. *A Concise History of Hong Kong*. Lanham, Md.: Rowman and Littlefield, 2007.

Carstairs, Catherine. *Jailed for Possession: Illegal Drug Use, Regulation, and Power in Canada, 1920–1961*. Toronto: University of Toronto Press, 2005.

Carty, R. Kenneth, and W. Peter Ward. "The Making of a Canadian Political Citizenship." In *National Politics and Community in Canada*, edited by Kenneth Carty and W. Peter Ward. Vancouver: University of British Columbia Press, 1986.

Chamberlain, Charles D. *Victory at Home: Manpower and Race in the American South during World War II*. Athens: University of Georgia Press, 2003.

Chan, Anthony. *Gold Mountain: The Chinese in the New World*. Vancouver: New Star, 1988.

———. "'Orientalism' and Image Making: The Sojourner in Canadian History." *Journal of Canadian Ethnic Studies*. 9:3(1981):37–46.

Chan, Sucheng. *Asian Americans: An Interpretive History*. Boston: Twayne, 1991.

Chang, Gordon. "Asian Americans and Politics: Some Perspectives from History." In *Asian Americans and Politics: Perspectives, Experiences, and Prospects*, edited by Gordon Chang. Washington, D.C.: Woodrow Wilson Center Press, 2001.

Chang, Iris. *The Rape of Nanjing: The Forgotten Holocaust of World War II*. New York: Penguin, 1998.

Chen, Shehong. *Being Chinese, Becoming Chinese American*. Champaign: University of Illinois Press, 2006.

Chen, Yong. *Chinese San Francisco, 1850–1943*. Stanford, Calif.: Stanford University Press, 2000.

Chen, Zhuojun, Yuzheng Chen, Jing Li, and Jianyun Huang. *Taishan Xianzhi*. Taicheng, Guangdong: Taishan Shi difang zhi bian zuan weiyuanhui, 1993.

Chew, Kenneth S. Y., and John M. Liu. "Hidden in Plain Sight: Global Labor Force Exchange in the Chinese American Population, 1880–1940." *Population & Development Review* 30.1 (Mar. 2004): 57–78.

Chong, Denise. *The Concubine's Children*. Toronto: Penguin, 1996.

Chow, Tse-tung. *The May Fourth Movement: Intellectual Revolution in Modern China*. Stanford, Calif.: Stanford University Press, 1967.

Chung, Sue Fawn. "The Chinese American Citizens' Alliance: An Effort in Assimilation, 1895–1965." *Chinese America: History and Perspectives* 30 (1988): 3–57.

Cohen, Lizabeth. *Making a New Deal: Industrial Workers in Chicago, 1919–1939*. Cambridge: Cambridge University Press, 1991.

Cole, Richard P., and Gabriel J. Chin. "Emerging from the Margins of Historical Consciousness: Chinese Immigrants and the History of American Law." *Law and History Review* 17.2 (1999): 325–359.

Con, Harry, Ronald J. Con, Graham Johnson, Edgar Wickberg, and William E. Willmott. *From China to Canada: A History of Chinese Communities in Canada*, edited by Edgar Wickberg. Toronto: McClelland and Stewart, 1982.

Creese, Gillian. "Exclusion or Solidarity? Vancouver Workers Confront the Oriental Problem." In *Canadian Working Class History: Selected Readings*, edited by Laurel Sefton McDowell and Ian Radforth. Toronto: Canadian Scholars' Press, 1992.

———. "Working Class Politics, Racism, and Sexism in the Making of a Politically-Divided Working Class in Vancouver, 1900–1939." Ph.D. diss., Carleton University, 1996.

Daniels, Roger. *Coming to America*, 2nd ed. New York: HarperCollins, 2002.

———. "A New Way of Thinking about Old Ways of Thinking." *H-Ethnic* (Oct. 2001). http://www.h-net.org/reviews/showrev.cgi?path=57201014227586. Accessed 4 Aug. 2007.

Davies, Bill. *From Sourdough to Superstore: The Kelly, Douglas Story*. Vancouver: Kelly, Douglas, 1990.

Delgado, Grace Peña, "At Exclusion's Southern Gate: Changing Categories of Race and Class among Chinese *Frontierizos*, 1882–1904." In *Continental Crossroads: Remapping U.S.-Mexico Borderlands History*, edited by Samuel Truett and Elliot Young. Durham, N.C.: Duke University Press, 2004.

Dhami, Singh. *Maluka*, 2nd ed. Patiala, India: Publication Bureau, Punjabi University, 1997.

Dikötter, Frank. *The Discourse of Race in Modern China*. Stanford, Calif.: Stanford University Press, 1992.

———. "Racial Discourse in China: Continuities and Permutations." In *The Construction of Racial Identities in China and Japan*, edited by Frank Dikötter, 12–33. London: Hurst, 1997.

Ding, Loni. *Ancestors in the Americas: Coolies, Sailors, Settlers: Voyage to the New World*. Berkeley, Calif.: Center for Educational Telecommunications, 2001.

Dyzenhaus, David, and Mayo Moran, eds. *Calling Power to Account: Law, Reparations, and the Chinese Canadian Head Tax Case*. Toronto: University of Toronto Press, 2005.

Eastman, Lloyd E. *The Abortive Revolution: China under Nationalist Rule, 1927–1937*. Cambridge, Mass.: Harvard University Press, 1974.

Elections British Columbia and the Legislative Library of British Columbia. "An Electoral History of British Columbia, 1871–1986" (1988). http://www.elections.bc.ca/docs/rpt/1871-1986_ElectoralHistoryofBC.pdf. Accessed 1 July 2009.

Esherick, Joseph W., and Mary Backus Rankin, eds. *Chinese Local Elites and Patterns of Dominance*. Berkeley: University of California Press, 1990.

Farkas, Lani Ah Tye. *Bury My Bones in America: The Saga of a Chinese Family in California, 1852–1996: From San Francisco to the Sierra Gold Mines*. Nevada City, Calif.: Mautz, 1998.

Farquar, Judith B., and James L. Hevia. "Culture and Postwar American Historiography of China." *Positions: East Asia Cultures Critique* 1.2 (Fall 1993): 486–525.

Finkel, Alvin, and Margaret Conrad with Victoria Strong-Boag, ed. *A History of the Canadian Peoples*, vol. 2: *1867 to Present*. Toronto, Ontario: Pearson Education Canada, 2008.

Fitzgerald, John. *Big White Lie: Chinese Australians in White Australia*. Sydney, Australia: University of New South Wales Press, 2007.

Foster, Hamar. "Romance of the Lost: The Role of Tom McInnes in the History of the British Columbia Land Question." In *Essays in the History of Canadian Law in Honour of R. C. B. Risk*, edited by Jim Phillips and G. Blaine Baker, 171–212. Toronto: University of Toronto Press, 1999.

Francis, Daniel. *National Dreams: Myth, Memory, and Canadian History*. Vancouver: Arsenal Pulp, 2002.

Friday, Chris. *Organizing Asian American Labor: The Pacific Coast Canned Salmon Industry, 1870–1942*. Philadelphia: Temple University Press, 1995.

Friesen, Darren. "Canada's Other Newcomers: Aboriginal Interactions with People from the Pacific." Master's thesis, University of Saskatchewan, 2006.

Fritz, Christian. "A Nineteenth Century 'Habeas Corpus Mill': The Chinese before the Federal Courts of California." In *Chinese Immigrants and American Law*, edited by Charles McClain, 55–80. New York: Garland, 1994.

Gabaccia, Donna R. "Is Everywhere Nowhere? Nomads, Nations, and the Immigrant Paradigm of United States History." *Journal of American History* 86.3 (1999): 1115–1134.

Gibbons, Alan O. "Foreign Exchange Control in Canada, 1939–51." *Canadian Journal of Economics and Political Science/Revue canadienne d'Economique et de Science politique* 19.1 (Feb. 1953): 35–54.

Gjerde, Jon. "New Growth on Old Vines—The State of the Field: The Social History of Immigration to and Ethnicity in the United States." *Journal of American Ethnic History* 18.4 (1999): 40–65.

Goodman, Bryna. *Native Place, City, and Nation: Regional Networks and Identities in Shanghai, 1853–1937*. Stanford, Calif.: Stanford University Press, 1995.

Gordon, Alan. "Patronage, Etiquette, and the Science of Connection: Edmund Bristol and Political Management, 1911–21." *Canadian Historical Review* 80.1 (Mar. 1999): 1–31.

Granatstein, J. L., and J. M. Hitsman. *Broken Promises: A History of Conscription in Canada*. Toronto: Oxford University Press, 1997.

Gray, Stephen. "Woodworkers and Legitimacy: The IWA in Canada, 1937–1957." Ph.D. diss., Simon Fraser University, 1989.

Greene, Victor R. *American Immigrant Leaders, 1800–1910: Marginality and Identity*. Baltimore, Md.: Johns Hopkins University Press, 1987.

Gross, Neil. *Richard Rorty: The Making of an American Philosopher*. Chicago: University of Chicago Press, 2008.

Gruen, Erich S. *Roman Politics and the Criminal Courts, 149–78 B.C.* Cambridge, Mass.: Harvard University Press, 1968.

Gutiérrez, David G., and Pierrette Hondagneu-Sotelo. "Introduction: Nation and Migration." *American Quarterly* 60.1 (Sept. 2008): 503–521.

Hamilton, Douglas. *Sobering Dilemma: A History of Prohibition in British Columbia*. Vancouver: Ronsdale, 2004.

Hansen, Marcus Lee. *Mingling of the Canadian and American Peoples*. New Haven, Conn.: Yale University, 1941; reprint, New York: Arno, 1971.

Hansen, Miriam. "Foreword." In *Public Sphere and Experience: Towards an Analysis of the Bourgeois and Proletarian Public Sphere*, edited by Oskar Negt and Alexander Kluge, ix–xli. Minneapolis: University of Minnesota Press, 1993.

Harney, Robert. "The Commerce of Migration." In his *If One Were to Write a History*, edited by Pierre Anctil and Bruno Ramirez, 19–36. Toronto: Multicultural History Society of Ontario, 1991.

———. "The Padrone and the Immigrant." *Canadian Review of American Studies* 5.2 (1974): 101–118.

Helly, Denise. *Les Chinois à Montréal, 1877–1951*. Quebec: Institut Québécois de Recherche sur la Culture, 1987.

Higham, John. "Introduction: The Forms of Ethnic Leadership." In *Ethnic Leadership in America*, edited by John Higham, 1–18. Baltimore, Md.: Johns Hopkins University Press, 1978.

Hirata, Lucie Cheng. "Free, Indentured, Enslaved: Chinese Prostitutes in Nineteenth Century America." *Signs: Journal of Women in Culture & Society*. 1979 5(1):3–29.

Hitsman, J. M. *Broken Promises: A History of Conscription in Canada*. Toronto: Oxford University Press, 1977

Hodgetts, J. E., William McCloskey, Reginald Whitaker, and V. Seymour Wilson. *The Biography of an Institution: The Civil Service Commission of Canada, 1908–1967*. Montreal: McGill-Queen's University Press, 1972.

Ho-Jung, Moon. *Coolies and Cane*. Baltimore, Md.: Johns Hopkins University Press, 2006.

Hsu, Madeline. *Dreaming of Gold, Dreaming of Home: Transnationalism and Migration between the United States and South China, 1882–1943*. Stanford, Calif.: Stanford University Press, 2000.

———. "Transnationalism and Asian American Studies as a Migration-Centered Project." *Journal of Asian American Studies* (June 2008): 185–197.

Huang, Belinda. "Gender, Race, and Power: The Chinese in Canada, 1920–1950." Master's thesis, McGill University, 1998.

Huang, Evelyn, with Lawrence Jeffery, eds. and comps. *Chinese Canadians: Voices from a Community*. Toronto: Douglas and McIntyre, 1992.

Huang, Kunzhang and Jinping Wu. *Huaqiao, Huaren Shi*. Guangzhou, China: Guangdong Gaodeng Jiaoyu Chubanshe, 2001.

Huttenback, Robert A. *Racism and Empire: White Settlers and Colored Immigrants in the British Self-Governing Colonies, 1830–1910*. Ithaca, N.Y.: Cornell University Press, 1976.

Ignatieff, Michael. *The Rights Revolution*, 2nd ed. Toronto: House of Anansi, 2007.

Innis, Harold Adams. *The Japanese Canadians*. Toronto: University of Toronto Press for Canadian National Committee for Mental Hygiene, Canadian Institute of International Affairs, 1938.

Ito, Kazuo. *Issei: A History of Japanese Immigrants in North America*, translated by Shinichiro Nakamura and Jean S. Gerard. Seattle, Wash.: Japanese Community Services, 1973.

Jagpal, Sarjeet Singh. *Becoming Canadians: Pioneer Sikhs in Their Own Words*. Madeira Park, B.C.: Habour, 1994.

Jiang, Qinghua. "Daonian jin zhi xianzhe Huang Wenfu xiansheng." In *Memorial Volume of Foon Sien Wong*. Vancouver: Privately printed, 1970.

Jupp, James. *The Australian People: An Encyclopedia of the Nation, Its People, and Their Origins*. Cambridge: Cambridge University Press, 2001.

Kealey, Gregory S. "The Canadian State's Attempts to Manage Class Conflict." In *Workers and Canadian History*, edited by Gregory S. Kealey, 433–437. Montreal: McGill-Queen's University Press, 1995.

———. "1919: The Canadian Labour Revolt." In *Workers and Canadian History*, edited by Gregory S. Kealey, 289–326. Montreal: McGill-Queen's University Press, 1995.

Kealey, Gregory S., and Douglas Cruikshank. "Strikes in Canada, 1891–1950." In *Workers and Canadian History*, edited by Gregory S. Kealey, 375–378. Montreal: McGill-Queen's University Press, 1995.

Keshen, Jeffrey A. *Saints, Sinners, and Soldiers: Canada's Second World War*. Vancouver: University of British Columbia Press, 2004.

Keyssar, Alexander. *The Right to Vote: The Contested History of Democracy in America*. New York: Basic, 2001.

Kim, Hyung-chan, and Richard W. Markov. "The Chinese Exclusion Laws and Smuggling Chinese into Whatcom County, Washington, 1890–1900." *Annals of the Chinese Historical Society of the Pacific Northwest* (1983): 16–30.

Kivisto, Peter. "What Is the Canonical Theory of Assimilation? Robert Park and His Predecessors." *Journal of the History of Behavioral Sciences* 40.2 (2004): 149–163.

Kiyama, Henry Yoshitaka. *The Four Immigrants Manga: A Japanese Experience in San Francisco, 1904–1924*, translated by Frederik L. Schodt. Berkeley, Calif.: Stone Bridge, 1999.

Kordan, Bohdan Stephan. "Ethnicity, the State, and War: Canada and the Ukrainian Problem: A Study in Statecraft." Ph.D. diss., Arizona State University, 1988.

Kuhn, Philip A. *Chinese among Others: Emigration in Modern Times*. Lanham, Md.: Rowman and Littlefield, 2008.

Kwong, Peter. *Chinatown*. New York: New York University Press, 1981.

———. *Chinatown, New York: Labor and Politics, 1930*. New York: Monthly Review Press, 1980.

——— & Dušanka Miščević. *Chinese America: The Untold Story of America's Oldest New Community*. New York: New Press, 2005.

Lai, David. "A 'Prison' for Chinese Immigrants." *Asianadian* 2.4 (1980): 16–18.

Lai, David Chuenyan. "The Issue of Discrimination in Education in Victoria, 1901–1923." *Canadian Ethnic Studies* 19.3 (1987): 47–67.

Lai, Him Mark. *Becoming Chinese American*. Lanham, Md.: AltaMira, 2004.

Lambertson, Ross. "The Black, Brown, White and Red Blues: The Beating of Clarence Clemons." *Canadian Historical Review* 85.4 (2004): 755–757.

———. *Repression and Resistance: Canadian Human Rights Activists, 1930–1960*. Toronto: University of Toronto Press, 2004.
Larson, Jane Leung. "Articulating China's First Mass Movement: Kang Youwei, Liang Qichao, the Baohuanghui, and the 1905 Anti-American Boycott." *Twentieth-Century China* 33.1 (2007): 4–26.
———. "New Source Materials on Kang Youwei and the Baohuanghui: The Tan Zhangxiao (Tom Leung) Collection of Letters and Documents at UCLA's East Asian Library." *Chinese America: History and Perspectives* (1993): 151–198.
Lee, Carol F. "The Road to Enfranchisement: Chinese and Japanese in British Columbia." *BC Studies* 30 (Summer 1976): 44–76.
Lee, Erika. *At America's Gates: Chinese Immigration during the Exclusion Era, 1882–1943*. Chapel Hill: University of North Carolina Press, 2007.
———. "Enforcing the Borders: Chinese Exclusion along U.S. Borders with Canada and Mexico, 1882–1924." *Journal of American History* 89.1 (June 2002): 54–86.
———. "Hemispheric Orientalism and the 1907 Pacific Coast Race Riots." *Amerasia Journal* 33.2 (2007): 19–47.
———. "Orientalisms in the Americas: A Hemispheric Approach to Asian American History." *Journal of Asian American Studies* 8:3 (2005): 235–256.
Lee, Jack Wai Yen, "Lee Mong Kow (1863–1924)" http://members.shaw.ca/leesassociationvictoria/mongkow.htm. Accessed 26 October 2006.
Leier, Mark. *Red Flags and Red Tape: The Making of a Labour Bureaucracy*. Toronto: University of Toronto Press, 1995.
Li Donghai. *Jianada Huaqiao Shi (A History of Chinese in Canada)*. [Yangmingshan]: Zhonghua da dian bian yin hui [Hua gang shu ju zong jing xiao, 1967].
Li, Julia Ningyu. *Canadian Steel, Chinese Grit*. Shenzhen, China: Shenzhen Baofeng, 2000.
Li, Peter S. *The Chinese in Canada*. New York: Oxford University Press, 1998.
Lim, Sing. *West Coast Chinese Boy*. Montreal: Tundra, 1979.
Ling, Huping. *Chinese St. Louis*. Philadelphia: Temple University Press, 2004.
Liu, Quan. *Guangdong Huaqiao Huaren Shi*. Guangzhou: Guangdong Remin Chubanshe, 2002.
Lo, Karl, and Him Mark Lai. *Chinese Newspapers Published in North America, 1854–1975*. Washington, D.C.: Center for Chinese Research Materials, Association of Research Libraries, 1977.
Louie, Emma Woo. *Chinese American Names: Tradition and Transition*. London: McFarland, 1998.
Low, Philip C. P. *Memories of Cumberland Chinatown*. Vancouver: Low, 1993.

Low, Victor. *The Unimpressible Race: A Century of Educational Struggle by the Chinese in San Francisco.* San Francisco: East West, 1982.

Ma, L. Eve Armentrout. *Revolutionaries, Monarchists, and Chinatowns: Chinese Politics in the Americas and the 1911 Revolution.* Honolulu: University of Hawaii Press, 1990.

Macauley, Melissa. *Social Power and Legal Culture: Litigation Masters in Late Imperial China.* Stanford, Calif.: Stanford University Press, 1998.

Macdonald, Ian, and Betty O'Keefe. *Canadian Holy War: A Story of Clans, Tongs, Murder, and Bigotry.* Surrey, B.C.: Heritage House, 2000.

Macdonald, Robert. *Making Vancouver, 1863–1913.* Vancouver: University of British Columbia Press, 1996.

Manela, Erez. *The Wilsonian Moment: Self-Determination and the Origins of Anti-Colonial Nationalism.* New York: Oxford University Press, 2007.

Mar, Lisa R. "Beyond Being Others: Chinese Canadians as National History." *BC Studies* 156–157 (Winter 2007–Spring 2008): 13–36.

———. "From Diaspora to North American Civil Rights: Chinese Canadian Ideas, Identities and Brokers in Vancouver, British Columbia, 1924–1960." Ph.D. diss., University of Toronto, 2002.

———. "The Mar-Sue Family's Quest for Survival in British Columbia, 1914–1949." Bachelor's honors thesis, Stanford University, 1992.

———. "The Tale of Lin Tee: Madness, Family Violence and Lindsay's Anti-Chinese Riot of 1919." In *Sisters or Strangers? Immigrant Women, Minority Women and the Racialized Other*, edited by Franca Iacovetta, Frances Swyripa, and Marlene Epp, 108–129. Toronto: University of Toronto Press, 2004.

———. "Yellow Peril: Images of Chinese Men with White Women in Toronto." Paper presented at the Association for Asian American Studies national conference, Ann Arbor, Mich., Apr. 1994.

Marlatt, Daphne, and Carole Itter, eds. *Opening Doors: Vancouver's East End.* Victoria, B.C.: Aural History Program, Province of British Columbia, 1979.

Marquis, Greg. "Vancouver Vice: Police and the Negotiation of Morality, 1904–1935." In *Essays on the History of Canadian Law*, vol. 6: *British Columbia and the Yukon*, edited by Hamar Foster and John McLaren, 242–273. Toronto: University of Toronto Press, 1995.

Matthews, Fred H. "The Revolt against Americanism: Cultural Pluralism and Cultural Relativism as an Ideology of Liberation." *Canadian Review of American Studies* 1 (1970): 4–31.

Mawani, Renisa. "Cross-Racial Encounters and Juridical Truths: (Dis) Aggregating Race in British Columbia's Contact Zone." *BC Studies* 156–157 (Winter 2007–Spring 2008): 141–161.

Maxwell, Judy. "A Cause Worth Fighting For: Chinese Canadians Debate Their Participation in the Second World War." Master's thesis, University of British Columbia, 2005.

McCaffery, Peter. "Style, Structure, and Institutionalization of Machine Politics: Philadelphia, 1867–1933." *Journal of Interdisciplinary History* 22.3 (Winter 1992): 435–452.

McCardle, Bennett. "The Records of Chinese Immigration at the National Archives of Canada." *Canadian Ethnic Studies* 19.3 (1987): 163–171.

McClain, Charles J. *In Search of Equality: The Chinese Struggle against Discrimination in Nineteenth-Century America*. Berkeley: University of California Press, 1994.

——— & Laurene Wu McClain, "The Chinese Contribution to the Development of American Law" In *Entry Denied: Exclusion and the Chinese Community in America, 1882–1943* (Philadelphia, Temple, 1991), edited by Sucheng Chan, 3-24.

McIllwain, Jeffrey Scott. *Organizing Crime in Chinatown: Race and Racketeering in New York City, 1890–1910*. Jefferson, N.C.: McFarland, 2004.

McInnis, Peter Stuart. *Harnessing Labor Confrontation: Shaping the Postwar Settlement in Canada, 1943–1950*. Toronto: University of Toronto Press, 2002.

McKee, Delber. *Chinese Exclusion versus the Open Door Policy, 1900–1906: Clashes over China Policy in the Roosevelt Era*. Detroit, Mich.: Wayne State University Press, 1977.

McKeown, Adam. *Chinese Migrant Networks and Cultural Change*. Chicago: University of Chicago Press, 2001.

———. *Melancholy Order: Asian Migration and the Globalization of Borders*. New York: Columbia University Press, 2008.

———. "Ritualization of Regulation: The Enforcement of Chinese Exclusion in the United States and China." *American Historical Review* 108.2 (2003): 377–403.

McLaren, Angus. *Our Own Master Race: Eugenics in Canada, 1885–1945*. Toronto: McClelland and Stewart, 1990.

McLaren, John. "Race and the Criminal Justice System in British Columbia, 1892–1920: Constructing Chinese Crimes." In *Essays in the History of Canadian Law in Honour of R. C. B. Risk*, vol. 8, edited by G. Blaine Baker and Jim Phillips, 398–442. Toronto: University of Toronto Press for the Osgoode Society for Canadian Legal History, 1999.

Meehan, John. *The Dominion and the Rising Sun*. Vancouver: University of British Columbia Press, 2004.

Miki, Roy. *Redress: Inside the Japanese Canadian Call for Justice*. Vancouver: Raincoast, 2005.

Mooney, Ralph James. "Matthew Deady and Federal Judicial Response to Racism in the Early West." In *Chinese Immigrants and American Law*, edited by Charles McClain, 241–317. New York: Garland, 1994.

Morales, Catalina Velázquez, "Differencias Politicas entre Los Immigrantes Chinos del Noroeste de Mexico (1920–1930): El Caso de Francisco L. Yuen." *Historia Mexicana* 55.2 (2005): 461–512.

Morley, Alan. *Vancouver: From Milltown to Metropolis*. Vancouver: Mitchell, 1961.

Morton, James W. *In the Sea of Sterile Mountains: The Chinese in British Columbia*. Vancouver: Douglas, 1974.

Morton, Suzanne. *At Odds: Gambling and Canadians, 1919–1969*. Toronto: University of Toronto Press, 2003.

Mosher, Clayton James. *Discrimination and Denial: Systemic Racism in Ontario's Legal and Criminal Justice Systems, 1892–1961*. Toronto: University of Toronto Press, 1998.

Mount, Graeme S. *Canada's Enemies: Spies and Spying in the Peaceable Kingdom*. Toronto: Dundurn, 1993.

Nanaimo Community Archives, Malaspina-University College, and Nanaimo Community Heritage Commission. "Nanaimo Chinatowns [*sic*] Project: Introduction." http://chinatown.mala.bc.ca/introduction.asp Accessed 9 April 2010.

Nasaw, David. *Schooled to Order: A Social History of Public Schooling in the United States*. New York: Oxford University Press, 1981.

Newell, Diane. "Beyond Chinatown: Overseas Chinese Intermediaries on the Multiethnic North-American Pacific Coast in the Age of Financial Capital." In *Finance, Intermediaries, and Economic Development*, edited by Stanley L. Engerman, Philip T. Hoffman, Jean-Laurent Rosenthal, and Kenneth L. Sokoloff, 247–271. New York: Cambridge University Press, 2003.

Ng, James. "Chinese in New Zealand, Past and Present." *Amity Center Publishing Project* (Oct. 2001). http://www.stevenyoung.co.nz/The-Chinese-in-New-Zealand/History-of-Chinese-in-NewZealand/Chinese-settlement-in-NZ-past-and-present.html. Accessed 2 July 2008.

Ng, Wing Chung. *The Chinese in Vancouver, 1945–80: The Pursuit of Identity and Power*. Vancouver: University of British Columbia Press, 1999.

Ngai, Mae. "History as Law and Life: *Tape v. Hurley* and the Origins of the Chinese American Middle Class." In *Chinese Americans and the Politics of Race and Culture*, edited by Sucheng Chan and Madeline Hsu, 62–90. Philadelphia: Temple University Press, 2008.

———. "Transnationalism and the Transformation of the 'Other': Response to the Presidential Address." *American Quarterly* 57.1 (2005): 59–65.

Nicol, Eric. *Vancouver*. Revised Edition. Toronto: Doubleday Canada, 1978.

Oiwa, Keibo, and Joy Kogawa, eds. *Stone Voices: Wartime Writings of Japanese Canadian Issei*. Montreal: Vehicule, 1991.

Okihiro, Gary. *Margins and Mainstreams: Asians in American History and Culture*, 31–63. Seattle: University of Washington Press, 1994.

———. *Teaching Asian American History*. Washington, D.C.: American Historical Association, 1997.

Oropeza, Gonzáles. "La Discriminación en México: El Caso de los Nacionales Chinos." In Cuademons del Instituto de Investigaciones Juridicas. *La Problemática del Racismo en los Umbrales del Siglo XXI*, Proceedings of SixthJornadas Lascasianas Conference, eds. José Emilio Rolando & Ordó ez Cifuentes, 47–56. Ciudad Universitaria, Mexico: Instituto de Invetigaciones Jurídicas, Universidad Nacional Autónoma de México, 1997.

Osborne, Jari. *Unwanted Soldiers*. Montreal: National Film Board of Canada, 1999.

Palantzas, Thomas. "A Chicago Reprise in the Champagne Years of Canadian Sociology, 1935–1964." Master's thesis, Lakehead University, 1994.

Patrias, Carmela. *Patriots and Proletarians: Politicizing Hungarian Immigrants in Interwar Canada*. Montreal: McGill Queen's University Press, 1994.

———. "Race, Employment Discrimination, and State Complicity in Wartime Canada, 1939–1945." *Labour/Le Travail* 59 (2007): 9–42.

Peck, Gunther. *Reinventing Free Labor: Padrones and Immigrant Workers in the North American West, 1880–1930*. New York: Cambridge University Press, 2000.

Persons, Stow. *Ethnic Studies at Chicago, 1905–1945*. Champaign: University of Illinois Press, 1987.

Pfaelzer, Jean. *Driven Out: The Forgotten War against Chinese Americans*. New York: Random House, 2007.

Powell, James. "A History of the Canadian Dollar." *Bank of Canada* (Dec. 2005), 53–55. www.bankofcanada.ca/en/dollar_book/dollar_book.fspdf. Accessed 13 Feb. 2009.

Raushenbush, Winifred. *Robert E. Park: Biography of a Sociologist*. Durham, N.C.: Duke University Press, 1979.

Ray, Arthur J. *I Have Lived Here since the World Began: An Illustrated History of Canada's Native People*. Toronto: Key Porter, 1998.

Reimer, Derek, ed. *Opening Doors: Vancouver's East End*. Victoria, B.C.: Provincial Archives of British Columbia, 1979.

Ren, Ronkang. "Canadian Trade Commissioners in Shanghai: Early Canada-China Trade Relations, 1908–41." Ph.D. diss., Carleton University, 1992.

Richter, Daniel K. "Cultural Brokers and Intercultural Politics: New York–Iroquois Relations, 1664–1701." *Journal of American History* 75.1 (1988): 40–67.

Roberts, Barbara. "Shovelling out the 'Mutinous': Political Deportation in Canada before 1936." *Labour/Le Travail* (Autumn 1986): 77–110.

Rowe, Allan. "'The Mysterious Oriental Mind': Ethnic Surveillance and the Chinese in Canada during the Great War." *Canadian Ethnic Studies* 36.1 (2004): 48–70.

Roy, Patricia E. *The Oriental Question: Consolidating a White Man's Province, 1914–1941.* Vancouver: University of British Columbia Press, 2003.

———. "The Soldiers Canada Didn't Want: Her Chinese and Japanese Citizens." *Canadian Historical Review* 49 (1978): 341–358.

———. *The Triumph of Citizenship: The Chinese and Japanese in Canada, 1941–67.* Vancouver: University of British Columbia Press, 2007.

———. *Vancouver: An Illustrated History.* Toronto: Lorimer, 1980.

———. *A White Man's Province: British Columbia Politicians and Chinese and Japanese Immigrants, 1858–1914.* Vancouver: University of British Columbia Press, 1989.

Rumbaut, Rubén G. "Assimilation and Its Discontents: Ironies and Paradoxes." In *The Handbook of International Migration: The American Experience*, edited by Charles Hirschman, Philip Kasinitz, and Josh DeWind, 171–195. New York: Russell Sage Foundation, 1999.

Salyer, Lucy E. *Laws Harsh as Tigers: Chinese Immigrants and the Shaping of Modern Immigration Law.* Chapel Hill: University of North Carolina Press, 1995.

Sangster, Joan. *Dreaming of What Might Be: Women on the Canadian Left, 1920–1950.* Toronto: McClelland and Stewart, 1989.

Schiller, Nina Glick. "Transmigrants and Nation-States: Something Old and Something New in the U.S. Immigrant Experience." In *The Handbook of International Migration*, edited by Charles Hirschman, Philip Kasinitz, and Josh DeWind, 94–119. New York: Russell Sage Foundation, 1999.

Seager, Allen, and David Roth. "British Columbia and the Mining West: Ghost of a Chance." In *The Workers' Revolt in Canada 1917–1925*, edited by Craig Heron, 231–267. Toronto: University of Toronto Press, 1998.

Shore, Marlene. *The Science of Social Redemption: McGill, the Chicago School, and the Origins of Social Research in Canada.* Toronto: University of Toronto Press, 1987.

Siu, Helen F. *Agents and Victims in South China: Accomplices in Rural Revolution.* New Haven, Conn.: Yale University Press, 1989.

Siu, Lok. *Memories of a Future Home: Diasporic Citizenship of Chinese in Panama.* Stanford, Calif.: Stanford University Press, 2005.

Smith, David E. "National Political Parties and the Growth of National Political Community." In *National Politics and Community in Canada*, edited by Kenneth Carty and W. Peter Ward, 87–91. Vancouver: University of British Columbia Press, 1986.

Smith, Robert Courtenay. *Mexican New York: Transnational Lives of New Immigrants*. Berkeley: University of California Press, 2006.

Snyder, Peter Z. "Neighborhood Gatekeepers in the Process of Urban Adaptation: Cross-Ethnic Commonalities." *Urban Anthropology* 5.1 (1976): 35–52.

Song, Jiaheng and Linfu Dong. *Zhongguo yu Jianada: Zhong Jia Guanxi de Lishi Huigu*. 1st Edition. Jinan, China: Qi lu shu she, 1993.

Stanley, Timothy J. "Bringing Anti-Racism into Historical Explanation: The Victoria Chinese Students' Strike of 1922–3 Revisited." *Canadian Historical Association Journal* 13 (2002): 141–165.

———. "By the Side of Other Canadians: The Locally Born and the Invention of Chinese Canadians." *BC Studies* 156–157 (Winter 2007–Spring 2008): 109–139.

———. " 'Chinamen, Wherever We Go': Chinese Nationalism and Guangdong Merchants in British Columbia, 1871–1911." *Canadian Historical Review* 77.4 (Dec. 1996): 475–503.

———. "Defining the Chinese Other: White Supremacy, Schooling, and Social Structure in British Columbia." Ph.D. diss., University of British Columbia, 1991.

———. "Lew, David Hung Chang," in *Dictionary of Canadian Biography Online*, Vol. 15. Edited by Ramsay Cook and Réal Bélanger. Toronto and Laval, Canada: University of Toronto Press and University of Laval Press, 2005. http://tinyurl.com/yftzqa4 Accessed 5 Feb. 2009.

———. "Schooling, White Supremacy, and the Formation of a Chinese Merchant Public in British Columbia." *BC Studies* 107 (1995): 3–29.

———. "White Supremacy, Chinese Schooling, and School Segregation in Victoria: The Case of the Chinese Students' Strike, 1922–1923." *Historical Studies in Education* 2.2 (1990): 287–305.

Starkins, Edward. *Who Killed Janet Smith? The 1924 Vancouver Killing That Remains Canada's Most Intriguing Unsolved Murder*. Toronto: Macmillan, 1984.

Sterne, Evelyn Savidge. "Beyond the Boss: Immigration and American Political Culture from 1880 to 1940." In *E Pluribus Unum? Contemporary and Historical Perspectives on Immigrant Political Incorporation*, edited by Gary Gerstle and John Mollenkopf, 33–66. New York: Russell Sage Foundation, 2001.

Stevens, Todd. "Brokers between Worlds: Chinese Merchants and Legal Culture in the Pacific Northwest, 1852–1925." Ph.D. diss., Princeton University, 2003.

Stevenson, Michael. *Canada's Greatest Wartime Muddle: National Selective Service and the Mobilization of Human Resources during World War II*. Montreal: McGill-Queen's University Press, 2001.

Stevenson, Michael. "The Mobilisation of Native Canadians during the Second World War." *Journal of the Canadian Historical Association* 7 (1996): 205–226.

Sunahara, Ann Gomer. *The Politics of Racism: The Uprooting of Japanese Canadians during the Second World War.* Toronto: Lorimer, 1981.

Szonyi, Michael. "Mothers, Sons, and Lovers: Fidelity and Frugality in the Overseas Chinese Divided Family before 1949." *Journal of Chinese Overseas* 1.1 (May 2005): 43–64.

Takahashi, Genshichi. "Footsteps: Autobiography of a Socialist." In *Stone Voices: Wartime Writings of Japanese Canadian Issei*, edited by Keibo Oiwa and Joy Kogawa. Montreal: Vehicule, 1991.

Takaki, Ronald. *Strangers from a Different Shore: A History of Asian Americans.* Boston: Back Bay, 1998.

Thomas, William, Florian Znaniecki, and Eli Zaretsky, eds. *The Polish Peasant in Europe and America.* Champaign: University of Illinois Press, 1996.

Torrance, Judy Margaret Curtis. *Public Violence in Canada, 1867–1982.* Montreal: McGill-Queen's University Press, 1988.

Toy, Eckard. "Whose Frontier? The Survey of Race Relations on the Pacific Coast in the 1920s." *Oregon Historical Quarterly* 107.1 (Spring 2006). http://www.historycooperative.org/journals/ohq/107.1/toy.html. Accessed 19 Nov. 2008.

Tsai, Jung-Fang. *Hong Kong in Chinese History: Community and Social Unrest in the British Colony, 1842–1913.* New York: Columbia University Press, 1993.

Tsang, Steve, and Steve Yui-Sang. *A Modern History of Hong Kong.* London: Tauris, 2007.

Van Dieren, The Response of the WMS to the Immigration of Asian Women, 1888–1942." *Not Just Pin Money: Selected Essays on the History of Women's Work in British Columbia.* Edited by Barbara K. Latham and Roberta J. Pazdro, 79–97. Victoria, Canada: Camosun College, 1984.

Vedder, R. K., and L. E. Galloway. "Settlement Patterns of Canadian Immigrants in the United States." *Canadian Journal of Economics/Revue Canadienne d'Economique* 3.3 (Aug. 1970): 476–486.

Wai-Man, Lee. *Portraits of a Challenge: An Illustrated History of Chinese Canadians.* Toronto: Council of Chinese Canadians of Ontario, 1984.

Waite, Peter. "Between Three Oceans: Challenges of a Continental Destiny (1840–1900)." In *Illustrated History of Canada*, edited by Craig Brown, 281–325. Toronto: Key Porter, 1997.

Walker, James W. St. G. *Race, Rights and the Law in the Supreme Court of Canada.* Waterloo, Ont.: Wilfrid Laurier University Press for the Osgoode Society for Canadian Legal History, 1997.

Wang, Guanhua. *In Search of Justice: The 1905-1906 Chinese Anti-American Boycott*. Cambridge, Mass.: Harvard University Press for Harvard University Asia Center, 2001.

Wang, Jiwu. *"His Dominion and the Yellow Peril": Protestant Missions to Chinese Immigrants in Canada, 1859-1967*. Waterloo, Ont.: Wilfrid Laurier Press for the Canadian Corporation for Studies in Religion, 2006.

Ward, W. Peter. *White Canada Forever: Popular Attitudes and Public Policy toward Orientals in British Columbia*, 2nd ed. Montreal: McGill-Queen's University Press, 1990.

Watts, Alfred. *History of the Legal Profession in British Columbia*. Vancouver: Law Society of British Columbia, 1984.

Whitaker, Reginald. *The Government Party: Organizing and Financing the Liberal Party of Canada, 1930-1958*. Toronto: University of Toronto Press, 1977.

Whynot, I. C. "Old Stamping Grounds." *Canadian Banker* 99.4 (July-Aug. 1992).

Williams, Michael. "Hong Kong and the Pearl River Delta *Qiaoxiang*." *Modern Asian Studies* 38.2 (2004): 276-277.

Wolf, Eric R. "Aspects of Group Relations in a Complex Society: Mexico." *American Anthropologist* 58.6 (1956): 1005-1078.

Wong, Foon Sien. "The Chinese." In *Strangers Entertained: A History of Ethnic Groups in British Columbia*, edited by John Norris, 209-219. Vancouver: Evergreen, 1971.

Wong, K. Scott. *Americans First: Chinese Americans and the Second World War*. Cambridge, Mass.: Harvard University Press, 2005.

Wong, Larry. "The Life and Times of Foon Sien." *British Columbia History* 38.3 (2005): 6-8.

Wong, Marie Rose. *Sweet Cakes, Long Journey: The Chinatowns of Portland, Oregon*. Seattle: University of Washington Press, 2004.

Wong, Marjorie. *The Dragon and the Maple Leaf: Chinese Canadians in the Second World War*. London: Pirie, 1994.

Wong, Sin Kiong. *China's Anti-American Boycott Movement in 1905: A Study in Urban Protest*. New York: Lang, 2002.

Woods, Lawrence T. "John Nelson (1873-1936) and the Origins of Canadian Participation in APEC." Institute of International Relations, University of British Columbia. Working Paper no. 18 (Oct. 1997).

Woods, M. "Rethinking Elites." *Environment and Planning A* 30.12 (Dec. 1998): 2010-2019.

Worden, Robert Leo. "A Chinese Reformer in Exile: The North American Phase of the Travels of K'ang Yu-Wei, 1899-1909." Ph.D. diss., Georgetown University, 1972.

Wynne, Robert. *Reaction to Chinese in British Columbia and the Pacific Northwest, 1850–1910*. New York: Arno, 1978.

Xiao-Planes, Xiaohong. "La Construction du politique dans la China du début du XXe siècle. L'action des élites locales du Jiangsu." *Annales* 55.6 (2000): 1201–1227.

Ye, Weli. *Seeking Modernity in China's Name: Chinese Students in the United States*. Stanford, Calif.: Stanford University Press, 2001.

Yee, Paul. "The Chinese in British Columbia's Salmon Canning Industry." In *Inalienable Rice*, edited by Garrick Chu et al., 9–11. Vancouver: Powell Street Revue and Chinese Canadian Writer's Workshop, 1979.

Yee, Paul Richard. *Chinatown: An Illustrated History of the Chinese Communities of Victoria, Vancouver, Calgary, Edmonton, Winnipeg, Toronto, Montreal, and Halifax*. Toronto: Lorimer, 2005.

———. "Chinese Business in Vancouver, 1886–1914." Master's thesis, University of British Columbia, 1983.

———. *Saltwater City: An Illustrated History of Chinese in Vancouver*. Vancouver: Douglas and McIntyre, 1988.

Yeh, Wen-Hsin. *Provincial Passages: Culture, Space, and the Origins of Chinese Communism*. Berkeley: University of California Press, 1996.

Young, Louise. "Rethinking Race for Manchukuo: Self and Other in the Colonial Context." In *The Construction of Racial Identities in China and Japan*, edited by Frank Dikötter, 158–176. London: Hurst, 1997.

Yu, Henry. *Thinking Orientals: Migration, Contact, and Exoticism in Modern America*. New York: Oxford University Press, 2001.

Yu, Renqiu. *To Save China, to Save Ourselves: The Chinese Hand Laundry Alliance of New York*. Philadelphia: Temple University Press, 1995.

Yun, Lisa. *The Coolie Speaks: Chinese Indentures, Laborers, and African Slaves in Cuba*. Philadelphia: Temple University Press, 2008.

Yung, Judy. *Unbound Feet: A Social History of Chinese Women in San Francisco*. Berkeley: University of California, 1995.

Zucchi, John E. *Italians in Toronto: Development of a National Identity, 1875–1935*. Montreal: McGill-Queen's University Press, 1988.

INDEX

Alternative public sphere, 4, 67–68, 89, 105, 132
American Federation of Labor (AFL), 55
Americanization. *See* Assimilation
Americas, 12, 18, 28, 65, 133. *See also* Transnationalism; Hemispheric History
Angel Island Immigration Station, 31
Anti-Asian movements, 5, 7, 18, 22, 23, 31–32, 70–71, 80–82, 85. *See also* anti-Chinese movements; Asiatic Exclusion League
Anti-Chinese movements, 6, 31–32, 55, 65, 70–71, 90. *See also* anti-Asian movements
Anti-Chinese laws, 3, 6, 8, 9, 15, 19, 30, 48, 50, 66, 104, 131, 133
Anti-Chinese movement, 55, 90
Anti-Colonial nationalism, 11, 69–72, 74–87, 96, 104, 131
Anti-Communism, 77–79, 102, 113
Anti-Conscription Movements, 12, 111, 114, 126–132
Anti-Imperialism. *See* anti-colonial nationalism.
Anti-Segregation Association (Victoria), 69, 76, 78, 79, 80

Anti-Segregation Movement, 11, 69–87, 103–104
Anti-Segregation Support Association (Vancouver), 81–83
Asia, 5, 7, 9, 18, 26, 75, 85, 104, 106, 120, 127. *See also* China; Japan; India; Southeast Asia
Asian Americans, 5–8, 11, 72, 89–91, 94, 99–100, 107–110, 131, 133, 169nn.6, 9, 10. *See also* Chinese Americans; Japanese Americans; Model Minority
Asian Canadians, 5–8, 11, 49–50, 70, 89–110, 114–115, 125–126, 130. *See also* Chinese Canadians; East Indian Canadians; Japanese Canadians; Model Minority
Asiatic Exclusion League, 22, 31–32, 92, 145
Assimilation, 8, 9, 11, 12, 71, 73–74, 84, 89–110, 131–132
Australasia, 12, 133
Australia, 106, 133

Bank of China (New York), 115, 117
Beer. *See* Full Glass of Beer Protest
Beijing, 74, 83, 100. *See also* China

Belgians, 30
Blacks (African Americans and African Canadians), 11, 62, 83, 89, 105–106
Blue Funnel Line, 25, 26, 39
Boggs, Theodore, 105, 106
Bootlegging, 47, 63, 64, 66
Borden, Robert, 47
Border controls, 10–13, 15–48, 64–66, 131, 133
Bowell, J. M., 24, 28–29, 39
Boycotts, 6, 12, 18–19, 30, 31, 34, 36, 37, 39–40, 69–88, 101, 103–104, 106, 128, 129, 130, 131, 144n.42, 151n.181
Bribery and graft, 6, 17, 18, 21, 22, 24–26, 30–32, 39, 44, 48, 54, 60, 62, 65–66, 92
Britain, 44, 83, 127. *See also* British Empire
Britishness, 101
British Asia. *See* British Empire
British Empire, 7, 9, 10–12, 28, 36–37, 45, 66, 72–76, 83, 85, 95, 97, 100–104, 106, 115, 131, 133
British imperial identity, 112
British Columbia Liquor Control Board, 64
Brokers and Brokerage
 Interpersonal dynamics, 7–8, 89–110, 131
 Party Politics, 15–48, 60–67, 115–117
 Second generation, 73–74, 93–94, 107–108, 126–130
 Theoretical conception, 3–14, 131–133, 137n.13
 *See* also Immigration Interpreters; Knowledge-Brokers; Legal Interpreters; Social Movement Brokers; Traditional Brokers; Worker-Brokers
Bumstead, J. M., 75

Business, 5–9, 11, 17, 20, 22, 26–30, 33, 37–38, 40, 44–47, 50–55, 58–61, 63–66, 74, 77, 79, 83–84, 86, 91, 93, 96, 100, 104, 112, 115–116, 129
Businesspeople, Chinese Canadian (Chinese Merchants), 3–7, 9–10, 16, 19, 21–27, 29–38, 40, 42, 44–47, 50–53, 55–57, 59, 61–66, 72, 76–79, 82–83, 86, 91, 95, 98, 100, 103–104, 112, 116, 121, 123–124
Businesspeople, Chinese American (Chinese Merchants), 30, 65
Business associations, 36–38, 46, 59, 73–75, 104. *See also* Chinese Board of Trade; Chinese Chamber of Commerce; Chinese Empire Reform Association; Chinese Freemasons; Chinese Peddler's Association; Chong Hoo Tong; Sei Yap Board of Labor and Trades; See Yip Benevolent Society; Vancouver Board of Trade; Yue Shan Society
Byng, Lord, 101

Cabinet of Canada, 17, 18, 29, 39, 44, 115
California, 18, 72, 89, 103, 105. *See also* San Francisco; Oakland; West Coast
Canadian-born, 9, 13, 24, 58, 74, 83, 97, 100, 116, 124, 128, 129, 132. *See also* Second Generation
Canadianization. *See* Assimilation
Canadian Oriental Wine and Liquor Company, 64
Canadian Pacific Railway (CPR), 9, 25–29, 35–39, 46–47, 64–65, 74, 120
Cantonese dialects, 37

Canton Merchants' Self-Governing Association (SGA, Yueshang Zizhi Hui), 31, 36, 47
Canton-to-Hankow Railway, 30
Catholic Church, 92
Chang, Toy (Sam Kee, Chen Daozhi), 22, 30, 37, 40, 62, 130
Chicago (city), 34
Chicago School (Chicago School of Sociology), 7–8, 11, 89–110, 131, 141n.59, 165n.32, 169nn.4–6, 9–10, 176nn.161–162
{Im Re} Chin Chee, 33
China, 4–12, 15, 17–37, 40, 42, 44–46, 49, 50, 53, 58–59, 62–64, 68, 70–77, 79, 80–84, 86–87, 90–91, 95–129, 132
    Extraterritorial rule, 113
    Gentry as emigration agents, 38
    Local elite-society relations, 137n.13
    Modernizing, 18–20, 30, 74, 95, 99–104
    Taxing emigrants, 116
    Registering emigrants, 116
    Relations with Canada, 6–7, 9–11, 12, 18, 19–20, 26, 28, 30, 34, 36–37, 73–76, 83, 100–104, 110, 113, 115–117, 119, 121–122, 125, 129
    Trade with Canada, 34, 36, 47, 53, 55, 66, 75, 83, 106, 116, 123, 125
Chinatowns, 4, 9, 11, 12, 40, 42, 49, 64, 70, 75, 76, 82, 91, 96, 98, 104, 107–109, 112, 117, 121, 123, 127, 128, 132
Chinese Americans, 3–4, 6–13, 16, 18–19, 28, 30–31, 36–37, 43, 47–49, 52, 54–55, 63–65, 72, 74, 75, 86, 89–92, 94, 99, 100, 104, 107–110, 111, 114, 131, 133

Chinese American Citizens' Alliance (CACA, Tongyuanhui, Native Sons of the Golden State), 74, 93, 104, 165n.35
Chinese Benevolent Association (Zhonghua Huiguan, Vancouver, CBA), 57–58, 73, 77, 81, 91, 93–95, 104, 117, 128
Chinese Board of Trade, 37–38
Chinese Canadian Club (CCC, also known as Tongyuanhui, Chinese Canadian Citizens' Alliance), 73, 74, 93, 103–104
Chinese Chamber of Commerce, 37–38, 73, 104
Chinese Consolidated Benevolent Association (Zhonghua Huiguan, Victoria, CCBA), 57–58, 73, 77
Chinese Empire Reform Association (CERA, Baohuanghui), 6, 20, 29–31, 33, 34, 47, 53, 99, 138n.19, 144n.41
Chinese Freemasons (Chee Kung Tong, Zhigongtang, CF), 30–31, 34, 37, 39, 47, 50, 57, 58, 62, 63–67, 136n.9, 138n.19
Chinese Immigration Act of 1923 (Canada, also known as the Forty-Three Harsh Regulations, and as the Exclusion Act), 11–12, 83–84, 86, 87, 100–101, 112, 130, 136
Chinese-language historical documents, 4, 136n.9. *See also* Newspapers
Chinese lawyers. *See* Legal Interpreters
Chinese Peddlers' Association (Caiye Gonghui), 59
Chinese Students Alliance (CSA), 74, 82, 93, 102, 103
Chinese United Church, 128
Chinese Workers' Party (Zhonghua Gongdang), 83

Chinese Youth Association (CYA, Huaqiao Qingnian Hui), 128, 129–130
Chong, Sing (Zheng Sheng), 58, 66–67
Chong Hoo Tong (Chang Hou Tang), 37
Christians, 67, 91–92, 94, 99, 102, 103, 108
Chung, Kwong, 38
Chung Hing, Company, 38
Citizens' Association (of Chinese Canadians), 166
Citizenship rights. *See* Rights politics
Civil disobedience, 69, 71, 74–75, 78–81, 83–86, 117. *See also* Boycotts; Non-cooperation Movement; India
Civil law, 54–55
Civil rights. *See* Rights Politics
Civil Service, 6, 15–18, 44–48, 60–61. *See also* Patronage
Clan and district associations (huiguan). *See* Chong Hoo Tong; *See* Yip Benevolent Association; Wong Kung Har Tong; Yue Shan Society
Clark, Colonel, 34
Class relations, 3–5, 9–12, 26–28, 37, 50–51, 53, 55–57, 64–67, 69–72, 75–80, 93, 95, 99–100, 102, 104, 107, 109, 112–114, 117–126
Columbia Clay Company, 55, 56
Columbia University, 75
Communist Party (of China), 12, 71, 72, 75, 76, 100, 101–102
  Hong Kong Seamen's Strike, 75
*Jianada Chen Bao*, 102, 137
Confucianism, 108, 164n.19
Consciousness, Ethnic. *See* Identity Studies.
Conscription, 12, 126–130
Consul, British, 36, 38
Consuls and Consulates, Chinese, 38, 116, 121, 123–125, 129

Conscription, 12, 111, 114, 126–130, 132
Conservative Party of Canada, 20, 29, 46–47
Cornett, Jack, 121
Coolidge, Mary, 47
Coolies (also known as "yellow slavery"), 4, 19, 57, 95
Corporations, Canadian, 16, 17, 18, 26, 33, 36, 47, 92, 121, 124, 125
Court challenges to anti-Chinese laws, 23, 73, 76, 155n.2
Cuba, 133
Culture and immigration studies, 108–110. *See also* Assimilation; Second Generation; Transnationalism
Cultural pluralism, 11, 71, 73, 74, 78, 82, 85 113, 131–132
Cumberland (British Columbia), 24
Cumyow, Gordon Won, 54, 157n.31
Cumyow, Won Alexander (Wen Jinyou), 17, 38, 51, 54–55, 82, 157n.31

*Da Han Gong Bao*, 102, 137n.9
*Da Han Ri Bao*, 137n.9
*Daily Colonist* (Victoria), 85
Deductions. *See* Income Tax.
Department of Trade (Canada), 28
Dependents. *See* Families of Chinese Canadians
Deportation, 24, 51, 83, 84, 93, 100
Despotism, 4, 55, 57, 95, 110
Detention building for immigrants, 149
Diaspora, Chinese, 3–14, 18–22, 29–31, 36–38, 43, 47–48, 50, 54–68, 69–87, 100, 112–126, 131–133
Discrimination against Chinese Canadians
  Gambling arrests, 62–63
  Immigration policy, 4, 15–18, 23–29, 31, 33–34, 44–48

Labor Unions, 22, 84
Legal System, 10–11, 49–55, 60–61, 66
Naturalization, 6, 136n.7
Public Schools, 11, 70–71, 72–73, 76, 84–86
Second World War policies, 111–131
As Transnational Migrants, 9, 13, 90, 96–97, 100, 107–110, 113, 115–126
Voting Rights, 4, 6, 125, 136n.7
Wages, 119
*See also* Head Tax
Disenfranchisement, 6, 9, 10, 12–14, 16, 46, 73, 90, 100, 109, 125–130, 132, 136n.7
Draft, Military, 38, 61, 126–130
Drugs. *See* Opium
Dock and Shipyard Workers' Union (DSWU), 122–125
Dominion Secret Service, 34–35, 38–40

East Indian Canadians, 32, 50, 54, 119, 125, 126, 128, 130
East Side of Vancouver, 11
Ecological theories of migration and race relations, 108–110
Economy of migration, 26–31, 64–65. *See also* Brokers and Brokerage; Businesspeople; Conservative Party of Canada; Immigration officials; Interpreters; Liberal Party of Canada; Political Machines; Social Movements; Steamship companies; Railway companies; Ticket Agents
Education, 53, 74, 69–87, 95, 99–100, 104, 106–110, 122
Education associations, 74
Employers, 55, 76, 79, 117, 118, 121, 123–125
Empress Steamship Line (of the Canadian Pacific Railway), 26, 35–37

Enfranchisement, 104–105, 125–130
England, 10, 99, 107. *See also* Britain; British Empire; London
Estates of Chinese immigrants, 56
Ethnic leadership. *See* Brokers and Brokerage
Ethnic studies scholars. *See* Chicago School.
Eugenics, 108
Exclusion Act, Chinese (Canada). *See* Chinese Immigration Act of 1923
Exclusion Act, Chinese (United States), 3, 8–9, 12–14, 16, 18–19, 25, 32, 34–35, 46–48, 114
Exclusion Era
　the Americas, 133
　Australasia, 133
　Canada, 3, 8–9, 12–14, 131–133
　Cuba, 133
　Mexico, 46, 133
　Pacific World, 12–14, 132–133
　Panama, 133
　Peru, 133
　United States, 3, 8–9, 12–14, 132–133

Families of Chinese Canadians, 6, 8–9, 12, 20, 24, 25, 28, 34–35, 44, 46, 59, 67, 71, 73–74, 79, 80, 82, 96, 98, 107–110, 112–113, 115–117, 125
Farris, John Wallace de Beque Farris (J. W. de B. Farris), 22, 44, 46, 62, 145n.59
Female Slavery. *See* "Slave Girl" Traffic
First Nations people, 5, 9, 13, 49–50, 50, 54, 68, 83, 125–130
First World War, 5, 11, 17, 70–72, 85
Fong, Kin Show, 38
Food, 62, 119
Foreign Exchange Control Board of Canada (FECB), 115, 116, 117, 181

Foshan, 113
Foster, Edward, 35, 36, 38, 40
Four Counties. *See* Siyi
Franchise, 9, 10, 12–13, 16, 46, 73, 92, 100, 109, 125–126, 128–130, 136n.7. *See also* Enfranchisement; Disenfranchisement.
French Canadians, 5, 12, 84, 104, 126
Frontiers, 9, 91
Full glass of beer protest, 119, 120

Gambling, 11, 47, 50, 56, 61–64, 66–67, 94, 95, 96, 108, 112
Gandhi, Mohandas, 75
Gardiner, John Vrooman, 17
Gender ratio of Chinese Canadian population, 67
Gentry. *See* China, gentry
Gompers, Samuel, 55
Grant, Gordon, 22, 44, 55, 145
Great Britain, 44
Great Depression, 12, 45, 112, 116
Guangdong, 7, 18, 27, 28, 30, 37, 38, 40, 43, 50, 63, 75, 100, 112, 113, 117. *See also* Guangzhou; Foshan; Pearl River Delta; Sanyi; Siyi; Taicheng; Taishan; Xinhui
Guangzhi School, 83
Guangzhou, 28, 30–31, 37, 46, 56, 74, 83, 84, 113

*Habeas corpus* cases, 33
Hastings, Harry, 52, 78, 103–104
Head Tax, Chinese (Canada), 3, 9, 10, 15–48, 136n.4
Hellaby, Hilda, 102
Hemispheric history, 12–14, 65, 91, 131–133
Hip Sing Tong (Xie Bang Tang), 63
Hong Kong, 6, 18, 20, 24, 27, 28, 30, 31, 35–36, 38, 41, 42, 44, 65, 74–75, 78, 102, 104

Hong Kong Seamen's Strike, 75, 78, 102, 104
Hope, Joseph (Liu Guangzu), 69, 73, 74, 77–82, 84
Hosang, Inglis, 157n.31
House of Commons of Canada, 84
Huang, Xia Sheng, 77
Huang, Zhuo Tang, 77
Hudson's Bay Company, 92
Human rights. *See* Rights Politics

Ideas about race and immigration, 12–14, 89–110, 131–133
Identity Studies, 109
Illegal immigration
 Chinese, 4–7, 10, 13, 15–48, 51, 63–66, 83, 96, 118, 120, 122, 131–133
 Italian, 26
 Japanese, 26, 45
Immigrant incorporation, 5–7, 11–14, 50, 71, 84, 107–110, 114, 131–133
 Legal system, 10, 49–68, 131
 Military service, 12, 128–130, 131–132
 Party machines, 6, 9–10, 15–48, 60–64, 131–133
 Organized labor, 12, 75–76, 117–126, 131–132
 As research subjects, 7–8, 11, 89–110, 131
 Social life, 11–12, 53, 94–100
 Social movements, 11, 69–87, 117–126, 131, 132
 *See also* Assimilation; Cultural Pluralism; Political integration; Second Generation; Transnationalism
Immigrant nation-building, 13, 11, 71, 73–74, 78, 82, 85, 113, 131–132
Immigrant youth. *See* Second Generation

Immigration, 3–13, 131–133
　Business, 6, 20, 38, 55–57, 115–116
　Global controls, 12–14, 131–133
　Ideas, 7–8, 11, 89–110, 131–133
　Illegal immigration, 12–48, 63–66, 112, 118, 122, 131–133
　Law, 3–4, 15–18, 23–25, 28–29, 32–33, 49–68, 83–84, 100, 118, 122, 130
　Myths, 8, 11, 107–110, 131
　*See also* Head Tax; Immigration Policy
Immigration Interpreters
　Canada, 6–7, 10, 15–48, 65, 131
　United States, 47–48, 52
Immigration Officials
　Canada, 6–7, 10, 15–48, 65, 131
　United States, 33–35, 47–48
Immigration Policy
　Canada, 3, 9–12, 15–48, 64–66, 83–84, 86, 87, 100–101, 130, 100–101, 112, 118–121, 130–133, 136
　United States, 3, 8–9, 12–14, 16, 18–19, 25, 32, 34–35, 46–48, 114
Immigration Studies, 7–8, 10, 12–14, 89–110, 131–133
Income tax, 114, 118, 119, 120–125, 127, 118–125
India, 11, 32, 50, 54, 75, 119, 125, 126, 128, 130
Institute of Pacific Relations (IPR), 106
Institute of Social and Religious Research, 92, 105
Integration. *See* Immigrant Incorporation
Intellectuals, 10, 11, 70, 77, 86, 87, 95, 89–110
Intellectual History, 7–8, 87–110, 131
Intermarriage, 94
International Woodworkers of America (IWA), 121–123, 125

Interpreters, 6–7, 10, 15–68, 96, 112, 119, 131, 157n.31
Interwar Era, 65

Jang, Jack, 58, 59
Jangze, Bevan, 128
Japan, 6, 11, 26, 31–32, 34, 36, 45, 50, 62, 68, 70, 73, 76, 90, 94, 97, 99, 105–106, 107, 108, 112–114, 116
Japanese, Americans, 90, 94, 105, 107–108, 169n.6
Japanese, Canadians, 11, 26, 31, 32, 36, 45, 50, 62, 68, 70, 73, 76, 90, 97–98, 105, 107–108
Jews, 11
*Jianada Chen Bao* (*Canada Morning Post*), 102
Jin, She, 122
*Jinshanzhuang*, 116
Judicial Committee of the Privy Council (British Empire, London, England, JCPC), 66

Kang, Youwei, 34
Kendall, F. W., 127
Kelly, Robert, 22, 31–32, 34, 38–39, 40, 44, 46
Kerr, David C., 65
Keshen, Jeffrey, 120
King, William L. Mackenzie King, 46
Knowledge-Brokers, 7–8, 11, 89–110, 131
Ko, Wing Kan, 96, 98
Ku Klux Klan, 85, 92
Kwong and Company, 55–56
Kwong Lee Tai Company, 51

Labor contractors, 5, 55–57, 56, 63–64, 75–76, 119

Labor unions, 11, 12, 18, 22, 43–44, 56, 67, 75–76, 85–86, 93, 114, 117–126, 129, 131–132. *See also* Dock and Shipyard Workers' Union; International Woodworkers of America; Overseas Chinese Workers' Friendship Union; United Chinese Workers' Union; Vancouver Trades and Labor Council

Language barriers, 118, 188n.2

Laurier, Wilfrid, 7, 18, 22, 33, 34, 39, 40, 47, 104

Law. *See* Chinese Immigration Act; Court Challenges; *Exclusion Act* (United States); Foreign Exchange Control Board; Head Tax; Immigration Policy; Interpreters; Lawyers; Legal System; School Segregation

Lawyers, 10, 22, 33, 38, 40, 40–46, 50–55, 58–60, 62, 65, 67, 81
   Chinese American, 52
   Chinese Canadian, 155n.2
   Exclusion of Chinese from legal profession, 49–50, 155n.4

Leadership. *See* Brokers and Brokerage

Lee, Cecil, 74, 98–99, 104

Lee, C. T., 123

Lee, Ghia, 51

Lee, Mongkow, 17, 37, 42, 52, 62, 65

Lee, Saifan (Lee Kee, Lee Shiqi), 22, 30, 37, 43, 62

(*Im Re*) *Lee Him*, 33

Leftists, 11, 69–72, 75–76, 93, 102–104, 117–126

Legal interpreters (Chinese lawyers)
   Canada, 10, 21–22, 33, 38, 49–68, 96, 112, 119, 131, 157n.31
   United States, 49, 52–55, 60, 157

Legal system
   Canada, 8–10, 23–25, 28–29, 33, 41–45, 49–68, 76, 114–126, 131–132, 155nn.2, 4
   Informal, 55, 57–59, 67–68
   United States, 47–50, 55, 155nn.2, 4

Lew, David (Liao Hongxiang), 7, 10, 15–46, 49–51, 53, 55–57, 58, 60–67, 145, 155n.2

Lew, Shong Kow, 99

Lew, Yick Pang (Liao Ye Pang), 58, 66, 82, 91, 94

*Lew vs. Lee* (1923–1925), 10, 63–64, 66

Li, Dao Wei, 117

Li, Donghai (David T. H. Lee), 116

Li, Yun He, 80

Liang, Qichao, 61, 62

Liangguang, Viceroy (China), 28, 36

Liberal Party of British Columbia, 60, 62, 64

Liberal Party of Canada, 6, 7, 10, 17, 18, 20–22, 26, 29, 30, 31–34, 36–47

Lim, Bang (Lin Bang), 17

Lim, Herbert, 120

Lin, Bao Heng, 82–83

Litigation masters, China (songshi, zhuangshi) 22, 53

Local elite-society relations. *See* China, local elite-society relations

London (England), 10, 66, 74. *See also* British Empire

Loo, Gee Wing, 22, 30

Louie, H. Y. (Hok Yat), 59

Lowe, Pany, 100

Lum, Ching Ling, 24–25

Lun Yick Company (Lianyi Gongsi), 63, 64, 66

Ma, Yu Ru, 81

Macau, 37

Macpherson, Robert, 31

Mah, Roy (Ma Guo Guan), 119, 123, 125, 129, 130

Mak, Wai, 27, 28

Manson, Alexander, 60

Marginal Men (i.e., Marginal Man theory), 8, 109
Martin, Joseph, 44
Mass Protests, 6, 18–19 112, 69–87, 117–130
May Fourth Movement, 71, 86–87
Mayors of Vancouver, 66, 83, 121
McCrossan, George, 40–43
McGill University, 75
McInnes, Thomas, 22, 31, 33–34, 46, 145n.59
McKenzie, Ian, 121
McRae, J. C., 60
Merchants. See Businesspeople
Mexico, 6, 30, 46, 63, 91, 133
Middlemen. See Brokers and Brokerage
Military service, 12, 112, 114, 120–121, 126–130, 185n.153
Minimum Wage Law (British Columbia), 86
Minneapolis-St. Paul, 43
Missionaries. See Christians
Model Minority concept, 8, 11, 104, 109–111, 130–131
Mon Keang School (Wenjiang Xuexiao), 102
Montreal, 33–34
Morgan, Nigel, 121
Morrison, Frank, 55
Mosaic, Canadian, 132
Multiculturalism, 13, 15, 59, 67–68, 71, 73–74, 105–110, 113, 131–133
Murphy, Denis, 40, 41

Nanaimo, 10, 17, 37, 40, 41, 45, 63, 64, 66
Nationalism, Chinese, 6, 18–20, 29–31, 62–63, 69–87, 96, 100–104, 106–108
Nationalist Party of China, 58, 62–63, 71–72, 75, 78–83, 86, 96, 100–104, 113, 115–117, 129

Nationalist Revolution (China), 62–63, 71, 83, 86, 97, 100–103
National War Labor Board of Canada, 121
Nativism, 71, 72, 85
Naturalization, 6, 24–25, 83, 100, 104, 129, 136n.7
Negro problem, 93, 106
Nelson, John, 92, 106
Newspapers, 4, 18, 39, 114, 136–137, 104. *See also Da Han Gong Bao*; *Da Han Ri Bao*; *Daily Colonist*; *Xin Minguo Bao*; *Jianada Chen Bao*; *Vancouver Sun*
New York City, 18, 30, 43, 47, 63, 92, 115, 117
New York State, 32
Ng, Yik, 28
Nippon Yusen Kaisha (NYK) Steamship Line, 26, 36
Non-cooperation movements, 75, 78–79, 128
North America, 4–7, 13–14, 18, 30, 37, 40, 63, 102, 107–109, 114, 125
  U.S.-Canada, 4–7, 13–14, 18, 30, 37, 40, 63, 102, 107–108, 109, 114, 125
  Canada, U.S. and Mexico, 4–7, 13–14, 18, 30, 37, 40, 63
North Vancouver, 70

Oakland, 72
O'Hara, Francis C. T. 28–29, 34
Ohashi, Chuichi, 105
On Leong Tong (An Liang Tang), 63
Opium, 40, 56, 61, 62, 95–96, 108
Ordinary Chinese, 4, 6, 55, 61, 70, 75, 77, 86, 91, 95, 99–100, 104, 131
Oregon, 52
Orientalism, 90
Oriental problem, 91–94, 89–110, 106
Ottawa, 15, 28, 33–36, 42, 43, 45–46, 84, 116, 122–124, 129

INDEX | 225

Out migration, 108
Overseas Chinese Workers' Friendship Union (OCWFU), 122–126, 129

Pacific World, 4–9, 11–16, 25–27, 30, 36–37, 46–49, 63, 65–66, 68–76, 81, 83–87, 91–93, 96, 106, 113, 131–133
Panama, 133
Panyu, 37, 43, 50, 62, 66
Paralegals. *See* Legal Interpreters
Park, Robert, 11, 89, 91–95, 99, 105, 107, 109, 169nn.4–6
Parliament of Canada, 11, 15, 17, 44, 55, 81, 83–84, 86, 100
Party Machines. *See* Political Machines
Patronage, 6, 9–10, 15–48, 60–65
Pearl River Delta of Guangdong, 28, 37. *See also* Sanyi; Siyi; Taishan; Xinhui
Peru, 133
Philadelphia, 28
Plant metaphors in migration theory, 108–110
Pluralistic approaches to immigrant incorporation. *See* Cultural Pluralism; Second Generation
Police, 34–35, 38–40, 44, 48–51, 53–64, 66–67, 76, 83, 96, 102
Political Economy. *See* Economy of Migration
Political Incorporation (Political Integration), 5, 13, 15–48, 60–68, 71, 73–76, 82, 85–86, 109
Political Machines
  Canada, 5–6, 10, 12, 15–48, 60–64, 92, 117–126, 131–133
  United States, 47–48
Poon, Shang Lung, 39–40
Popular democracy. *See* Social Movements
Portland, 52

Prentiss, P. L., 34
Prostitution, 50, 56, 63, 65, 95–96
Provincial Party (of British Columbia), 92
Punjab (India), 125. *See also* East Indian Canadians

Quebec, 126

Race relations, transnational, in Canada, 3–14, 131–133
  Civil rights and human rights movements, 69–87, 114–115, 117–133
  Law, 49–68
  Politics, 15–48
  Public discourse, 89–110
  War time, 114–115, 117–133
Race relations cycle, 108–110
Railway companies, 9, 25–29, 32, 35–39, 46–47, 64–65, 74, 120
Raushenbush, Winifred, 78, 92–95, 97–99, 101–108, 169n.6, 171n.34
Registration of Chinese Canadians
  By China (1940), 116
  Under Chinese Immigration Act (1924), 83
Relief aid groups, Sino-Japanese war, 117
Relief remittances. *See* Remittances
Religious beliefs of Chinese Canadians, 94, 96
Remittances, 9, 12, 115–118, 122–123, 181
Researchers, 7, 8, 11, 89–110
Rightist politics, 56, 69–72, 76, 78–79, 86, 100–101, 104, 119
Rights politics (Civil Rights and Human Rights), 10, 23, 33, 69–88, 90, 104–105, 109, 111–114, 117, 118, 120, 122, 125–130, 132
Riot, anti-Asian (Vancouver, 1907), 23, 32, 81
River Han, 80

Robinson, Oscar, 61
Robinson-Mansfield Detective Agency, 60–61
Roosevelt, Theodore, 19, 34
Royal Commission on Chinese immigration frauds (1910–1911), 15, 18, 36, 39, 40–47
Russell, Joseph Ambrose, 51, 52, 53
Russia, 106

Sam, Joe, 120
Sam, J. P., 67, 157n.31
Sam Kee Company, 57
San Francisco, 11, 31, 36, 47, 54, 72, 74, 86, 91, 99, 100, 104, 107, 108, 117
Sanyi (Sam Yap, the Three Counties, Guangdong, China), 37, 40, 43, 63–65
Saunders, Charles, 123
School boards
  North Vancouver, 70, 82
  Vancouver, 70
  Victoria, 72–73, 75–76, 78, 81–85
School boycotts
  China, 73
  *See also* Anti-Segregation Movement
Schools
  British Columbia, 11, 69, 70, 72–76, 81, 82, 84–85, 89, 103, 106–109, 131
  California, 72–73, 86
  Chinese community, 76–77, 83, 102
  Teachers, 74–77
  Principals, 70, 73, 83
School strikes. *See* Anti-Segregation Movement
School Segregation
  Canada, 11, 69–86
  U.S., 71–72, 86
Science. *See* Social Science
Seattle, 11, 34, 91, 99–100, 104

Second Generation Immigrants, 9, 71, 73–74, 86, 98, 104, 107–108, 155
Second World War, 5, 12, 111–130
  Conscription and Military Service, 126–130
  Foreign Exchange Control Board and Immigrant Remittances, 115–117
  Income Tax Protests, 117–126
  Industries, 114–125
  Labor Unions, 117–126
  *See also* Sino-Japanese War
See Yip Benevolent Association (Siyi Huiguan), 37
(Pro) Segregation Movement, 70–73
Sei Yap Board of Labor and Trades (SBLT, Hong Kong), 36
Seid, Gain Back, Jr., 52
Senate of Canada, 84
Sending money to relatives. *See* remittances.
Senkler, Harry, 41, 44
Settlement nations, 12–14, 19, 46, 65, 132–133
Seto, Ying Shek (Seto More, Situ Mao), 80, 82, 84, 91, 94
Sex-trafficking. *See* "Slave Girl" Traffic
Shanghai, 6, 74, 83–84
Shen, Man, 22, 166
Sherwood, Percy, 34, 39
Shingle Mills, 76, 118–125
Shipyards, 118–125
Sino-Japanese War, 112–113, 115–117
Siyi (Sei Yap, the Four Counties), 37, 38, 40, 43, 63–65, 117
Siyi Board of Trade (British Columbia), 37
"Slave Girl" Traffic, 65–66, 162n.114
Slavery, African, 83
Smith, Janet case, 60, 61
Social Darwinism, 108

Social Movements, 6, 18–19, 11–12, 69–87, 51, 111, 114, 131, 117–130, 131. *See also* Anti-Conscription Movements; Anti-Segregation Movement; Labor Unions; Taxpayer Rights Movement
Social Movement Brokers, 10–11, 70–87, 111–112, 114, 117–132
Social Science, 7, 11, 74, 89–100, 89–110, 169nn.4–6, 10, 176nn.161–162
Socialism, 71–72, 75–76, 78, 102
Sociologists, 7, 11, 89–110
Sojourners, 9, 79, 95, 99, 118–120, 122, 125, 132
Soldiers' rights. *See* Anti-Conscription Movements
Southeast Asia, 18, 26, 127
Special Operations Executive (SOE, Great Britain), 127
Steamship Companies, 9, 25–28, 32, 38, 65. *See also* Blue Funnel Line; Empress Line of the Canadian Pacific Railroad; Nippon Yusen Kaisha Line; Weir Line; CPR, Weir, Blue Funnel and NYK lines
Steveston (British Columbia), 53
Strikes, 31, 56, 71, 73, 75–76, 78, 79, 80, 83, 102, 104, 118, 120–125
Student groups, 73–75, 81–84, 93, 102–104
Sun, Yat-Sen Dr. (Sun Zhongshan), 31, 46, 100, 101, 108
Sung, Lambert (Song Langbi), 82, 91, 94
Survey of Race Relations, 7–8, 11, 78, 89–110, 131, 176nn.161–162

Taicheng, 113
Taishan, 27–28, 38, 117
Tammany Hall (New York), 47
Taxes
Canada (*see* Head Tax and Income Tax)
China, 116
Tax Office, 118, 121–122, 124–125
Taxpayers' Rights Movement, 12, 111, 114, 117–126
Taylor, S. S., 38, 42
Templeman, William, 17–18, 39
Theories of immigration, 108–110
Thom, Tom Chue, 40
Thomas, William I., 92
Three Counties. *See* Sanyi
Ticket Agents, 26, 32, 64–65
Tongs, 30, 37, 61–67, 94–95, 100, 108
Toronto, 40, 67, 128
Torreon (Mexico), 6, 30
Toy, Eckard, 107
Traditional Brokers, 5–12, 15–48, 53, 55–57, 61–67, 70, 72, 75–79, 82, 86–87, 91, 93, 95, 111–112, 115–117, 121, 123–124, 127–128
Transcontinental Railway (Canada), 9
Transnational Life. *See* Transnationalism
Transnationalism, 5–6, 8–14, 15–49, 52–53, 55–57, 60–61, 63–66, 69–87, 89–110, 112–113, 115–118, 121–122, 131–133
Transpacific Ties. *See* Transnationalism

Unions. *See* Labor Unions
Unionist Government (Canada), 46
United Chinese Workers' Union (Overseas Chinese Workers' Friendship Union), 129
United States, 3–15, 18–19, 23–26, 29–32, 34–37, 43, 46–49, 50, 52–55, 57, 60–61, 63–65, 68, 71–75, 77, 86, 89–94, 99–100, 103–111, 114–115, 117, 131–133, 136
University of British Columbia, 67, 91–92, 97, 98, 105, 106

University of Chicago, 11, 75, 89. *See also* Chicago School

Vancouver (Canada), 6–12, 15–46, 49–67, 69–70, 72, 74–75, 77, 79–85, 87, 89–106, 111–112, 113–130
Vancouver Board of Trade, 46
Vancouver General Hospital, 57
Vancouver Island, 56, 63. *See also* Cumberland; Nanaimo; Victoria
*Vancouver Sun*, 61, 92
Vancouver Trades and Labour Council (VTLC), 22, 43–44
Vegetable-peddling truck dispute, 58–59
Vermont, 32
Veterans, Chinese Canadian, 114, 130
Veterans' benefits, 129–130
Victoria (Canada), 11, 17, 25, 35, 41–42, 45–46, 52, 57, 62–63, 65–66, 70–85, 91, 98–99, 103–104, 116
Voting rights. *See* Enfranchisement; Disenfranchisement

Wang, Herbert, 98, 99
Washington, Booker T., 93
War. *See* First World War; Second World War
War industries, 114–125
Warlords, China, 83
War Measures Act, 115
Washington state, 35, 93. *See also* Seattle
Weir (Steamship) Line, 26
West Coast (Canada and U.S.), 4, 7, 8, 30, 31, 47, 71–72, 86, 89, 90–91, 94, 96, 104–105, 107–110
Whaun, Thomas Moore (Huang Song Mao), 67, 96–97, 98, 101–103, 106, 124
Wickberg, Edgar, 25
Wing, Lee (Rong Li), 64, 66

Wing Sang Company (Yong Sheng Gongsi), 46, 58, 116
Winnipeg, 60, 75
Winnipeg General Strike (1919), 75
Withholding. *See* Income Tax
Women, Chinese Canadian, 4, 61, 64–67, 70, 74, 80, 90, 93, 98, 124, 128, 129
Wong, Bing, 120
Wong, Frank, 130
Wong, Lung, 38, 53
Wong, Foon Sien (Huang Wenfu), 23, 24, 51, 59, 60–61, 79, 82–83, 117, 119, 124–125, 127, 129, 157n.31
Wong, Foon Sing (Huang Huan Sheng), 60–61
Wong, Ming Choo, 61
Wong, T. S., 128
Wong Kung Har Tong (Huang Jiangxia Tang), 102
Woodworkers. *See* Shingle Mills; International Woodworkers of America
Worker-Brokers, 10, 12, 69–72, 75–76, 117–126, 129
Workers, 3–5, 9–12, 18–19, 25–28, 35, 37, 43–45, 55–57, 62, 67, 70–71, 75–81, 83–84, 86, 93, 95–96, 99, 102, 104, 107, 111–114, 117–126, 129
Workers' Movement. *See* Labor Unions
Workers' Rights, 75–76, 111, 117–126
Working-Class. *See* Class Relations; Workers

Xian Xiang Theatrical Society, 83
*Xin Minguo Bao*, 137n.9
Xinhui, 38

Yellow Slavery, 4, 57, 95
Yin, Lung Tong, 38
Yip, Kew Him (Yip Kew Ghim, Ye Qiu Jin), 46

Yip, Kew Mow (Ye Qiu Mao), 46, 95
Yip, On (Ye En, Ye Huibo, Yip Wai Pak, Yip Ting Sam), 6, 7, 10, 15–47, 85, 144nn.28, 41, 42
Yip, Quene (Yip Kew Quene), 58–59, 129
Yip, Sang, 26, 35, 46, 95–96, 129
Yip, Sue Poy, 35
Yip, Yen (Charlie Yip Yen, Yip Yuen), as immigration interpreter, 26, 35, 42

Yip Family (Ye Family), 6–7, 10, 15–47, 62–65, 85, 95–96, 116, 129
Yom, G., 58, 59
Yong, Jung Sum, 44
Yu, Henry, 90
Yue Shan Society (Yushan Zongxinju), 62–65, 67

Zhongshan, 59
Zhou, Chi Zhu, 19, 87
Zhou, Qi Lian, 83
Zhu, Bo Ran, 83–84